Objects Untimely

Objects Untimely

Object-Oriented Philosophy and Archaeolgy

Graham Harman and
Christopher Witmore

polity

First published in 2023 by Polity Press

Polity Press
65 Bridge Street
Cambridge CB2 1UR, UK

Polity Press
111 River Street
Hoboken, NJ 07030, USA

ISBN-13: 978-1-5095-5654-0
ISBN-13: 978-1-5095-5655-7(pb)

A catalogue record for this book is available from the British Library.

Library of Congress Control Number: 2022943168

Typeset in 10.5 on 12pt Sabon
by Cheshire Typesetting Ltd, Cuddington, Cheshire
Printed and bound in Great Britain by TJ Books Ltd, Padstow, Cornwall

The publisher has used its best endeavors to ensure that the URLs for external websites referred to in this book are correct and active at the time of going to press. However, the publisher has no responsibility for the websites and can make no guarantee that a site will remain live or that the content is or will remain appropriate.

Every effort has been made to trace all copyright holders, but if any have been overlooked the publisher will be pleased to include any necessary credits in any subsequent reprint or edition.

For further information on Polity, visit our website:
politybooks.com

MIX
Paper from
responsible sources
FSC   FSC® C013056
www.fsc.org

Contents

Acknowledgments

This book has benefited from conversations with Levi Bryant, Ewa Domanska, Gavin Lucas, Laurent Olivier, Bjørnar Olsen, and Michael Shanks. We are grateful to Gavin and Bjørnar for their comments on Chapters 1 and 2. We also thank two outside readers for their invaluable feedback on the book as a whole: one of them Jon Cogburn at Louisiana State University, the other still anonymous.

Figures

(All photographs by Christopher Witmore)

Preface

The spark for this book originated during a visit by Harman to Lubbock, Texas in February 2014 to give the prestigious Haragan Lecture at Texas Tech University. Over the two-day course of this visit, we conversed on a number of occasions about philosophy, archaeology, and the concept of time, the challenge posed by object-oriented ontology (OOO) to anthropocentrism, and the various ways in which archaeology was engaging with OOO while taking leave of a modernist historicism. Witmore invited Harman to discuss time in relation to OOO, while contemplating a few archaeological examples, in an open interview that was audio recorded. As the conversation went on, it became patent that we shared an understanding of time as *generated* by objects rather than encompassing them.[1] By the interview's end, we agreed that this axiom – objects generate time – warranted a deeper exploration in light of both archaeology and OOO. The first fruits of this endeavor appear here as *Objects Untimely*.

That we consider the objects to which the present book is devoted as *untimely* can be justified on multiple grounds. Against the current and pervasive conviction that reality consists of an unceasing flux, associated in philosophy with New Materialism, OOO asserts that objects of all varieties are the bedrock of reality from which time emerges.[2] Against the narrative convictions of time as the course of historical events, the objects and encounters associated with archaeology resist the very temporal delimitations which have defined the field and its objects ever since its professionalization in the nineteenth century. Against the current tendency to treat time as deep, this book articulates a time that is counterintuitively superficial; as Chapter 1 will explain, this has nothing to do with Plato's contrast between time and eternity. Finally, it is also anything but timely to consider a field routinely defined as "the study of the human past through its material remains" on the grounds that all that exists are objects here in the present, and that they cannot be reduced to their pasts.

It is true that within the history of ideas, there is a sense that the exchange between philosophy and archaeology has been far from balanced. For the archaeologist who holds that philosophy seems to have rarely concerned itself with the archaeological endeavor, it would be easy to cast blame upon their fellow practitioners. Not only could they argue that archaeologists – laboring in the shadows of history – have given philosophers little cause to see their soil-encrusted objects as anything other than yoked to the past, burdened by allegory and historical expectation. They could also resign themselves to the all-too-common opinion that theoretical concerns within archaeology are little more than derivative, insofar as the archaeological application of philosophical ideas rarely comes back to impact philosophical developments.[3] The philosopher who comes to ponder this imbalance could just as easily denounce their own field for an overemphasis on the human subject, one that has contributed to a neglect of things. This is a neglect that, in the case of archaeology, was further intensified by the tarnish of entropy, the banality of random detritus, the grimy dregs of oblivion, or the treatment of downcast ruins as a canvas where deeply held fantasies might be satisfied. To be sure, a closer look would reveal the inadequacies of these exaggerated impressions. One could contend that the allure of archaeology is critical to modern philosophical thought.[4] But more than this, there are also numerous philosophers who have given serious consideration to the field – R.G. Collingwood, Merrilee Salmon, and Alison Wylie, among others – in terms of the philosophy of history, science, or language.[5] This book does not seek to balance scales. But if forging connections and mutual understandings comes about by actively engaging in generous and open-minded conversation, it will already help to pique curiosity by showing that both fields are not what one expects them to be.

Objects Untimely takes shape over the course of five chapters. In Chapter 1 we explore the grounds for the book in more detail, with a brief discussion of time and objects in archaeology and philosophy. We move from a consideration of archaeological clockmaking through the example of Ancient Corinth to the place objects hold with respect to the past. Turning to philosophy, we find a recapitulation of Harman's longstanding thesis that Martin Heidegger possesses no conception of time at all; the Heideggerian temporality of thrown projection is contrasted, in particular, with the philosophy of time found in Henri Bergson. Against the New Materialist conception of reality as being in constant flux, there is a discussion of the occasionalist tradition in which reality consists of a series of static though ephemeral poses that quickly pass away into something else. As another way of accounting for the irreversibility of time, the discussion moves on to the views of Lynn Margulis on serial endosymbiosis: when two previously autonomous organisms form a symbiotic union, we know we have stepped forward into a new world. Against this philosophical background, we contemplate a number of archaeological examples in which time arises from objects rather than the reverse.

In Chapter 2, "The Antiquity of Time," Witmore explores the fraught relation between archaeology and history, both of which ostensibly deal with the past, to offer a different understanding of archaeology and the time that is generated by things. Over the course of six discrete sections, Witmore moves through the line of disciplinary history, following a path whose route complicates the sequential model of time: through a temporal topology of the storied citadel of Mycenae, with the times of things found in the course of the citadel's excavations, onward into Michel Serres' notion of time as percolation, and finally towards a different definition of archaeology as exploring the antiquity of time alongside objects themselves.

In Chapter 3, Harman and Witmore shift to a dialogue format to discuss the implications of Chapter 2, beginning with the idea of an archaeology that is not primarily the study of the human past. For Witmore, archaeology is very much a discipline of the present that works with what is still available to us in order to imagine what might have been. The discussion ranges from the traditional Three Age System of Stone, Bronze, and Iron, to James G. Frazer's apparently linear conception of magic and then religion giving way in turn to science, to a possible tension between the notions of time as percolation and as topology found in the writings of Serres. Among other topics, Harman and Witmore discuss how periodization is established in archaeology, the discursive topography of the discipline, and how a situation where politics has become first philosophy drove some kindred spirits twenty or so years ago to return to things, under the influence of Serres and Bruno Latour. In closing, the authors discuss Harman's assessment that archaeology is best viewed as a "cold" medium in Marshall McLuhan's sense, since certain aspects of the discipline are lacking in completeness of detail.

In Harman's Chapter 4, "Objects as the Root of Time," he presents his view that time belongs to the surface rather than the depth of reality. This implies no denigration of time, since for OOO the surface of the world is the only place where anything can happen. After a summary of the fourfold model at the heart of OOO, of which time is one part, Harman responds to three specific critiques of the OOO model of time, as formulated respectively by Peter Wolfendale, Peter Gratton, and Arjen Kleinherenbrink. From there the chapter shifts to the much-discussed theory of the unreality of time proposed by J.M.E. McTaggart, supplemented by the OOO critique that his perspective shares too many of the assumptions of classical Empiricism. After giving an analogy of intermittently moved chess pieces to depict how objects are not actually in a state of constant flux, the chapter closes with a discussion of so-called "process philosophies," a term that mixes two very different types of theories: (a) the true philosophies of constant temporal flux, as with Bergson and his later devotees Gilbert Simondon and Gilles Deleuze, and (b) those of Alfred North Whitehead, Latour, and even Heidegger, who are fully aware that reality changes frequently, but whose models of time focus instead on the internal complexity of individual instants.

Chapter 5 returns to dialogue format, recapitulating some of the alternatives to linear or sequential time already discussed: percolating, topological, and cyclical. What, Witmore asks, might OOO add to these alternatives? Harman offers three answers: (1) an epochal conception of time grounded in the constant change of human generations; (2) the possibility of a calmer relation to time (given that much of what happens proves to be unimportant) as opposed to the almost crazed models of constant flux that are currently in fashion; and (3) a conception of time as frequently reversible, given the constant possibility of reviving or retrieving seemingly dead past realities. Pressing forward into the central problem of how changes along the surface of reality can have retroactive effects on its depth, it is argued that all causation can be interpreted as the retroactive effect of a whole on its parts.[6] Against the recent tendency to favor change and flux as the basic constituents of reality, it is argued that we need to turn our focus to the surprising stability of the cosmos. The book closes with a summarizing note on the various conceptions of nonlinear time that have been introduced.

I

Time and Objects

Graham Harman and Christopher Witmore

Objects generate time. This axiom grounds the exploration that follows, and while it constitutes the basis of a shared understanding between archaeology and OOO, it inverts what is currently conceivable, due to the primacy both fields tend to bestow upon time. Such an axiom cannot avoid stoking the flames of present-day controversy in either archaeology or philosophy. Still, when considered in relation to the history of these disciplines, the importance of this principle becomes clear. Archaeological thought has always endeavored to situate human societies *in time*, which ultimately was also a matter of situating ourselves. We who live in the present were secure in our position at the end of the long sequence of events whose distance from us was measured in years, centuries, and millennia. For two hundred years, modern archaeology built its trade on foundations laid through its own clockmaking, in the form of a periodization established on the basis of old things, treated as proxies for the past to which they were assumed to belong.[1] In seeking out the age of extant remains, nineteenth-century archaeologists – following in the footsteps of antiquarians – fixed the contours of historical epochs to temporal coordinates derived from texts, themselves regarded as *sources*. While the chain of successive historical events served as the model for earlier periods and non-textual traditions – worked out stratigraphically on the basis of differences in found objects – the historical text as an intermediary (equally valid when copied, multiplied, or digitized) served as an exemplar for how archaeological things were treated as sources for a particular past.[2]

In recalling the circumstances of early archaeological clockmaking, one recognizes how it was (and continues to be) bound foremost to specific localities. By searching for what had become of a particular past, nineteenth-century archaeologists (in Greece, for example) ventured to those places where they already knew

1

The Archaic temple at Corinth

what might be found. Prefigured in a long tradition of antiquarian readers of ancient texts, archaeologists pushed beyond what remained on the surface at sites like Ancient Corinth.[3] Beginning with excavations in the shadows of Doric columns, they worked to reveal what had (according to Benjamin Powell, a fellow of the American School of Classical Studies at Athens) "survived the changes and chances of time unto our own day."[4] On either side of what is believed to have been a synoecism in the eighth century BCE, archaeologists eventually found evidence of Prehistory – Neolithic, Helladic, and Early Iron Age – as well as History. The latter followed the familiar cadence of the Archaic, Classical, and Hellenistic down through the Roman destruction of 146 BCE, which was trailed by the founding of a Roman Corinth in 44 BCE, and so on. Each period formed a separate link in a chain of terminations and replacements that gauged time's passage up to the present.

Through archaeology's own labors, time displayed the familiar features we now associate with modern historicism.[5] It was linear: for the past, which was held to be separate, demarcated, and distinct, remained at a measured distance. It was successive: for periods were arranged sequentially, and tethered to their locations, while the objects they contained continued to sink deeper into the abyss of the past. The arrangement of archaeological objects into their temporal compartments expanded beyond matters of chronological metrology, for it invited us to contemplate their erstwhile existence over yonder; it tied what was found at places like Ancient Corinth to the circumstances of a given historical period; it suggested limits to their being within a specified timeframe, impacting the circumstances within that capsulized past, and perhaps affecting subsequent periods up to a definitive terminus-transition, such as the coming of Christianity.

Of course, there is a great deal of truth to this image of succession in a fossilized city like Ancient Corinth, where the oldest levels of abandonment tend to be buried below more recent accretions. In effect, the superposition of heterogeneous structural forms lent itself to the notion that the true identity of archaeological objects belonged to an arbitrary sliver cut from the continuum of time.[6] The questions posed by archaeologists reinforced this image. To what era does the Doric temple standing at the center of Ancient Corinth belong? Do transformations around the bases of its columns relate to the Roman resettlement of the site? The first question seeks temporal coordinates, and the answer keeps them there. To label a ruin "Archaic temple" suggests to us that the seven columns and other remains on Temple hill belong to a particular block of time. To link a nearby surface to the "Roman resettlement" suggests that it is only knowable in historical terms.

To be sure, archaeologists posed questions of time in other ways. Were those surfaces revealed around the bases of its columns residues of a particular event, or aggregates of multiple events? How long did it take to produce the vestiges that were encountered here by archaeologists? These questions suggest that whatever old things happen to persist in the present are to be understood as consequences or products of activities in the past, thereby according a separate past primacy over what is found here in the present. Are archaeological surfaces and vestiges derivative of a particular moment or sequence of events long passed? Do they owe their existence solely to the efforts of those who lived at another time? By situating objects in time, archaeologists reinforced the old Platonic notion that time was independent from those things that were placed within it.

Archaeological clockmaking would widen to encompass larger areas, whether in Greece or elsewhere, first by comparing the results from the excavation of different sites, and later by surveying the areas in between. Yet the tenacity with which modern historicism was maintained by archaeologists was tied to the structural organization of the field. Primal and external, the continuum of time took on definitive shape through archaeological labors, while those different compartments structured their own divisions of labor, as practitioners continue to be defined by their specific period of study. This, of course, is not without good reason: for without the toil of period specialists, changes over the long term of millennia would be far less comprehensible, whether in Greece or elsewhere. Nevertheless, while practitioners were beneficiaries of *how* they structured history, the *way* history was measured reinforced the notion of time as a basic structural dimension of reality. Given how archaeologists were consigned to their various periods from deepest prehistory down to the present, who among them did not regard their craft as the study of the past through its material remains?

We will return to these points in Chapter 2. For our purposes here, it is worth noting briefly that archaeologists came to recognize their objects less as offering glimpses of the past as it was, and more as affording suggestions as to what might have been, on the basis of what had become of it.[7] Lewis Binford gave the name the "Pompeii premise" to the assumption that material vestiges speak to the moment of their deposition.[8] By classifying objects solely in terms of the making, use, and activity associated with human beings, archaeologists neglected the processes of formation, entropy, and accretion that have transformed sites like Ancient Corinth into what they are today.[9] While this processual emphasis opened a way to conceive of their objects beyond the confines of any one moment or period, an entropic time served as a counter to the steady and consistent image of a homogeneous clock time.[10] The pavement of the Lechaion Road – the *cardo maximus* of Roman Corinth – was buried under episodes of sporadic deposition where rates of formation varied between slow accumulations with a few centimeters of soil accruing over the course of centuries, and rapid accretions with catastrophic avalanches of debris amassing in the span of but a few hours. Complete gaps are not infrequent. Just as "great quantities of earth and mud" were left after an extraordinary rainstorm in August of 1906 reburied the excavated hollow of the Lechaion Road below the Archaic temple, subsequent clearing work by the Greek government removed any archaeological indication of it apart from what is now referenced in publication.[11] In addressing the different temporal rhythms associated with the sporadic formation of the archaeological record, archaeologists emphasized time perspectivism (the latter refers to Geoff Bailey's notion that different timescales relate to different

The Lechaion Road, Corinth

features of behavior) and nonlinear dynamics (James McGlade and Sander van der Leeuw have, for example, sought to emphasize the variability of persistence and change).[12]

Formational theories were, by and large, the rearguard of an archaeology that continued to grant primacy to a past consisting of static stratigraphic units regarded as derivative of those dynamic processes that gave rise to them.[13] In many ways, these theories anticipated a pervasive emphasis among archaeologists today on process-first philosophies where the stability of objects, human or otherwise, takes a backseat to that incessant kinesis on the carousel of becoming. We have more to say about these theories below in relation to their philosophical background. But the second-rate status granted yet again to things more than legitimates the need for a conversation between archaeology and philosophy.

Returning to Ancient Corinth, we may note a few more points with respect to archaeology and time. First, change can only stand out against a stable background. The seven standing columns that continue to uphold a portion of the architrave above the archaeological site of Ancient Corinth have constituted parts of the peripteral temple now associated with Apollo; they have persisted where others were quarried as stone; they lingered to delimit an estate in Ottoman Corinth; they offered themselves as objects of antiquarian scrutiny and modern Greek heritage. Even as Roman surfaces were buried, the road persisted in form, impacting the orientation of medieval buildings and enduring as the route to the coast, which is said to have remained in use until the earthquake of 1858. Stone columns and buried road surfaces can neither be reduced to a particular moment nor to a protracted portion of a continuum, for they persist as objects amidst change. Second, when one ponders archaeological considerations of time, at root the most basic question pertains to the age or duration of a particular object. How old are the Doric columns and remaining portion of the architrave?

For how long did the form of the Roman road persist? Neither question can be posed without the objects that elicit them, but it is also the case that these objects do not retain unequivocal chronicles of their age: this requires the work of archaeology. We will return below to the issue of how archaeology seeks to answer such questions by explaining such objects in terms of those that do offer a measure of their duration, which is translatable into calendar time. Here we have simply provided some ground for understanding the place of objects in relation to time in archaeology. In order to begin the task of understanding how time is generated on the surface of objects, we will now turn to philosophy.

Here it is appropriate to first say a word about Heidegger and his theory of time. Heidegger is often seen as a champion of dynamic temporality in opposition to stasis, as someone who converts sluggish nouns into active verbs, and as a general advocate of ceaseless historical flux and becoming. After all, his major book is called *Being and Time*, and this title seems to hint at a replacement of the Ancient Greek tradition of motionless being with a more processual conception of reality.[14] In fact, the real situation is quite different.[15] We can see this by contrasting Heidegger's position with that of a true champion of the ever-flowing river of change in philosophy: Bergson, whose ideas reached a new vogue in the late twentieth century through the influence of Deleuze.[16]

Heidegger is often associated with the phrase: "Time is not a sequence of now-points," which is one way he puts it in *Being and Time*. This also sounds like something that Bergson might conceivably have said, given his constant critique of the model of time as a cinematic sequence of frozen, statuesque poses. Nonetheless, if they had ever met and conferred on this point, issuing a joint press release saying that "time is not a sequence of now-points," they would have meant very different things by this phrase. For it turns out that the two have nearly opposite models of time. From the Bergsonian standpoint, of course, one can never really break time down into "nows." Imagine choosing two successive instants of time, as close as you want to make them. For Bergson, something would always happen between these two instants; in fact, there are no instants of time at all. Motion is ongoing and cannot be reconstructed through any series of poses, no matter how tightly we might try to pack them together. One could say the same for Deleuze, or for any other philosopher who makes "becoming" primary. Another good example would be Deleuze's fellow Frenchman Gilbert Simondon, who is gaining in popularity now that his major book is finally available in English.[17]

There are surprisingly ancient roots to this model of time. For although Bergson often has critical things to say about Aristotle, the Aristotelian conception of time is the same as his own on this particular point. The *Physics* is where Aristotle discusses time in greatest depth.[18] He argues there that time is fundamentally a continuum, meaning that one cannot break it up into individual points except "potentially." How many distinct moments are there in the reading or writing of this book? Are there three? Are there a thousand? Or are there a million? For Aristotle it is entirely arbitrary how we decide to cut up this stretch of time, because time does not consist of any definite number of units. Among other things, this is the method he uses to dispose of Zeno's famous paradoxes, in which Achilles can never catch up with the turtle and an arrow can never move towards its target. But there are other continua for Aristotle as well. Space is also a continuum: for example, you cannot say that there are exactly five parts or seven parts of the room in which you are currently sitting, since the room is a single continuous space that can only be carved into parts in a more or less arbitrary way. Becoming, too, is a continuum. No one can slice up the development of an organism into any definite number of parts, although, interestingly, Aristotle adds that this does not mean that all becoming is gradual: the dam bursts *suddenly* after a long build-up of pressure. And finally, number is a continuum for Aristotle. How many numbers are there between 0 and 100? The answer is once again arbitrary, since it depends on how large our intervals of counting are. We can count by integers, halves, tenths, or any increment as large or small as we please.

Yet, crucially enough, Aristotle does not say the same thing about substances, which are the key topic of his *Metaphysics*, and which survive – in heavily modified form – as the real objects of OOO.[19] How many people are in your room right now, yourself included? The real answer is one, two, seven, or some other definite number. We cannot proclaim that some arbitrary number of people are present, in the manner we do when speaking of space, time, or number. This is one crucial way that Aristotle differs from many philosophers of becoming, who also want to absorb what used to be called substance into a continuum as well. They might speak of a "pre-individual" realm as Simondon does, or they might suggest, in the manner of the anthropologist Tim Ingold, that objects such as landscapes are "continually in formation, shaped by concurrent processes – of work and rest, of seasonality, of growth and decomposition, building and ruination, erosion and deposition – that are going on now as they have ever done, and that their rhythmic resonances describe the passage of time."[20] One might venture even further in the manner of Bergson or Karen Barad, saying that the world is carved up into objects only by means of practical activity: by making an "agential cut," in Barad's terminology.[21] Others agree that there is initially a swirling, turbulent whole and that our minds are what cuts things up into parts, as in the early Emmanuel Levinas or the mature work of Jane Bennett.[22] But how is it that our minds are separate enough from this whole to be able to carve it up in the first place? This is a question that such positions cannot really answer. To summarize, Aristotle notes a central duality that later philosophers try to erase: on the one hand reality consists of continua, while on the other there are also chunks, quanta, substances, distinct entities. Aristotle addresses the problem taxonomically, in the sense that he holds certain kinds of things (time, space, number, becoming) to be naturally continua and others (substances) to be naturally chunky.

At any rate, for Bergson it is impossible to break time into instants; time simply cannot be constructed from a series of instantaneous moments, since no such moments exist.[23] Although it is widely assumed that Heidegger is making the same point, he is not. What Heidegger aims to show instead is that any given instant *already* has an ambiguous threefold structure made up of what he does call past, present, and future, but which no longer have the usual temporal sense of these terms. Far from dismissing the model of time as made of moments, he provides a new and fascinating basis for theories of time as made up of frozen poses. "Past" for Heidegger simply means that which is both given to us and partially concealed, that into which we are always already "thrown," as he puts it. "Future" simply refers to the "projection" of possibilities that we humans make upon that past. When the authors of this book first met in a room on the campus of Texas Tech University, they were both thrown into the same situation in the same room, but they were projecting it differently, to use Heidegger's term. The conversation meant different things for the two of them. Texas Tech was Witmore's home institution, while for Harman it was his first-ever visit to Lubbock, Texas; one was host, the other was guest. This factor and many others made the situation very different for the two of them, despite their discussion of a common project. In short, that room on the Texas Tech campus was made up of a shared thrownness but with very different projections. The Heideggerian present is simply the combination of those two aspects, which is why "thrown projection" is another phrase that Heidegger uses to denote the now. Note the significant difference from Bergson here. For Bergson it is impossible to analyze an instant of time; for Heidegger, by contrast, the analysis of instants is the whole point. Orthodox Heideggerians usually assume that the threefold instant is somehow the "ground" for time in the usual sense of flowing alteration, but Heidegger never actually shows us how such a transition can occur. Although Heidegger the person was surely no advocate of a motionless universe, the Heideggerian *philosophy* never actually does the work of taking us outside the ambiguous threefold instant and establishing how it leads to change. If the universe were simply halted in its tracks and never altered again, the Heideggerian analysis of time would still be operative, whereas for Bergson such a thought experiment would be nonsensical and absurd. Historically speaking, Heidegger can be linked with the polar opposite of Bergsonian temporality: an appropriately discontinuous and heterogeneous group of thinkers belonging to the so-called "occasionalist" tradition, which originated in medieval Islam before returning in force in seventeenth-century Europe.[24] It originated around the year 900 CE in Basra, in the thought of al-Ash'ari. The powerful Ash'arite theological tradition followed directly in his wake, and included the better-known Persian figure al-Ghazali (known as Algazelus or Algazel in Europe). This school of thought affirmed two central doctrines. The first was that God is not just the only creator in the universe, but the only causal agent at all. Although it appears that fire burns cotton, the meeting of these two materials is really just the "occasion" for God to burn cotton. This notion never caught on in medieval Europe, no doubt because of the serious consequences that follow for human free will and the corresponding rewards or punishments in the afterlife; the point awakened debate in Islam as well, but the Ash'arites managed to hold their own or even prevail in that controversy. The second, related doctrine ingeniously held that one moment of time also has no causal link with the next, so that a continuous re-creation of the universe by God is needed in each instant.

With the seventeenth century the hour of occasionalism finally dawned in Europe.[25] The Cartesian thinker Nicolas Malebranche is usually the key European name listed under the occasionalist heading.[26] But traces of God as an all-powerful causal agent are ubiquitous in early modern European thought, including in such central figures as René Descartes, Baruch Spinoza, G.W. Leibniz, and George Berkeley.[27] For a long time thereafter this current of thought lost all respectability in European philosophy, and it would be easy to assume that this was due primarily to Enlightenment

skepticism regarding the very existence of God, let alone his purported causal monopoly on all events in the world. But in a sense
occasionalism has never left us. What happened was that God's
causal monopoly was simply converted into a monopoly of the
human mind. For David Hume, causation is something that appears
only in experience and cannot be projected beyond its givenness
to us, through "habit" formed from "customary conjunction."[28]
Immanuel Kant continued along these lines, treating causality as
nothing more than a category of the human understanding, so that
we cannot speak about causal relations in the hidden world of the
thing-in-itself.[29]

Occasionalism might still have been left to some dusty volume
of the history of philosophy, if not for its astonishing return in the
twentieth century. The key figure here is Alfred North Whitehead,
who revived *both* of the central doctrines of occasionalism at the
heart of his own philosophical system.[30] Whitehead boldly rejected
Kant's assumption that the thought–world relation is the only one
we can speak about clearly; for Whitehead the thought–world
duality is just one relation, no different in kind from the causal
impact between inanimate beings. This is already enough to make
him the rare non-Kantian among the post-Kantians. Yet Whitehead
took even more radical steps in the occasionalist direction. For one
thing, he also rejected direct causal influence, claiming that one
entity can only "prehend" (relate to) another through God, who
Whitehead conceived as the repository of all "eternal objects"
(roughly, universal qualities). For someone to perceive someone
else's purple shirt, for instance, it is necessary to pass through God,
who contains the eternal object "purple"; nothing can interact
directly with anything else. But Whitehead was also an occasionalist on the question of time. Note that his term for things that exist,
"actual entities," is doubled with what he treats as a synonymous
phrase: "actual occasions." Much like the original occasionalists, Whitehead insists that entities cannot "become," since they
instantaneously "perish" instead, and must be replaced by close
successors that are different things altogether, even if very similar
ones. There is little point worrying about the immortality of the
soul, since each of us already dies every microsecond, or whatever
we choose to call each isolated frame of time. Unfortunate confusion arises from the fact that Whitehead is widely and rightly called
a "process philosopher." After all, the word "process" certainly
sounds a lot like "becoming."[31] Doesn't this put Whitehead on the
same side of the fence as Bergson and Deleuze, as a philosopher of
radical flux? Not at all. Recall that for Bergson, to speak of time

in terms of discrete cinematic frames is outright forbidden. But Whitehead – like Heidegger, in Harman's reading – speaks of time precisely as consisting of moments. This is why the present-day tendency to link Whitehead with Deleuze – even by as formidable a reader of Whitehead as Isabelle Stengers – is off target.[32] Thomas Nail is a rare exception among the present-day champions of flux, one who openly recognizes that Whitehead is not his ally.[33] When it comes to the philosophy of time, Whitehead and Heidegger belong with the occasionalists in opposition to the Bergsonian school, which can ultimately be traced to the pre-Socratic philosopher Heraclitus, with his famous maxim that no one can step in the same river twice.

Enter Latour, who along with his close colleague Stengers is one of today's great admirers of Whitehead. Latour like Whitehead incorporates both aspects of classical occasionalism into his philosophy, though with an important twist as concerns the first. This pertains to the topic of causation, which the classical occasionalists and Whitehead all route through God. Although Latour is a practicing Catholic who defends religion openly, he foregoes any divine solution to the problem of causal relations.[34] For this reason he can be called the first "secular occasionalist" in the history of philosophy, whatever his religious commitments.[35] In an especially brilliant chapter of his book *Pandora's Hope*, Latour examines the case of Frédéric Joliot-Curie, son-in-law of Marie and Pierre Curie. The question at hand is what possible connection there could be between politics and neutrons, especially since neutrons were discovered by James Chadwick only in 1932. In a French context, at least, it was Joliot who first insisted on the crucial link between them, in his ultimately failed effort to gain funding for a French atomic bomb project.[36] This does leave open the question of how Joliot can touch both neutrons and politics if they cannot touch each other, thereby leading to a possible infinite regress. But the important point is that Latour is the first to enable the possibility of *local* indirect causation not mediated by either God or the human mind, a topic that OOO has pursued with vigor.[37]

Latour is no less an occasionalist when it comes to the doctrine of time. Just as Whitehead tells us that entities perish instantly without ever really becoming, Latour also declares that everything happens only once, in one time and one place only.[38] This idea is no stray artifact of Latour's early career. Even in the 2013 *An Inquiry Into Modes of Existence*, the masterwork of his later period, Latour introduces as one of his fifteen modes "[REP]" (or "reproduction"): the radically anti-Bergsonian principle that everything must be brought back into existence continuously.[39] In some sense you the reader may be the "same" person from infancy through childhood through maturity and old age, but only in a derivative, occasionalist sense: throughout your life you are actually perishing over and over again, and it would take some external observer to trace various similarities across your lived trajectory as a whole, even if you yourself act as that observer. To summarize, Latour could hardly be more of an occasionalist than he already is; he is as anti-Bergsonian and anti-Deleuzean as one can be. Perhaps someone could establish an important debt on the part of Latourian Actor–Network Theory (ANT) to the "rhizomes" of Deleuze and Félix Guattari's *Anti-Oedipus*, but that debt could have nothing to do with the concept of time, on which Latour and Deleuze are diametrically opposed.[40] In passing we should also note that while Whitehead and Latour accept both major aspects of classical occasionalism, OOO endorses only one of them.[41] As concerns causality, Harman endorses what he calls "vicarious causation" and holds that occasionalism was rather profound in discovering a problem with direct causal relations.[42] The same does not hold for time, which OOO does not see as made up of discontinuous and disconnected instants; time is a continuum, just as it is for both Aristotle and Bergson. Yet OOO inclines towards Aristotle, insofar as it endorses the existence of discrete individuals that remain partly robust in the face of temporal change. For Bergson, by contrast, individual objects are highly derivative, being generated primarily by human practical needs.

Most archaeologically inclined readers will no doubt be familiar with how Latour challenged the modern conception of linear time, in which the past was dramatically separated from us by Copernican revolutions and epistemic ruptures. By contrast with time as a succession of distinct eras where the past is posited as outside the present, he famously asserts in *We Have Never Been Modern* that "it is the sorting that makes the times, not the times that make the sorting."[43] Thus, for Latour, what we call time is not an empty Newtonian container moving forward with regularity regardless of what happens inside it. Instead, time is produced by the creation of an "asymmetry." Time happens, for instance, when Antoine Lavoisier shows that water is not an indivisible element, but a compound made up of hydrogen and oxygen combined in fixed proportions of two to one. The history of France looks very different after the Revolution than it did before, or after de Gaulle's triumphant re-entry into Paris following the dark years of Nazi occupation. But this does not imply total irreversibility;

purportedly extinct forms often return to haunt us, long after being declared dead and buried. For the modern history of science, Louis Pasteur put a permanent end to the misguided idea of the "spontaneous generation" of bacteria inside sealed flasks. But this same idea, now dismissed as reactionary superstition, could well make a comeback in connection with prebiotics, as Latour himself has noted.[44] There are other ways in which ancient things can persist amidst their supposed disappearance. Latour and Emilie Hermant's book *Paris, Invisible City* gives the eye-opening example of the Rue Saint-André des Arts on the Left Bank in Paris, which follows the same curve as the Neolithic path along the edge of the former marshes.[45] Of course, Paris is saturated by such examples. The Rue Saint-Jacques follows the *cardo maximus* of Lutetia, the old Roman town. Le Petit-Pont crosses the Seine at precisely the same site as the Roman bridge. The streets of the Latin Quarter and the Île de la Cité, today the 5th and 4th Arrondissements, hold memories of the ancient street grid as well as the ramparts, along with the shape of the forum and the amphitheater. Likewise, a building inhabits many different environments in its history, or even different civilizations if it is an especially durable building – such as the structure known as the Hagia Sophia in Constantinople and later the Aya Sofia in Istanbul, which has passed from church, to mosque, to museum, and now back to functioning mosque. By analogy, think of the Egyptian spring festival that began as the Shemu in Pharaonic times, which continued to be held by Coptic Christians on the day after their Orthodox Easter, and which even now is a national holiday in majority-Muslim contemporary Egypt. Schopenhauer says somewhere that we should never visit sites from our own past: they will always be disappointing, because what we are really nostalgic for is a time rather than a place. But is this really true? Visiting sites from one's own past, or even humanity's past, is rarely disappointing even if all the people are gone or dead, or still there but transformed in important ways.

The Acropolis is one such example: one might feel closer than ever to Ancient Greek philosophy when standing on the Acropolis. One can also still visit the house in Virginia where the Confederate general Stonewall Jackson died. At least in the late 1990s (and perhaps still today) the Virginia tour guide there would tell visitors: "Here is your connection to the past: this ticking clock is the same one that was next to Jackson's bed when he died." It is a remarkable experience to hear this clock, the last sound the notorious general heard on earth. And in Cairo there is the tourist attraction El Fishawy Café, which claims to have been in continuous twenty-four-hour operation since the time of Napoleon. Still, that the Acropolis stands today unencumbered by those things that accumulated there in post-Classical eras speaks to how the wreckage of the past piles up and is redistributed. In the case of the Acropolis, for example, one past advanced at the expense of many others. Its proximities to the Athens of the Classical period result from scouring away what had become of subsequent pasts. On the Acropolis we do not find the seventeenth-century equivalent of philosophy's books: the material things of various succeeding eras (Roman, Byzantine, Venetian, Ottoman, post-independence) were all removed in the nineteenth century without, in many cases, even the most rudimentary catalogue. On the Acropolis it is all Plato. On some level, it is true that having all Plato is not such a bad thing: after all, Whitehead did describe philosophy as a series of footnotes to him.[46] We may or may not agree as to the importance of some of these footnotes, so one question here is who decides which footnotes to carry forward. The sanctioned present state of the Acropolis, which amplifies the proximity of the fifth century BCE, demanded a destructive selectivity, one that has robbed us of those objects that would have stood as our own archaeological footnotes. To frame objects as belonging to a particular past requires that we downplay not only their post-history, but also the complete novelty of the present moment in which we encounter them, for a past never existed in the same way as what becomes of it in our present. Nietzsche penned the motto of those who, through a hatred of greatness within their own age, embrace the monumental conception of the past as "let the dead bury the living."[47]

For those readers who are engaging with this book in the traditional paper format, there is also the longevity of the medium before you: in the form of codices, books usurped scrolls over a protracted period of time, between the first and fourth centuries CE. We can also understand this in terms of composition: paper dates to the beginnings of Imperial China, over two millennia ago, while for example the sans-serif typeface Arial was introduced only in 1982. Again, for Latour, time does not produce this sorting; rather, this sorting produces time. Yet there is no "time" for Latour in the flowing sense of Aristotle or Bergson. For Latour, whose notion of time as asymmetry was probably borrowed from Serres, there is no particular reason to see anything as flowing either backwards or forwards: it's just that a particular asymmetry is created, so that irreversibility is the essence of time.

But here a great deal of caution is needed, since Latour also negatively links the idea of irreversibility with modernity: a period in which time is understood as a unidirectional movement towards either progress or decadence. Against this notion, whirlpools, eddies and countercurrents also make up the turbulent flow of time. This turbulence, in turn, can be linked with Serres' idea of a proliferation of quasi-objects. For Serres, time does not simply pass away, but flows in an astonishingly complex and turbulent manner.[48] Marked by periods of calm, thunderous accelerations, and countercurrents and eddies, time "percolates."[49] What might be very distant in linear time can be quite proximate from the standpoint of percolating time. Serres offers the image of an ironed and perfectly flattened handkerchief:

> You can see in it certain fixed distances and proximities. If you sketch a circle in one area, you can mark out nearby points and measure far-off distances. Then take the same handkerchief and crumple it, by putting it in your pocket. Two distant points suddenly are close, even superimposed. If, further, you tear it in certain places, two points that were close can become very distant.[50]

This crumpled and torn manifestation is analogous to Paris, the house where Stonewall Jackson died, or the Athenian Acropolis. Archaeologists work with and contribute to such cases in their practice. Still, across all these examples, percolating time does not manifest itself as a true anachronism, such as would happen with placing anything from a codex to a MacBook Pro in Plato's Athens.

Returning to Heidegger, we can clarify the situation in his case by contrasting him briefly with two of his most important historical neighbors: his former teacher Edmund Husserl (founder of phenomenology) and his later admirer Jacques Derrida (founder of deconstruction). Husserl has his own theory of time, as explained in his marvelous work *The Phenomenology of Internal Time-Consciousness* – edited for publication by the young Heidegger, of all people.[51] Husserl's primary motivation in this work was to push beyond the theory of time of his own mentor, the brilliant Austrian philosopher Franz Brentano, who was also the one-time teacher of Sigmund Freud. Brentano's model of time was transmitted mostly in oral form, but showed the clear tendency to think of time as consisting only in the "now," with past moments existing only insofar as they somehow leave traces in it. Husserl was more on the Bergsonian side of this debate, offering a theory in which the now also consists of a "retention" of the past and a "protention" of the future. Indeed, Husserl's credentials as a thinker of continuous time are unimpeachable, as recognized even by his critic Derrida.[52]

But, in an important sense, Derrida gets both Husserl and

Heidegger wrong when it comes to time. Let's begin with Husserl.
The main difference between him and his teacher Brentano, the
very insight that makes full-blown phenomenology possible at all,
is his discovery that experience consists of *objects* rather than *contents*. For Brentano, every mental act aims at certain experienced
contents. Imagine that you are watching a horse running in a field.
At any given point in time, you are seeing the horse from some particular angle and distance, with the sunlight reflecting off its coat in
one specific way and no other. From the Brentanian standpoint the
horse is effectively a "bundle of qualities" in the manner of Hume
and British Empiricism. The horse as an "object" is nothing more
than a series of family resemblances that remain invariant across
time: the horse is always chestnut-colored, and always has a tail, but
each momentary view of the horse is primarily a matter of detailed
content that is constantly changing. This is why Brentano can think
of time only in terms of a "now"; the horse is defined solely by all
of its properties *right now*. The radical step taken by phenomenology is to say that the horse-object precedes the horse-content. The
horse is primary; it has certain core qualities that can never change
without our ceasing to recognize it as this horse. On top of that it
has many qualities that we might call accidental: it does not matter
if the horse stops reflecting the sun in exactly the way it does now,
because you the viewer still see the same horse, regardless of these
inessential details. The phenomenological analysis of a horse is supposed to strip away all these peripheral, shifting features in order to
get at the essence of the thing (or *eidos*, as OOO will call it, since
essence turns out to be something different). It is a lot like Aristotle's
distinction between essential and accidental, but applied purely to
the phenomenal realm rather than the world of real substances.

Returning to Derrida's assessment of the situation, he claims
that Husserl – notwithstanding his solid Bergsonian credentials as
a philosopher of constant change – remains stuck in the "now,"
despite adding "retention" and "protention" to his account of time.
But this is not the case. The fact that Husserl analyzes the "now"
of time does not mean that it is a now of isolated, cinematic frames
as with the occasionalist tradition. Instead, Husserl's now is the
so-called "specious present," referring to our own sense of the now
as we go about living: not a single instant, but a rather small duration that many researchers have tried to measure more precisely in
various psychological experiments, though their conclusions have
varied widely.[53] In other words, for Husserl it is already the case
that time is something generated by objects, which endure for a
greater or lesser stretch but are always displaying different surface-

properties as they move, or as we move while looking at them. Derrida cannot concede this point due to his more general polemic against identity, so that for him it is already naive to talk about enduring objects of experience. Since Derrida opposes "difference" to identity, he thinks that a thing's difference from its own self is all that is needed to generate time. Yet there are two problems with this assumption: (a) Husserl is right about the existence of durable objects of experience, which are found at the heart of his theory of time; (b) Derridean difference (or *différance*, as he prefers to spell it) is not yet the same thing as time. The famous "square circle" of logicians, for instance, cannot possibly be identical with itself, since it has contradictory properties, yet that does not mean that the square circle is already a case of flux. Even Bergson saw clearly that contradiction and flux are not the same thing. The same point was made more recently, with different motivations, by Quentin Meillassoux, who notes that "it is profoundly inaccurate to associate the thesis of real contradiction with the thesis of sovereign flux."[54] After all, if something is contradictory – like the square circle – then it is contradictory in a specific way rather than all ways: it is both square and circular at the same time, not both red and green, or both good and evil at the same time and in the same respect. But this means that the square circle never changes at all; it always contradicts itself in exactly the same way. The same holds for all imagined non-self-identical things.

Derrida's mistake with respect to Heidegger is similar, despite all the differences between Heidegger and his teacher. But in this case, unlike the first, Derrida is wrong because he thinks that he and Heidegger agree. The key passage occurs in *Of Grammatology*: "Heidegger's insistence on noting that being [*Sein*] is produced as history only through the logos, and is nothing outside it, the difference between being [*Sein*] and the entity [*Seiendes*] – all this clearly indicates that there is nothing outside the signifier, and that, in the last instance, the difference between signified and signifier is *nothing*."[55] Here Derrida thinks he is speaking about Heidegger, though he is really projecting his own views onto the German philosopher. Heidegger is by no means an opponent of the hidden self-identity of anything: self-identical is precisely what Heideggerian Being is. It withdraws from us, always remaining concealed, and it always remains one and the same Being. It is certainly true that Heidegger has difficulty accounting for individuals within this framework, and in fact he never quite gets there; for him, individual beings or entities are always primarily a matter of appearance. But he does make an important effort to go beyond this limitation, in his late meditations on "the thing."[56] The jug does not exist because it holds wine, but holds wine because it exists, a formula that begins to empower individual entities in the way that they deserve. This means that despite Heidegger's rather Kantian attempt to make time a property of human existence, which he calls *Dasein*, time is only manifest in the ambiguous status of specific beings: the wine jug hides its reality from us ("past") even while reaching out and partly manifesting itself to us in accordance with this or that purpose ("future"). But this means that time for Heidegger is just as object-oriented as it is for Husserl. The main difference is that for Heidegger time is always co-produced between a withdrawn reality and its manifest surface, while for Husserl there is nothing outside the manifest surface. Thus, time unfolds along a different, purely phenomenal axis: the horse that remains one and the same, and the horse that consists in specific qualities at any given moment. OOO sides with Husserl on this point, preferring to link Heideggerian temporality with what is usually called "space." This will be discussed further in Chapter 4 below. But what is interesting is that Derrida's model is incompatible with both of the earlier figures, precisely because he disregards the possibility of both kinds of objects: the Heideggerian sort that hides and only reveals hints of itself, and the Husserlian object that never hides but only slips in and out of various accidental profiles even while remaining one and the same thing.

There is an understandable tendency to speak of time and space in the same breath, as if the two taken together made up a unique framework for the whole of the cosmos. Throughout both Western and Eastern philosophy we can find various meditations on the two, about whether they are real or illusory, and related issues. In recent Western science, under the influence of Albert Einstein and Hermann Minkowski, as well as in more recent analytic philosophers such as Ted Sider, there have been attempts to collapse time and space into a single, four-dimensional "space-time."[57] In a sense, Aristotle might have been tempted to go along with this modern conception, given that he treats both time and space as arbitrarily divisible continua, thereby making them basically commensurable. But OOO argues the contrary. For reasons to be explained in Chapter 4, the OOO model recognizes two kinds of objects and two kinds of qualities, meaning that there are four possible types of object–quality pair.[58] Two of these four are identified with time and space, and this has a pair of consequences. First, it entails that time and space are basically *incommensurable* (since they occur along different axes of reality) and thus cannot be collapsed into a single continuum; indeed space for OOO is not a continuum at all, but is filled with holes. Second, it means that there are still two unnamed spaces on the grid for other cosmic frameworks that are not usually mentioned in the same breath as time and space. OOO calls these "essence" and "eidos," another topic left for Chapter 4. But rather than speaking of four-dimensional space-time, we should speak instead of a four-dimensional conclave of time, space, essence, and eidos.[59] In all of these cases, even as concerns time, the object is central.

To skip ahead a bit, OOO ends up agreeing with Husserl that time is something unfolding entirely on the surface of reality, though for Husserl this is because the surface is all there is: no "deep" layer of reality exists, so that anything can in principle be the object of an adequate mental act that directly beholds it. Yet for OOO as for Heidegger, there is a depth to reality that can never adequately be translated into something directly accessible. This has led to criticism of OOO by certain Derrideans. Peter Gratton has said, both on his blog and in his book on Speculative Realism, that OOO remains stuck in the most traditional concept of time insofar as it reduces time to an epiphenomenon, a step that he likens to the Platonic tradition.[60] But Gratton knows perfectly well that the destructibility of objects is central to OOO; furthermore, his complaint quickly boomerangs back onto his own position. In other words, although Gratton says that OOO reduces time to an epiphenomenon, that is exactly what he and his model Derrida do. Unlike OOO, that is, they simply do not think there is anything "deeper" by comparison with which time would be superficial. Instead they think that time (which they wrongly equate with difference) is all that there is, and this is the only sense in which their model would not be epiphenomenal. Stated differently, time is simply phenomenal for them, even if they would drop the prefix "epi-." It is OOO rather than Derrida which adds something that is not epiphenomenal, though without calling it time.

Aside from all that, there is nothing wrong with locating time on the surface of reality, since the surface of the cosmos is just as real as anything else. In fact, the surface for OOO is the only place where anything can ever happen, given that the depth of things is too deep ever to affect or be affected by anything else – in opposition to Deleuze, who speaks only of "sterile surface-effects" and treats the deeper virtual as the place where everything occurs.[61] We can even speak in this sense of a "revenge of the surface," which OOO has often done when speaking of Heidegger, the media theorist Marshall McLuhan, and the pivotal art critic

Clement Greenberg.[62] All three figures are primarily theorists of *depth*.

For Heidegger, the present-at-hand phenomena are completely superficial, and what really matters is Being as that which *withdraws* from presence. For McLuhan, "the medium is the message," meaning all that counts is the background condition in which we find ourselves at any moment. The content of good or bad television shows is irrelevant compared to the effect of the medium of television itself.[63] He says in his famous *Playboy* magazine interview that the content of any medium is of no more significance than the stenciling on the case of an atomic bomb.[64] For Greenberg, academic art is art that is unaware of its medium, which is something McLuhan could also have said, or even Heidegger for that matter. Greenberg discusses the point in an important late lecture in Sydney, where he defines academic art as "art that takes its medium for granted."[65] It is hard to imagine a more McLuhanian phrase than this.

Nonetheless, all three authors end up strangely reliant on the derided surface, since it is the only place where change can occur. For Heidegger, the withdrawal of Being always remains what it is, so that nothing can happen there, and whatever occurs must be a matter of Being revealing itself to *Dasein* in specific historical configurations. For McLuhan, media in their own right simply persist as powerful backgrounds and change only because of the side effects they produce, which can happen in just two basic ways: reversal and retrieval, both of which play out exclusively on the level of the content that he otherwise tries to downplay.[66] In the case of retrieval, in which a now dead medium is revived by some "artist," the situation is even under direct human control. For even if we cannot avoid the effects of hidden background media on us, we do have an extensive role to play in the retrieval or invention of new media, which is why Raymond Williams and the Birmingham School are wrong to accuse McLuhan of "technological determinism."[67] As for Greenberg, who claims to despise pictorial content and treats it as a form of mere "literary anecdote," even the flat canvas background of modern painting is not enough.[68] After all, the task of the modern artist is to signal awareness of the hidden deep background through various indications on the surface, whether in the manner of Picasso, Braque, Mondrian, Miró, or Pollock.

If the background is withdrawn or absent, as some would say, then there is no point in speaking about it at all. This was already the German Idealist argument against Kant: since Kant *speaks* about the hidden thing-in-itself, then it is not really hidden after all; the thing-in-itself is merely a special case of what appears. The long tradition of Hegelian philosophy (including its politicized heir the Frankfurt School) hinges on this very point. What it misses is that we can also have a sense of the background that is *indirect*: there are ways that the absent signals itself within the sphere of presence. The complaint is often made that this amounts to nothing more than a "negative theology," one that enables nothing but empty poetic fancies about the absent. But to say this is to assume in advance that direct access is the only kind of access there is, so that the only alternative would be empty gesticulation. In the celebrated words of the early Ludwig Wittgenstein: "Whereof one cannot speak, thereof one must be silent."[69] But these oft-quoted words display a premature triumphalism. For we frequently speak of things indirectly without being able to state them directly in discursive prose form, the latter being the means used by every form of knowledge.[70] We gain indirect access to things through metaphor, for example: there is no way to translate Homer's "wine-dark sea" into a literal comparison of colors. We do it through rhetoric, as in Aristotle's example that "this man has been three times crowned with laurel," which does not have the same effect as its literal equivalent: "this man has won three times at the Olympic games."[71] We even do it with names: "Roman Corinth" does not refer to any given bundle of definite properties, but points to Roman Corinth even if everything we thought we knew about it was wrong, as shown by Saul Kripke's influential theory of naming.[72] This sort of indirect discourse is typical of the humanities, and admittedly this means that these fields run the risk of pretension or inexactitude in a way the hard sciences do not. It does not follow that indirect access to the real is nothing but empty gesticulation; there is no philosophy, for instance, without a built-in element of Socratic ignorance. Latour saw this in his own way, with his powerful maxim that there is "no transport without transformation."[73] Stated differently, reality is never fully commensurable with any of our models of it, whether they be linguistic or mathematical.

We have been speaking about the way in which incidents on the surface of reality are often able to lead to changes in its depths. A possible term for this would be "retroactivity," which provides us with yet another model for a nonlinear sort of time. But here we need to distinguish between critical and positive uses of the term. The best example of the critical kind can be found in Chapter 5 of

Latour's book *Pandora's Hope*, which asks the question "where were microbes before Pasteur?"[74] A scientific realist would say that microbes always existed and then were simply discovered at last by Pasteur in 1864. But Latour's response is to say "*after 1864* the microbes had been there all along" (this is one of the places where he closely resembles Quentin Meillassoux's "correlationist").[75] Latour's gesture here amounts to a straightforwardly anti-realist version of retroactivity, however complex his relation to realism may be in other respects. But there is another sense of retroactivity, one in which thought can modify the past decisively without seeming to summon it *ex nihilo*. Such a case is found in the French philosopher Alain Badiou's theory of "events," which for him are happenings that break with any given mediocre situation and put us in contact with a "truth" that exceeds all situations. Since Badiou is on the hard Left politically, for him revolution and communism are typical cases of political truth. Yet what is most interesting in Badiou's account is that a given occurrence is not *inherently* either evental or non-evental. This can only be determined through the "fidelity" of a subject who ratifies a past incident as an event. For instance, the Egyptian Revolution of 2011 (which Harman witnessed in person) looks now to have been largely a failure. But from a Badiouian standpoint, the Arab Spring would still count as an event if an ongoing group of Egyptian activists, today, live in remembrance of it while awaiting their next opportunity. This sort of retroactivity is more mind-independent than Latour's, since it involves a radical change of status for the past without positing its radical creation by human thought. There are even examples from science itself. Thomas Kuhn asks whether Max Planck really discovered quantum theory in 1900 with his solution of the black-body radiation problem.[76] While it might seem so at first, Kuhn thinks that the discovery of 1900 occurred only retroactively, from the standpoint of 1909. For at the time of his initial discovery, Planck thought of the smallest units of energy in his theory only as convenient mental subdivisions, not as actual physical quanta. But after taking on board some criticisms of his work made by Albert Einstein and Paul Ehrenfest in 1906, Planck recognized by 1909 that the quanta had to be genuine units of reality. In Kuhn's words:

> After those alterations, Planck's argument was both radically different and very much the same. Mathematically it was virtually unchanged, with the result that it has been standard for years to read

Planck's 1900 paper as presenting the subsequent modern [quantum theory] argument. But physically, the entities to which the derivation refers are very different.[77]

This too is an example of retroactivity in the more positive sense. Planck's 1900 paper looked at the time (even to Planck himself) like a clever solution to an outstanding problem, but not like some sort of world-historic discovery. Only from the standpoint of 1909 was 1900 revealed to have been a revolutionary year in physics: not according to the usual picture of a great genius needing nine years to defeat professional resistance, but in the more interesting sense that the very genius in question needed nine years to recognize he had done something ingenious in the first place.

This retroactive aspect of time brings us back to the theme of objects, though in an indirect way. For it turns out that one of the features of real objects more generally is their ability to have retroactive effects on their own parts. Manuel DeLanda offers some interesting criteria for what constitutes a real assemblage, which is the Deleuzean-sounding term he uses for "object."[78] One of DeLanda's central concerns is to defend the philosophical notion of "emergence," meaning cases in which something is "more than the sum of its parts," to use a familiar phrase.[79] Water cannot be reduced to a sum total of the properties of hydrogen and oxygen, since both of the latter are gases that fuel fire, while water itself is a liquid that extinguishes it. Even if advanced quantum chemistry enables us to "predict" the properties of water from those of its two ingredients, the point is that water (however predictable) is something over and above its ingredients added together. In DeLanda's terminology, water is not subject to micro-reduction (OOO's "undermining"). Conversely, we cannot understand water as nothing more than a sum total of uses or relations, since water can change its relations or (at least in a thought-experiment) be removed from relations with other entities altogether, while still remaining the same water that it is. Stated in the language of DeLanda, water is not subject to macro-reduction (OOO's "overmining"). One consequence of the fact that water cannot be undermined is that it can actually exert downward force on its components, or even replace them with new ones, which might be easier to see in the case of social objects: a city relies on its subordinate pieces, but can also change or replace them.

A special case of emergence is found in what Lynn Margulis calls "endosymbiosis," in which two previously independent organisms enter into physical union.[80] According to her theory, this is actually the major mechanism of biological evolution, rather than the slow drift of genes in a population due to natural selection. Harman applied this theory to historical objects in his book *Immaterialism*, taking as his case study the Dutch East India Company.[81] This was partly in response to the philosopher G.W. Leibniz, who once wrote to Antoine Arnauld that the officers of the Dutch East India Company taken together could not possibly be a real thing.[82] What *Immaterialism* tried to show, contra both Leibniz and Actor–Network Theory, is that not all actions and passions of the Company belong on the same footing. Many incidents in its history, including some of its noisiest battles and commercial transactions, were of no significance at all to the internal structure of the Company itself. According to the argument of the book, there turn out to have been just a half-dozen or so "symbioses" with other objects that transformed the Company irreversibly, somewhat in the spirit of Latourian asymmetry.

Before closing, we should return to the question of what value object-oriented ontology might hold for archaeology, and vice versa. In the present book we find common ground – against the notion of time as a container – in the proposition that objects generate time. We believe that OOO provides productive avenues for understanding how time arises from the surface of objects. Still, there is far more to the conversation. Archaeology is bizarre.[83] It is composed of diverse fields: genetics and art history, physics and sociology, mathematics and epigraphy, economics and ethnography. Given this heterogeneity, what do archaeologists hold in common? Objects, we submit, are the common ground of archaeology, and this is a key attribute of OOO, which is why the authors came together to write this book in the first place. Of course, not all archaeologists would agree with this approach.

Many practitioners continue to hold to a definition of archaeology as the study of the human past through its material remains. For us and others, this definition points to why the field has long been estranged from its empirical grounds. When seen solely as intermediaries to what was, the objects of archaeology can never be plainly what they are. If archaeology is the study of what has become of the past in the present – with an aim to learn more about these things and what they suggest concerning their pasts – then it must concern itself with far more than the human. Archaeology deals as much with unstable slopes and buried wall forms, nitrogen-fixing bacteria and olive wood, wine residues and sealed amphorae as it does with historical objects like an Argive citizen, Roman soldier, or Ottoman child. There has been a tendency to regard the

nonhuman object interlocutors of archaeology with embarrass-
ment, and to understand them only in terms of their relation to the
human.[84] In this respect, archaeology runs the risk of a crisis of
identity between science and humanity – it wavers between the "I"
and the "it." Good philosophy helps break this cycle.

Another species of this cycle is the old dialectic of a culture of
presence asserting itself against a culture of the imagination. Upon
this, archaeology also continues to turn.[85] Fundamental to so much
of the discipline's self-identity is its emphasis on a practical set
of relations with things, and rightly so. The differences between
cutting turf or defining a feature and writing about these things
are legion. However, such differences are often evoked in terms
of the old, overdramatized struggle of practice and theory, which
– much like the separation of a purified past from the present
– needs to be put to rest once and for all. As OOO has long contended, both theory and practice equally tend to caricature things.
And here it should be emphasized that ideas, imaginations, values,
psycho-political commitments are also objects, no more and no less
important than temple columns or buried road surfaces.

We may echo Latour's point that "philosophy is the calisthen-
ics necessary to be as subtle as the case at hand."[86] In the case of
archaeology, this requires imagination and invention. If an engagement with philosophy helps keep one lucid, and OOO happens to
shed light on a number of issues that archaeologists and philosophers currently face in common, then thinking through archaeology
in terms of how objects generate time also provides precisely the
kind of friction that good philosophy demands.[87]

2

The Antiquity of Time: Objects Greek

Christopher Witmore

Without archaeology, at least for those curious enough to question the written traditions, the broader durations of humanity and the emergence, stability, and transformation of its objects would have remained shrouded in a thick fog.[1] For over two hundred years modern archaeology has labored in the shadows of history, gauging distances and bringing form to previously opaque depths. With this came a taxonomic definition of archaeology's purpose and domain as the study of the human past, with the additional and necessary caveat of working, unlike talkative history, almost exclusively with non-textual material remains. Yet taxonomic distinctions would prove superficial. Pasts were always situated over yonder, across a distance maintained by a linear approach to history with its succession of eras framed by decisive events, and it was through what had remained, things treated as intermediaries to what was, that those pasts were assessed.[2] Indeed, what so many archaeologists regarded as their empirical domain, the material past, was also history's domain: for insofar as both fields have been concerned, artifacts, remnants, vestiges, by their very definition, point to something outside of themselves. For so many archaeologists – albeit from a position among the lower echelons in a hierarchy of value where the written word reigned supreme – that "something outside" was often assumed to be fundamentally historical.[3] Thus, for two hundred years archaeology has been left by and large with a definition of those remains, those relics, as subsidiary to the written past over which history holds the monopoly. *This past* is understood here not only as a continuous narrative record of successive human events, but also as the lived actions that generated what remains. Thus, what is confronted by the archaeologist in the present was held to exist as a consequence of the former, where the past is framed in the perfect tense as something that is completed.[4] The past was and continues to be confused with this History, and archaeology helped make it so.

Now that much of the haze seems to have lifted over large portions of the expanse of human existence, in both the cartographic and chronographic sense, now that taxonomic definitions of archaeology's objects have fallen by the wayside with respect to history, things, with all their strange (metaphysical) quirks, appear to be making new demands. Or to put it another way, their persistent and taken-for-granted realities seem to have acquired a new relevance.[5] Yet such a melodramatic assessment misses a more fundamental point: by always relegating things to the role of intermediaries to a past that is elsewhere, archaeologists maintained for themselves the rather enigmatic position of dealing with their "sources" here in the present.[6] Because what archaeologists did and that with which they engaged existed in opposition to what they claimed to be doing – articulating a past defined by its finitude – questions of what archaeology, its objects, and its past actually are (their ontological status) remain vastly unexplored.[7] This book offers some answers to these questions, specifically in a way that recognizes archaeology as an alternative and complement to history.[8] But more generally the aim is to develop a different theory of time, one that arises through a productive and ongoing conversation with object-oriented ontology.[9] Whereas time is often honored with astounding primacy by history and archaeology as an inexorable agent of change, actual things are not cast upon present shores by time's unrelenting waves. This particular form of modern historicism can no longer obscure the true grounds of archaeology, which are found above all in things: cyclopean bridges that have endured since the Bronze Age and cart roads given new form in the nineteenth century, stonemasons and ashlar masonry, potters and ancient ceramic forms, soil and rubble walls, along with the rapports, exchanges, and mergers between legion such objects that are generative of time.

The steps this chapter takes towards this purpose are six in number. The first, "Line," plots the journey from an archaeology operating in the shadows of history to an archaeology that, in beginning with things, is poised to generate fresh alternatives to history, at least in the sense of a continuous thread of human events that – although already completed – retain their causality. Second, "Segment(s)" moves along a fourteen-kilometer stretch of road through a valley in Greece in an effort to coax forth a sense of times otherwise. Working through folds and proximities, tears and lacerations, irrespective of the distances gauged along a line, the third section, "Pleats and Rents," offers a *topology* of Mycenae, the citadel of Homeric renown. Fourth, "Things: Contiguities, Symbioses, Emergence" expands from a way of generating associations through what is contiguous to, sharing the insights of OOO, a more lively set of symbioses. Fifth, "Time/Percolation" reconfigures these foregoing objects into a different model of time. Finally, the sixth section, "An Archaeological Paradox," reveals grounds for a positive dialogue with philosophy in shared and mutual speculation along another, no less bewildering path.

A. Line: History, Archaeology, Time

Archaeologists are effects of the times they craft, at least in part. This is as true for our labors today as it was for those initial escapades at the roots of our disciplinary history. By confronting an open question ("How deep is the well of the past?") archaeologists began to make explicit (that is, measurable and comprehensible) what in the wake of biblical certainty had come to be obscured by a thick fog.[10] In this pursuit, loquacious history could only take us so far in the articulation of prehistoric continuities.[11] With its larger loyalties to ruins, reliquiae, and material artifacts, silent prehistory made it possible to cast light into the opaque, potentially bottomless well.[12] Out of these circumstances there developed a diverse toolkit, which included stratigraphy (the coincidence of layers in the soil), typology (the arrangement of mute objects on the basis of common characteristics), and seriation (the sequential sorting of artifacts, and a division of labor geared towards the meticulous definition and burdensome organization of material remains into their various compartments).[13] Lending form to the continuum of the human past, the depth of the well was gauged by the serial ordering of these divisions.

Peripheral to Northern European developments in the early nineteenth century, prehistory came late to Greece. Here history, as understood in the latter half of the same century, proved more obstinate. Captivated by the written traditions, Heinrich Schliemann (that famed magnate turned archaeologist) sought to put what he regarded as historical truth to the marvelous ruins of Mycenae and Tiryns, which stood as proof of the powers that produced them. Yet in ignoring the line drawn between history and myth by the scholarly community, Schliemann merely repeated the familiar shift from the contemplation of ancient texts to the acquisition of evidence in support of them.[14] In the act of searching for the graves of Agamemnon and his companions, he inadvertently removed the cap from the well of Greek prehistory.[15]

Almost immediately, archaeologists in Schliemann's wake would set his follies right, by gauging the depth of this abyss. The length and character of each temporal unit – period and phase, epoch and era – expanded or contracted in step with the idiosyncratic and located labors of practitioners and the introduction of newly devised techniques. Few now recall how much effort Panaiotis Stamatakis, Georg Karo, Antonios Keramopoullos, and Alan Wace put into carefully working out what Schliemann had confused at Mycenae. Few now remember how scholars, in an era prior to radiometric clocks, would, despite the distance, connect the workmanship of Stonehenge to that of Mycenae in hopes of establishing an absolute chronology.[16] Archaeologists would eventually situate the *arche* for the shaft grave burials 250 years before the likely time of Homer's great king; the sarsen stone circle at Stonehenge would predate Mycenae's double ring of slabs by over a millennium. Along a linear course, chronology (as information management towards the definition and measurement of the temporal units) stretched in its proportions, and with it a very particular image of time acquired form.[17]

The past was separated out in myriad ways in accordance with the ongoing definition and refinement of latent realities. National and regional museums developed to hold the material exemplars of various eras and epochs. By arranging art and artifacts within cases, into rooms, and along corridors, late nineteenth-century museums staged a peripatetic itinerary through time. Through the layout of galleries and the organization of holdings, the Greek National Archaeological Museum materialized the historical text, spatialized the continuity and discontinuity of human achievement, and normalized time as a chain of successions for a general public.[18] It simultaneously appropriated the alien other of the ancient past to a museal narrative of national patrimony while maintaining its temporal distance from the present.[19] The National Muses sheltered two visions of the past, for when the size and nature of the displays are taken into consideration not all periods were treated with equal interest. Absent were post-Roman periods, for here the Classical, and what fell on either side, held far more potency.[20]

Accumulation and articulation were counterbalanced by appropriation and alienation. Unique and losable, the spatial loci of the explicit past were both opened to public engagement and severed from everyday experience: shepherds gave up their favorite enclosures, stonemasons relinquished their preferred quarries, inhabitants were evicted from their "ramshackle" dwellings, aristocrats were barred from inscribing their names in hallowed stone. At the Athenian Acropolis, Delphi, Mycenae, Olympia, and Corinth, what had become of their pasts was cordoned off from their present milieux as archaeological sites. Situated within a detached and antecedent domain, their pasts were closed, purified of their mixed, polychronic entanglements, and even severed from the labors that gave rise to them.[21] Nothing else could occur over there, in the past, which made it ripe for "discovery."[22] Ultimately, this discrepancy between self-representation and practice was both to the profession's benefit and detriment.[23] Despite the spatial implications of these separations and estrangements, time (which acquired further shape as a chain of successions) held primacy in the realm of archaeological achievement.

Developments in European (and particularly Scandinavian) pre-history remained at a distance of 2,400 kilometers. Oscar Montelius, Curator of the Museum of National Antiquities in Stockholm from 1868 to 1907, sought to develop a morphology of types akin to biological understandings of species evolution.[24] As the evolution of types, typology stood as an alternative to a sequential time, with its emphasis on what had happened in a given period.[25] In Greece, labors oriented towards the explication of discrete allotments – a life-long pursuit in itself – came to operate within the allotted portion. Even the Northern European tradition would fall back into such a "historicist kind of approach."[26] It almost went without saying in twentieth-century professional circles that archaeologists were defined by their particular period: Aegean prehistory – the Paleolithic, Mesolithic, Neolithic, and Bronze Age – the Early Iron Age – prelude to history – Archaic, Classical, Hellenistic, Roman, Byzantine, and so on.

Fieldwork generated massive amounts of "material" for which practitioners worked out the temporal coordinates of successive periods. Excavate down. Collect from surfaces. Sort out. Write up. The cadence of disciplinary production was maintained by training and routinized procedure. From Olympia to Corinth to Samothrace, excavation volumes and reports documented what had been covered by the veil of detritus and accumulation subsequent to what had been by detailing things "discovered" in map, plan, photograph, and description, with all finds deemed to be of relevance dutifully catalogued.[27] What had become of the past was fixed to temporal coordinates. Following a path blazed by Johann Winckelmann and Eduard Gerhard, descriptive accounts traced the developmental trajectories of architectures, lithics, metals, objects of art, and ceramics in exhaustive detail.[28] By progressing, there was a refinement of labors, instruments, techniques, and narratives; gaps were filled to create an unbroken continuum, a trajectory along which human history was further defined. Following the path of least resistance, time was maintained to be linear, and elevated into an ontology of history.[29] Like beads strung into a rosary, pasts appeared to compartmentalize along this line.[30] Outwardly speaking, ruptures, terminations, and replacements came to delimit each era, which seemed to contain the circumstances for its own existence. Inwardly, demarcations were reinforced by disciplinary boundaries, institutions, and divisions of labor.[31] The past was cordoned off into a distant realm, and archaeology's objects were the *vehicles* used to get to it.[32]

For most, "the adequate explanation of events that flowed naturally from their full description" fell short of past lives and their experiences.[33] The correlation between the sequences generated by archaeologists and a given historical phase was (and remains) always less than straightforward. Apprehended as partial and incomplete, the found objects were nonetheless seen as intermediaries to what had happened in the past. In many eras, the historical leitmotif that "this happened here" continued to prevail as the guideline for how to approach a given site.[34]

It is characteristic of those archaeologists considered to be literate participants in the field of Classics to have worked their way through the relevant books of antiquity before venturing into the field. Against this background, there was tremendous value in projecting those eventful details recorded in ancient literary documents – the Persians obliterated Athens in 480/479 BCE, the Argives destroyed Mycenae in 468 BCE – onto what remained. Repeatedly, historical expectations – where those changes detected in the excavation of a particular site should be explained in terms of such recorded events – proved to be archaeological fallacies, as the differences between found objects, understood as "material culture," and what was inscribed in texts were as often ignored as acknowledged.[35] Anthony Snodgrass called the tendency to equate "archaeological prominence with historical importance" the "positivist fallacy."[36] Such flawed reasoning repeats the association lying behind Schliemann's confusion of what was found in the shaft graves at Mycenae with what was recorded in written traditions. For Snodgrass, the problem was not with history *per se*, but with the wrong kind of history. By this, he was speaking of a history that emphasized moments lived at the expense of what could be gleaned from archaeological objects – "event-oriented history" centered on "man the doer" was "incommensurable" with "true archaeology" which is suggestive of "man the maker."[37] For Snodgrass, archaeology is not history (that is, a *recorded* narrative of events) but that does not mean that archaeology could not shed light on historical processes.[38] Still, the view that history encompassed the totality of the past that is archaeologically explicable (or "that the past that lies outside of recorded history" is, as Laurent Olivier put it, anything other than "historically knowable") was not questioned.[39]

Gradually – though at times abruptly – as the temporal background was rendered sufficiently explicit, archaeological narratives began to zoom in to the level of the quotidian, and zoom out to trace the human adventure within and through the successive compartments at the level of site, region, and beyond. Focused on sites in relation to their encompassing milieu and wider region, the organizational base of landscape projects was spatial.[40] New methods were devised for approaching the countryside, and with them a new range of objects was brought under scrutiny.[41] After initial forays defined by chronological frames (i.e. limited to a particular period: the late Bronze Age, for example), intensive surveys expanded to generate long-term histories in the vein of Fernand Braudel, placing emphasis on durations measured in millennia and medium-term fluctuations in contrast to short-term events.[42] In reaching across the tableau of human life, archaeologists gave primacy to diachronic processes in hopes of understanding changes and durations in settlement, political forms, land use, and the environment over time. As a consequence of a larger loyalty to the multitemporal character of landscape, they fueled research into voids left in between and at the margins: postmedieval archaeology (Frankish, Ottoman, and Venetian) and even the archaeology of the early modern period.[43] In marking out what had been covered, surveyed areas stood out against the white ground of *terra incognita*, thus implicitly pointing to areas of future interest.[44] To some degree, all points in space and time came to hold equal value, though within Greece the present would continue to be regarded as non-archaeological territory.[45]

Through such labors, archaeology (now understood as a cross-disciplinary and collaborative endeavor) achieved a certain sovereignty over the "fourth dimension" of regions and their multiple temporalities. The success of these efforts can be measured in how these achievements are seen as advantageous to other disciplines. Partly as a consequence of having been worked out to a sufficient degree, history expands and enters into where it had always implicitly been.[46] Archaeology, which cleared the fog from where history once dared not go, has become what Shryock and Smail call *paleohistory*.[47] Of course, such a development has as much to do with the discipline of history shedding its own preoccupations (by questioning what counts as the study of history) as it does with occupying new territory.[48] Still, that territory had already been well mapped by archaeologists as essentially historical. From Childe to Renfrew to Hodder to Graeber and Wengrow, by way of far-reaching stories, archaeologists broke old compartments and expanded into broader temporal and spatial domains.[49] Even while archaeologists worked through the dregs left behind, what history passed over due to its incoherence, banality, and erratic partiality, Ian Morris proclaimed what he held to be a self-evident truth: "archaeology is culture history or it is nothing."[50] With the temporal content of the deep past defined for historical inclusion, archaeologists returned to the medium of the past in order to open other possibilities.

It is more than coincidental that when old taxonomic differences between archaeology and history fall away, new distinctions become explicit.[51] In beginning with the background of a separate past, reinforced by a linear and externalized time, the archaeological object could never simply be what it is.[52] These *a priori* frames began to loosen to some degree as new understandings of archaeology's role emerged with respect to the present. At the same time that ethnoarchaeology and middle-range studies were gaining traction as ways to use analogous situations in the present to better understand pasts unseen, unvoiced, and unwritten, practitioners trained within anthropology argued for archaeological studies of the present in itself.[53] Initial forays pressed the issue not in an effort to lay claim to the last domain of the timeline, but to raise the question of what qualifies as an object of archaeological concern.[54] Despite these efforts, it was not enough for the present to lose its taboo status as non-archaeological ground; it was not enough for practitioners to recognize that they engage the past here and now.[55] Since the dawn of prehistory's definition archaeology has excavated, sorted, and measured its things; by modeling its past on the historians' use of the textual record, it prepared the ground for history. Whether they be sealed deposits, burials, or terrace walls, things have always been weighed with the expectation that they speak to a past sealed off in another realm, and thus archaeology held its things to be derivative of something other than themselves.[56] For two centuries, the truth of archaeology's objects remained at a length that it itself had gauged.[57]

What was latent in soil-encased slabs, in buried walls, in forgotten bowls was not human history, not the past that was, but what had become of it, and what had become of it were actual things here in the present.[58] This latency (as Olivier, Bjørnar Olsen, and others have observed) is related more to a species of memory that is involuntary, banal, idiosyncratic, and unique to things.[59] But what is latent cannot be fully encapsulated by memory, either; for memory is but one of many qualities possessed by threshold stones, abandoned road segments, or former tholos tombs, which are in possession of a surplus reality that exceeds *their pasts*. Indeed, the memory these things hold, the erstwhile existence that they stabilize, belongs to them, and their pasts are objects generated out of contact and exchange with thresholds, road fragments, emptied tombs, archaeologists, and myriad other things deployed along the convoluted path of their articulation.[60]

Through tremendous effort, the past (with its now appraised depths as the historical milieu) pivots from the well before us – which draws us to contemplate its anterior extents, separated by well-measured distances – to pasts as orientations, memories, and achievements with us and ahead of us. If these pasts emerge as tentative outcomes of working with and among things, then their heterogeneity increases through a fidelity to the sheer specificities of what remains, while the leeway for creative possibility widens significantly. It is here that another understanding of archaeology and another sense of time are revealed. It is here that a different definition opens for archaeology, which had hitherto been exclusively defined as the study of the human past through its material remains. Archaeology now constitutes the study of things with an aim to generating stories, allegories, lessons, or understandings that are in service to the past, the present, and the future.[61] Archaeology expands from sorting out the time of antiquity to openly working with the sorting that is itself the antiquity of time.[62]

B. Segment(s): From Nafplion to Kazarma 2012

National Road 70 (Ethniki Odos 70; henceforth EO70) runs between the town of Nafplion, a former capital of modern Greece, and the erstwhile sanctuary of Epidaurus, sacred to the hero-healer turned healing-god Asclepios. To traverse the first five kilometers of this route is to pass from a headland, named after a son of Poseidon, of importance as a port for several millennia; over former marshes filled with debris from dismantled Venetian bastions; across open spaces laid out according to nineteenth-century designs for a short-lived capital city; along the foot of the Palamidhi, an uplifted mass of limestone 120-plus million years in the making, crowned by a massive late seventeenth-century fortress; by the old neighborhood of the Pronoia and the myriad shops, restaurants, and apartments of the New Town, an area bustling with traffic, commotion, noise; past roadside soils contaminated with heavy metals, discharged with the exhaust of automobiles burning lead gasoline prior to the 2000 EU ban, or from catalytic converters; past the former Anthos/Kyknos canning plant turned cultural center; past Agios Vlasios, where archaeological excavations in the 1980s unearthed the remains of a Neolithic-to-Early-to-Late Helladic settlement; skirting the northern end of a low limestone ridge, Vouno-Arias; across the canopied plain of Asini, where soil has been turned for four hundred generations in plots formerly unencumbered by water-loving citrus trees; along a portion of road delineated by broken clusters of cypresses; through a patchwork of citrus orchards, olive groves, farm plots and their boundaries, tacit agreements between farmers upheld by berms, fences, or tree lines; among new walled estates, illicit garbage dumps, and borehole wells that tap deep aquifers now partially inundated by seawater; alongside an ascending drainage ravine, below Pirgiotika, a village settled by displaced shepherding families in the late nineteenth century; to a low, olive-studded hill known as Kastrakia, whose apex is crowned with the remains of a 2,400-year-old square tower, enrolled in the 1990s by a local farmer as a stone envelope for a concrete cistern.[63] From the oblique angle permitted by an archaeological perspective, the bewildering diversity of things that gather along this five-kilometer section of road may be considered as what has become of various pasts and apprehended in terms of their longevity. Coextensive with this stretch of road, these things form a polychronic composite of various durations, and from them and their rapports we may gain a different sense of time. To understand this, let us follow along this old road, with its objects (including their encompassing lands), in the course of a journey undertaken by an archaeologist a decade ago.

Beyond Kastrakia, the road to Epidaurus passes through an area known as Asprovrisi. Dispersed on either side of its tarmacked course, I encounter derelict longhouses, with their tile roofs and mudbrick superstructures, juxtaposed with new concrete villas. The old and the abandoned crowd the road; set back among agricultural plots, many now planted in olive trees, most neglected, the new and the concrete keep their distance. Along here the asphalt

Kastrakia

road had been recently widened and straightened. A section of
the old paved surface, which followed the wide curve dictated
by gradient, relief, and bedrock, is severed from the linear course
of traffic. From this abandoned arc, the road ascends on a slight
incline towards a low spur of Kakó Tsouroúmi. A few unkempt
agricultural plots lie beyond margins bristling with the forsaken
progeny of those guided flora once nurtured in this valley. Carved
out as terraced surfaces, these plots mark the extent of recent
agrarian efforts to reclaim a few soil-holding creases from the
maquis-covered limestone slopes.

Farther east, past the road to Kandia – now traveled less often
because of improved roads in the south, and increased heavy traffic
associated with aggregate quarries – I take note of how exposed
road scarps on the left are bracketed by more relinquished portions of the former EO70 on the right. The latter relics provide
more than indications of defunct early- to mid-twentieth-century
road design, for this is an old way. Following the path of the
nineteenth-century cart road to Epidaurus, the modern car road
modified the older infrastructure and inherited most of its course.
This pattern of abandonment is repeated a few hundred meters
east. Here, the EO70 passes through a low depression between two
spurs, where there are two more straight roadcuts, and with them
two more severed, oxbow sections of the old road. Casualties to

Trans-European Highway standards, impatient travelers on large tour buses take little notice of arcs of rejected pavement now left to the convenience of the few farmers who still use the abandoned tarmacked surfaces to access their agricultural plots, and to those who dump garbage illegally along their out-of-sight margins.

If the time delays demanded by curvature came to be experienced as excessive from the angle of automobility, then road fragments suggest that a different pace and intensity once characterized movement along these slopes. Immediately on the left, four hundred meters up a ravine in an area known as Galousi or Asprochroma, a bridge of cyclopean construction crosses where the cleft thins in exposed bedrock.[64] Dated to between 1400 and 1200 BCE on the basis of its strange form, with its corbeled arch and abutment of giant stones, over this span the Greek Archaeological Service opened a four-hundred-meter-long pedestrian path by clearing maquis and other overgrowth in 2005.[65] Portions of the ancient road bed were reclaimed. Once again, a Bronze Age roadway upholds the pedestrian traffic of the occasional tourist or trekker.

From this depression the new motorway veers off to Epidaurus. Striking a direct line across the maquis-covered slopes of Vounokorfi, just above the agricultural bottomlands, this new motorway bypasses the remaining stretch of the EO70, severing

The cyclopean bridge at Galousi

any direct link with the villages, churches, monuments, and olive groves it integrates.[66] A break with geography, the motorway jumps from the valley center to the edge and thereby inverts the foreground and background associated with an ancient pattern of movement. It eliminates obstacles and disrupts an iterative experience of those places along the EO70. In moving from the superfluous to the optimal, what was formerly an obligation now comes to be experienced as an option. With accelerated movement to the sanctuary of Asclepios, or to points farther south, the time it takes to travel through the valley is compressed. If the automobile road reduced by five-sixths the time it once took to travel from Nafplion to the sanctuary on foot, then with the new motorway what once required forty-five minutes to an hour to travel by car will now take less than half as long. Though generative of an object of infrastructure, bulldozing straight lines through such diversity has proven to be utterly destructive.[67]

Along here we encounter what might be glossed by that familiar story of improvement through work, of progression measured in speed and efficiency: upgrading farming plots by moving from grains or tobacco to olive trees; the installation of an irrigation system by co-opting an ancient tower. New houses made of concrete are constructed at a distance from a raucous road. The abandoned houses made of mudbrick recall a time when traffic was not comprised of noisy automobiles. Along "improved" roads – straightened, macadamed, smoothed, widened, maintained without potholes – speed increases. Were archaeologists to look here, they might find indications of another story, now equally familiar, of fluctuation – swings in demography, ebbs and flows in agricultural lands or pastoral modes of existence. Were they to attend to present ground, they would confront a profound rupture with an agrarian *modus vivendi* for the majority, a close of agrarian humanity capping off multiple durations within objects and their iterative relations measured in millennia.[68] Local seed and stores, unique cereals and pulses, seasonal variations in the moisture content of different soils, earth worked with hoes, fields furrowed by ox-pulled plow, movement from village to plot or grove and back, such objects and rapports have been all but eliminated from this valley.

From the entrance to the new motorway, the EO70 returns to its old path, upheld by a thinner paved surface with abundant curvature. At the top of the hill, the bare heights of Arachneo appear in the distance. On this mountain, according to the Roman traveler Pausanias, there were altars to Zeus and Hera. Upon these altars,

Kazarma Hill with the bare heights of Arachneo in
the background

farmers sacrificed in times of drought. Ahead the road continues to
turn, with slopes covered in a patchwork of olive groves. Beyond,
in a gulley near the village of Agios Ioannis, just off to the left, is
a second cyclopean bridge, Kazarma.[69] The placement of these
bridges intimates a Bronze Age roadway that avoided incline and
obstacle by following even contours along these hills. Its course
was dictated by slope, bedrock, and drainage. Its compacted surfaces were shored up by terraces of large boulders. What this road
gained in uniform grades it sacrificed in speed between the locales
it connected.

From the gully, the road passes in a tight turn over a ravine
on a single lane bridge and sweeps around the southern foot
of a hill. Covered in ruins and potsherds, this hill is crowned
by what Sir James Frazer, famed author of *The Golden Bough*,
described as "one of the best preserved fortresses of antiquity in
all Peloponnese," and from this the place name for the area is
derived: Kazarma or Kasarmi (perhaps from the Venetian "Casa
di Arma").[70] There, limestone outcrops from the Triassic-Jurassic
support polygonal ramparts, reaching heights of six meters, from
perhaps the fourth century BCE, which in turn substantiate walls
of a much later fortress, one whose precise dates have yet to be
made explicit through sustained archaeological intervention. Not

The Kazarma Fortress

far ahead (some four hundred meters, within the small village of
Agios Ioannis) the remnants of a collapsed Mycenaean tholos
tomb survive on the southern slopes of Kazarma. Exposed to
sun and rain, overgrown with oats and knotgrasses, black mus-
tard and milk thistle, this ruin lies emptied of the burials it once
contained.

Following the path of the old, nineteenth-century carriage road
from Nafplion, the proximity of the EO70 to the line of cyclopean bridges, old citadels, and watchtowers suggests a persistence
and integrity with which shepherds and sheep, pilgrims and yoked
oxen, travelers and their mounts, reckoned over several millennia.
The lay of the land provided an enduring envelope of organization
for the journeys of ancient Argive masons and the black stone of
Argos, legion Argive pilgrims, and later Pausanias, the Antonine-
era author of the *Periegesis Hellados* or *Description of Greece*,
on the straight road from Argos.[71] Known to history, Northern
Europeans, with Pausanias' guidebook in hand, retraced this old
way: Sir William Gell, Edward Dodwell, William Martin Leake,
Puillion de Boblaye, and Ernst Curtius, among others. Frazer, in
writing his exhaustive commentary on his translation of Pausanias'
guidebook (published in 1898 in six volumes), took the high
road from Nafplion, as would archaeologists including Gertrude
Bell and Panayiotis Kavvadias, the excavator of the sanctuary of

Asclepios. Along here they all passed, and through the cascade of
their recorded descriptions runs a mobile image of differences in
this old route, which reveals discrepancies indicative of time.

Agrarian communities from the villages of Agios Ioannis,
Arkadiko, and Giannouleika, those who never participated in
history, also passed along this ancient route. Through their iterative engagements, they detected durations and changes missed
by others. Through their repetitions, they encountered formerly
unseen stones exposed in the course of their labors. In the late
1990s, Yiannis Pikoulas, professor at the University of Volos,
walked through this area and queried villagers in local cafés – are
there more memories of forgotten towers, roads or stones overgrown?[72] Through such work, something of their pasts returns to
history.

The fact that abandoned curves are no longer linked to a route
taken, the fact that cyclopean bridges no longer carry through
traffic, the fact that old towers no longer facilitate observation or
that an erstwhile fortress is composed of strange masonry – all suggest changes and metamorphoses. And yet these suggestions come
about as contrasts to those things/objects which endure, which
persist, which stand stubborn, all the more obvious in the face of
transformation. Indeed, is it not striking that the route of the old
EO70 has managed to deviate so very little from a course, as suggested by overlapping filaments, that has remained remarkably
consistent for at least three millennia? This wreckage conditions
the present and makes it intelligible. From objects and metamorphoses there follows our sense of a deeper time, but here there is
far more to be considered.

The juxtaposition of a Mycenaean bridge and an asphalt road
is generative of time, not because these are two material things of
different durations in close proximity, but because the late Bronze
Age bridge makes a difference in the line taken by the old carriage
road which gives form to the paved National Road, and because
the new courses of these later roads render the rough bridge, set
in a wide curve, obsolete with respect to carrying traffic. A Bronze
Age bridge impacts paths several thousand years removed from
its construction. A new object disrupts an older ecology of movement and association with respect to wheeled traffic, and the speed
of movement increases in two directions simultaneously over a
smooth, horizontal surface. There are also retroactive effects on
the Mycenaean bridges, which are no longer worn down through
daily traffic. They may come to be used as quarries, or experienced as singular and losable and thereby elevated to the level of

The Kophino Valley

an exception as protected heritage. These are the oldest standing bridges in Europe. In accordance with Trans-European Highway standards, the flat, continuous surface of a new motorway, being the same as everywhere else, seems evacuated of locality. Along its route, few take note of the fading and tattered harlequin patchwork of erstwhile agrarian labor. Still, though the new bypass breaks with the old pattern – influenced by primordial slope, bedrock, and ravine, ancient landholding, settlement, and religiously charged ground – the southern boundary of olive plots and the enduring envelope of the Kophino Valley as a whole continue to orient and direct late twentieth-century infrastructure. Though the bypass will render a major change in movement *through* the valley, it reconstitutes the expectation of movement *to* a destination: the ancient sanctuary of Asclepios, which had been a major draw in antiquity for pilgrims and the infirm, returns as an attraction for locals and tourists.

C. Pleats and Rents: Mycenae 2014

Edges of a limestone outcrop, the formation of which began with the unrelenting, submarine precipitation of dead microorganisms to the sea floor some 200 million years ago, cradle the course of colossal walls erected in the thirteenth century BCE. Bedrock and cyclopean walls orient the concrete path all visitors must take to enter Mycenae through the Lion Gate. Over its massive threshold, under its enormous lintel, lies bygone tumulary ground. After having been interred some ten generations earlier, a cluster of graves was severed from a much larger cemetery. Marked with stelae, encircled by a double line of standing slabs, encompassed by a new enceinte of the citadel, this delimited domain of the dead served to legitimate the locus of the living over three millennia ago. Above, the innermost heights of the citadel, fashioned as the seat of the "kingly" self, divinely favored, perhaps in the line of the Atreidae, provided foundation for a temple sacred to forgotten gods, erected a millennium after the lords of Homeric renown relinquished their well-built halls. Today you, me, or anyone may walk by these walls, through this gate, within this enclosure, along these routes. Directed by unyielding geologic forms rooted in the early Jurassic, by architectural forms laid out in the late Bronze Age, which stabilize achievements for over a millennium of subsequent inhabitation, we visitors move.

War and/or fires destroy what could not be borne away: archival records, stores of oil and grain, wooden basins, dried fruits, stale bits of bread, ovens, bureaucratic positions, livelihoods, treasuries and their ransacked riches, hallowed halls with high columns, frescoes, cherished heirlooms, esteem-infused garments, sumptuous fabrics and looms, beds once occupied by lovers, family homes, ivory-inlaid furniture, boots, well-wrought shields, painted figurines and sacred altars, goats, horses and chariots, oxen and carts, musical instruments, children's dolls. With the desolations of ca. 1200 BCE the palatial culture of Late Helladic Mycenae comes to an end. After a period of reoccupation, another calamitous episode follows around 1100 BCE. There is evidence of occupation across the Early Iron Age, through the Archaic and into the Classical, when a spiteful Argos would destroy another Mycenae in 468 BCE. Later, in the third/second centuries BCE, the citadel is reoccupied as a *kôme* (quarter or ward) of Argos. What a succession of dates situates as closed, distant, proximate, or coextensive on the line fails to grasp is what is torn from, distant, proximate, or coextensive within the fabric of the citadel itself. Indeed, this can be considered not so much an issue of time as one of space: what is and is not present, what is and is not contiguous.

Formerly buried and obscured, old stones have returned. Though visitors now traipse through the Lion Gate, this experience was buried under earth and stone for untold generations until 1841, when Kyriakos Pittakis oversaw the clearance of the passage on behalf of the Archaeological Society of Athens.[73] Likewise, a view to the exposed shaft graves within the tumulary circle was distant by many meters of fill from the families of the eighty hoplites sent to the Battle of Thermopylae in 480 BCE.[74] Deposits and accumulations just under the ground grazed by tinkling goats of the late-eighteenth century are now lost to Lethe. Though they held their own idiosyncratic memories more tenaciously than any texts, they were deemed insignificant, destroyed without being made explicit as the stratified contexts they were, and displaced into spoil tips in the wake of late nineteenth-century excavations.[75] Things now displaced are things no longer proximate, no longer coextensive with the things now extant. In total, these examples are suggestive of topology.

Topology is commonly associated with an area of mathematics that deals with the properties of forms or spaces resistant to, or unchanged by, continuous deformation.[76] Topology highlights invariant loci that retain pleats or folds between points distant in two dimensions. Rather than delineate stable and well-defined temporal distances, a topology specifies junctures of contact and the passages between points held to be distant on a plane, even when the fabric is as torn and tattered as Mycenae. Topology involves all manner of *topoi* or places: a room in a house, a part of the body, a position in the zodiac, a site of burial, a passage in a text, or even a topic or theme within rhetoric.

Tethered to the actual ground of being-there, a visitor bears witness to how Mycenae today is not severed from the present within an epoch removed by the distance gauged along a measured line. Across the last century, the foot traffic of millions of visitors wore away at the great conglomerate threshold, adding to the imperceptible abrasions of sandals, shoes, and buskins, paws, hooves, and carts in the millions of crossings from antiquity. Beneath scuffs and scrapes, the protracted wear of antiquity's throng, two to three million years of cementation, are undone over a millennium. A slow creep speeds up with the new and increasingly frequent traffic of the last century, only to stop. Wooden platforms, including a ramp recently added in the course of renovations, put a pause to the long wearing-away of stone, repeating the effects of the debris that accumulated in the wake of the abandonment of the Argive *kôme*. Whether covered by soil or wood, the threshold is wholly insensitive to the through traffic of passersby above. And yet, both the bonds of cementation and the memories of slow wear were abolished in drainage grooves carved over the course of hours by a tenacious stonemason with mallet and metal chisels. These things and their rapports are suggestive of pleats and folds, lacerations and tears in the fabric of time.

Between 1886 and 1902, Christos Tsountas labored to expose the enduring features of the Achaean capital. Faithful to an image of Mycenae under the Pelopid line, he cut through taken-for-granted overburden at the summit to expose the mixed accumulation of centuries.[77] By dismantling the southwestern portion of the Hellenistic temple foundation, Tsountas revealed the northern

Shaft graves, Mycenae

wall of a court and adjacent corridor associated with Mycenaean overlords. Undone by decades of exposure to wind, rain, and sun, the remainder of the temple platform and other structures dating to the Geometric period (ca. 900 to 700 BCE) were removed from the court between 1920 and 1923.[78] Just as prior to Schliemann the slab circle and the shaft graves were never synoptically contiguous, before Tsountas the foundations of palatial halls were never exposed to the touch of sun and rain on the same day as the base of the Hellenistic temple. What are perfect anachronisms from one perspective are perfectly synchronistic from another: new folds, zones of contact and overlap, occur in the wake of rents. By removing volumes of fill or stratigraphy archaeologists participate in shaping Mycenae as others have done. Pleats held by earth and stone are kneaded by archaeology with its spades, trowels, institutions, practitioners, allegiances, and stories. Different times unfold at Mycenae as old things resurface to be preserved, displaced, or destroyed.

Stones raised in the thirteenth century BCE, a wonder attributed to the work of the Cyclopes, are pulled down in key areas, in all probability by the Argives in or shortly after 468 BCE. These portions are rebuilt, with little doubt, as part of the reoccupation of the citadel as an Argive *kôme*. Differences in form – cyclopean, ashlar, polygonal – suggest differences in the stonemasons' craft. Dislodged by tremors, roots, and millennia of neglect, stones are reset by the Greek Archaeological Service in 1950.[79] Folds held by stone, reinforced by written history, make the late Bronze Age coterminous with the Hellenistic, coextensive with the mid-twentieth century.

The multitemporal walls of Mycenae

Again, Schliemann went against scholarly consensus by ignoring the line between history and myth.[80] With the loquacious Homer standing at the beginning of the European tradition, Schliemann reached across an undisclosed distance to embrace a previous unknown in an effort to breathe new life into these well-built walls. What was supposedly lost is nonetheless here, but when? Scholars would eventually come to see Homer as relating stories put to longstanding yet silent stones, rather than preserving tenacious memories of forgotten exploits in an earlier Bronze Age.[81] They would connect the text to a Greece forming in the Early Iron Age among ruins associated with a heroic past, four to five centuries and more after the great king.[82] Still others would regard the text equally as a composite diversity.[83] It too is pleated and riven through with an assortment of times.[84]

Sacred to the Muses, Mycenae today is a museum. Prescribed paths, viewing platforms, information signs, maps with numbered itineraries, site guards with whistles, exhibition space, all condition the crowds.[85] Here, estrangement and exclusion are after-effects of curatorial responsibility. Here, distance is maintained by cordoned enclosures, the timeline with its terminations and replacements, the space of exposition and dubbed overlay. Here, topological folding occurs with forms of estrangement. The megaron, a word meaning the "great hall" characteristic of Mycenaean "palaces," the Hellenistic temple, and the exhibition space of a museum – all stage and separate, delimit and divide off. All three uphold hierarchies: an area for concentrating observers over here and an area for affirming the position of strength over there. Over the hearth sits the lord on the throne. Over the cella is shielded the statue of the goddess. Over the page is fixed a past that was. All too familiar, these repetitions of form create a common *topos* between the Mycenae of today, the Mycenae of the Hellenistic *kôme*, and the Mycenae under Bronze Age overlords.

D. *Things: Contiguities, Symbioses, Emergence*

Legion are those things that object to a modern historicism in which the past is held to be completed, circumscribed within the boundaries of its own delimitation, and thereby detached from the present.[86] Though uninterrupted progress and unrelenting advancement seem to occur along a linear and supercessive trajectory, neither the march of technology nor the unremitting pace of development manifests a definitive break with the past.[87] At Mycenae, coextensive with the present, a compulsory past stands still, driven by the tenacious propensity to persist of limestone outcrops, monumental walls, stone circles, soil-encased foundations, or buried pots. Against such an obstinate background, change may be witnessed through the juxtaposition of that which gathers and disperses. While overburden (whose accretions were laid down in leaps and drags over millennia) was displaced from within its high walls, new paths, signs, cordons, and synoptic juxtapositions between formerly unassociated things have multiplied within the citadel, bestowing upon the present an increasing diversity of pasts, erratic, fragmentary, and unruly though they are.[88] These pasts are not successive. They are not ordered within a series of replacements along a line which is not time, but its measurement.[89] They are simultaneous, coincidental among the legion things that hold on to something of their pasts, that are suggestive of changes and generative of time. Let us return, once again, to the beginning.

Schliemann's confusion of recorded traditions with the things he found at Mycenae opened a path for others to articulate the contours of the continuum that linked their present to what had been. After the turn of the century, Karo undertook the comprehensive and detailed analysis of the grave circle, shaft graves, and particularly the finds (in the German tradition of *Altertumwissenschaft*), drawing on subsequent excavations by Stamatakis.[90] Later, Tsountas, Keramopoullos, Wace, and others scraped through the hollows, under stones formerly unturned, and between walls in an attempt to make sense of what was left. Through the tedious work of typology, ceramics were organized on the basis of similarities in shape, fabric, and decoration.[91] With the verification of these

materials against stratigraphically ordered contexts, archaeologists built developmental sequences along which ran the stylistic
evolution of pottery.[92] As these sequences were further refined,
they used imports found throughout Mycenae and elsewhere to
establish correlations with Egypt, where calendrical dates were
more secure. The Bronze Age of Greece was divided into three
stages, Early, Middle, and Late, in rough correspondence with
the Kingdoms of Egypt: Old, Middle, and Late.[93] Giving contours to the continuum, relative chronologies followed, and the
development of Mycenae was mapped out across the Middle and
Late Helladic periods. Against this periodization, every object at
Mycenae, whether present or subsequently unearthed, would be
framed.

Though necessary for the construction of knowledge, the division of a continuum, whether in the partitioning of Late Helladic
into a tripartite scheme or a day into twenty-four hours, is in
some sense arbitrary insofar as a system of division is concerned.[94]
However, one cannot divide the Late Helladic period into twelve
or twenty phases in the same way as a day, which can be arbitrarily reshuffled into ten or thirty hours. The fidelity of Late Helladic
phases pertains to subtle changes in ceramic typology (the technology and form of pottery, both durable and pervasive) and not to
the sequential ordering of a measured, homogeneous time into
which, through association with datable objects, it nonetheless
translates.[95] On some level typologies respond to changes in form,
which are specific to ceramic bowls, amphorae, or other objects.
Forms are created through negotiations with actual objects, and
this is less a matter of a date than of a practice of dating through
intermingling durations.[96]

Space can also be conceived as an arbitrarily divisible continuum; the distance between the reconstituted Land Gate in
Nafplion and the ancient tower on Kastrakia is five kilometers
or 3.1 miles. From the two-dimensional space of the mapmaker's
table, the spatial is underwritten by a representational system of
gridded points and measured lines, again an arbitrary compact
with a history. Indeed, a segment is one of the simplest forms of
geometric space. Here, however, the segment is taken as a portion
of a thing: the EO70. Seg-ment: *seg*, from the Latin *secare*, to cut,
and *ment*, the production of this action. A segment of the EO70
seems arbitrary on some level, and yet a town and a collapsed
tholos tomb are involved in the movement of an archaeologist
from one to the other in 2012. At root, this is the segmentation
of an actual thing (the EO70) through a rapport between actual

entities: the town of Nafplion, the erstwhile tomb at Kazarma, an archaeologist, the author of this chapter, with an automobile and a research project.[97] While the gauged division of any continuum can be executed in many different ways, this does not follow for specific objects (see Chapter 1).[98]

Rather than the homogeneous, arbitrarily divisible units of measured, two-dimensional time and space, along the EO70 one encounters specific things: terrace walls, an old stone tower transformed into a cistern, actual plowed furrows, property boundaries, kermes oaks, perennial streams, one cyclopean bridge at Galousi, another at Kazarma, a footpath reconstituted by the Greek Archaeological Service, thirty-three olive trees in the grove immediately south of the Kazarma bridge, one ancient fortress on the limestone heights above the village of Agios Ioannis, an empty ruined tomb at its base, or a smooth tarmac surface that connects Argos with Epidaurus with Corinth via the Saronic Gulf. Each of these actual entities has its own duration, as do the rapports between each of these things. Whereas Bergson gives priority to movement over the things that move, perhaps these things are not derivative of some underlying current or flux, but rather give rise to it.[99] Is it not from specific things and the rapports between them that time wells up for the archaeologist?

The Latin word *stratum* denotes "something spread out," "laid down," or "prostrate"; this word suggests both spatial presence and formation. To form stratigraphy, a level must *extend* above, below, or through another stratum. To apprehend strata as stratigraphy, one should give due attention to the *graphos*, which requires the perpendicular profile, an exposure crafted through seismic uplift, erosive winds or waters or excavation; or one must excavate every stratum individually, as a context in phase, planned from above and linked to other contexts diagrammatically. Either way, the recognition of stratigraphy, of phasing in single-context recording (a mode of removing and documenting every context/stratum in phase), is guided, which is to say dominated, by the page. Writing, drawing, planning, photography; this is the two-dimensional ground of synoptic contiguity. This synoptic contiguity of strata through profiles, or the graphic representation of strata as contexts and phases in open-area excavation, falls to archaeologists or geologists with their instruments and labors.

From the contiguous (above, below, next to) or the discontiguous (apart from) follows the stratigraphic, which may or may not suggest the contours of a continuum. "This below that"

translates into "this before that." "This above that" translates into
"this after that." Such plain translations end here. It requires the
work of archaeology to go further. Thickness of deposits and consistency of intervals do not equate to rates of sedimentation or the
pace of stratification. Established by other means, a deposit may
form through slow accretion, persist as a stable and unchanging
object, or accrue abruptly in the wake of fire or the earthquakes
that seem to have occurred at Mycenae towards the end of the
thirteenth century BCE. Fills, accumulations, strata are displaced
through renovations, through excavations (rents and lacerations
that bring them into contact with other things) which create new
pleats and folds. The intervention makes two formerly separate
things coextensive by virtue of the cut, the exposure, translated to
the plan. Contiguity shares its Latin root *tangere* (to touch) with
contingency, the accidental.

Returning to stratigraphy, "this next to that" cannot plainly
translate into "this contemporary with that." Contemporaneity,
outside of the present – necessary for eventful history – is far
more difficult to establish, as discussed by Gavin Lucas.[100] An
unpainted bowl with horizontal handles contains 137 glass beads,
fifty-eight carnelian beads, six beads of amber, thirty decorated
glass plaques, an ivory comb, and more.[101] Within a room, among
other sundry items, seventeen kylikes, nine cups/bowls, twelve
anthropomorphic figurines, seven coiled terracotta snakes, three
tripod tables, one ivory box, and three conical bowls (including the one which contained the cache of miscellaneous items)
are gathered together. The contiguity of items contained in and
with the bowl, labeled 68-1402, with and within Room 19 of
the temple complex at Mycenae, is what allows these things to
be sealed off in their own time; that is, the assumed time of their
supposed use and abandonment based on ceramic typologies in
stratified deposits, that of Late Helladic IIIB2.[102] Are the items
placed in the bowl iteratively, or as one group? Is the bowl part of
a collection of other things abruptly hidden away in the room, or
is it among other items that are stored intermittently, thus accu-
mulating over a protracted period of time? While the collection
of these things might suggest a single moment in time, different objects have different durations, with some items already
several generations old in comparison with others less than a
decade in age at the time of their abandonment.[103] The fact that
these objects confronted archaeologists in the late 1960s, and
that they continue to do so today, challenges any expectations
that their time is limited to lived relations sealed off in another

period. What times, the question must be asked, are peculiar to them?

Despite being encased within the same deposit, these contiguities do not reveal differences in their collation that can be translated into a minute, hour, day, month, year, or even a human lifetime.[104] The pace of their accretion in the bowl has passed into oblivion. *What was* is not there. What remains are these assembled things and their plain and simple contiguities with each other, the bowl, and the earth that encompasses it. And to these things (which subsist) belong durations, their *continua*.[105] Whereas the *con-tem-pus* situates something as belonging to time, "contiguity" from the *contiguus* simply denotes that something touches something else.[106] It does not, however, specify *how* something coexists with something else, and if contiguity simply situates things together without specifying that dynamism that surfaces in how a bowl, beads, soils affect each other and merge into new things, then it does not go far enough.

Archaeologists have long conceived of change in terms of dynamic processes, where what becomes of the past is regarded as a product of a protracted course of entropy and accumulation. According to these precepts, widely understood in terms of formational processes (that is, the ways by which archaeological objects come to be as they are), old things encountered in the present are the result of continual shaping and transformation: corrosion and compaction, decomposition and deposition, erosion and aeolian accretion.[107] Yet ruins, walls, buried deposits, or bead-laden bowls change because they exist rather than existing because they change, to borrow an expression from Harman.[108] Organic remains, bacteria, and rubble walls are things rather than processes, and things change depending on their interactions with other things. A ceramic bowl and encasing soils stabilize a collection of beads and other items for millennia. A cooking pot turned upside down persists in withholding waters from its contents. A rock-cut cist prevents the dispersal of a burial with its items, including bronze daggers, which having formed a layer of copper oxide resist the corrosive forces of water-saturated soils.

Formational processes assume a gradualist image of change. Whether over the short or long term, it is implied that every instant should be accorded equal interest. Yet not all instants are the same. Some changes are of more consequence for the formation of what becomes of the past than others.[109] Whether through an earthquake or wanton destruction, terracotta figurines and coiled snakes, tripod tables and faience beads, sundry items of

ivory and bronze are sealed in a room left to a darkness formed
under earth and stone. Released from human use and interaction,
they persist in themselves and together, bringing their own idiosyncratic otherness to excavators working under Lord William
Taylour at the moment of the encounter in the late 1960s.[110] Here
is another fold, and through encounters such as those that occur
in the course of archaeological excavation, change is more sporadic, the transformations that occur over the life of a thing more
saltatory.

By positioning a past (destructions associated with the fall of the
Bronze Age citadel) behind what remains at Mycenae, one renders
that which remains as a derivative effect or consequence of an historical cause, a supposed reality that has already passed. Yet that
which is present is not here in a resultant, causal relation to the
past that was; for that would situate the old things of Mycenae as
derivative of a past no longer present. Rather, things present are
what make the past, including processes, possible. Understanding
how things give rise to pasts demands a different understanding
of causation. Here, an *emergent* understanding of causation takes
over from the *resultant* sort.[111] Emergence specifies how objects,
whether an unpainted bowl containing numerous items, the buried
remains of a series of rooms, or a tumulary circle, exceed the
components that gave rise to them in such a way that once formed
they retroactively define their ingredients as well as their own mor-
phogenetic history.[112] After organic objects are fully consumed by
bacteria, new soils emerge to enter into their own chthonic adventures with ivory combs, ceramic bowls, or relic walls.[113] After
Bronze Age stonemasons (with hammer and chisel) work unhewn
areas of conglomerate, former extrusions of bedrock emerge as a
quarry that has retroactive effects on outcrops of stone.[114]

The coexisting together of different living things, which generates
novelty by their fusing and forming (rather partially or entirely)
into new entities, has been called *symbiosis*.[115] This term took on
a new level of meaning in the work of Lynn Margulis, who recognized symbiosis as the engine of evolutionary novelty.[116] Since then
it has expanded even more through the work of Harman, who sees
symbiosis metaphorically as the engine of all significant change
(see also Chapter 1).[117] Just as the merger of work crews with
wall stones generates breaches in polis ramparts eight centuries
old, the fusion of polygonal cut stones with ashlar and cyclopean
masonry yields a renewed circle of security in a Hellenistic *kôme*.
Just as the fusion of encompassing deposits with structural remains
secures walls of rubble and mud mortar for millennia, the merger

of archaeologists with the marvelous miscellany of the chthonic realm beyond the grave circle and inside the citadel leads to the formation of the "Cult Centre." From this exchange and partial merger through translation, objects are generated (finds are documented, illustrations are produced, photographs are taken, papers are written, objects are put on display in museums) and these have post facto effects on their makers.

By situating what was found in a particular moment – their deposition – correlated to particular era (LHIIIB2), these things come to be anchored at a measured distance from the present, which bestows significance upon them by locating their deposition in the aftermath of catastrophe: the downfall of Mycenae. This is necessary for showing how these objects operate within the development of Mycenae as a whole. However, this act of consigning what remains to a separate era overshadows what is otherwise coextensive in experience and emerges in its wake. The question for the archaeologist is not simply *to what era these things belong*, but rather, *for how long have they endured in themselves and in relation to other things?* For over three millennia, walls have stood on foundations 200 million years in their punctuated formation. Under the feet of other Mycenaeans, Argives, and visitors to storied ruins, a chthonic domain has shielded objects in dark perdurance since they were abandoned in the waning days of the Bronze Age. If archaeology makes explicit such object durations and initiates new contiguities, then it is through the symbiosis of a ruined citadel and archaeology that a different object, Mycenae, emerges on present grounds.

A biology of forms is how Olivier has conceived of the evolution of ceramic typology, which does not proceed as a continuous or consistent march of changes through time, but as the negotiation between different durations of form.[118] Form can respond to whatever is present or whatever returns to presence.[119] The unpainted bowl's label (1968) indicates the year excavated, and 1402 indicates its find number. The present of the intervention among things undated is another contemporary moment in archaeology; this is the moment of a return, not in the sense of *anamnesis* (of remembering again) but in the sense of *anamorphosis* (the recurrence of form). Something of the Mycenaean past is present as an excavated object whose form, now present, may multiply yet again, returning to wider circulation through replication, another symbiosis. *Skeuomorphs* – from the Greek *skeuos*, vessel or implement, and *morphe*, or form – are available for purchase in the museum shop at Mycenae. Through persistence, contiguities, and symbioses, other objects emerge to proliferate among old things released from the soil. Alongside things with their durations, their symbioses, archaeology opens another time.

E. Percolation/Time

Archaeologists choose to embrace the past as history in seeking out the explicit, in hitching time to human change and interaction. This mortal time grounds our humanity, yet archaeology opens on different grounds. Plaster at Mycenae is preserved through contact with soil and lost through exposure to rain. What Schliemann interpreted to be half-burnt portions of wood from the funeral pyre were likely meal scraps left by microbes.[120] Lost to Lethe, it was only after Schliemann's excavations that what became known as the shaft graves were regarded as always having been there in their earth-filled underground cavities. Not being seen, not being apprehended by human observers, they were at some times locked in stable fills and strata and at others undergoing adventures with water, soil, and roots. Through archaeology, the soft has been displaced. What was movable has found new homes. How does one weigh the loss of these things and their unrealized pasts?

It is the tenacity of ashlar walls that do not shift in the wind, the persistence of stone circles that do not rot, the obstinacy of ceramics within soils that allow change to be glimpsed through their comparative presence. Interactions of specific entities perturb, transform, and give rise to processes that are only apparent as strange differences indicative of change, as the look of age suggesting metamorphosis, as forms without their completions, as memories held in things. Typological studies of ceramics from the excavated grave circle, stratigraphic associations with other fragmented ceramic forms, comparative examples from other portions of the citadel, intuitions gained through hindsight – as new things arise they illuminate and obscure other things. The last shaft-grave burial seems to have entered the earth nearly four centuries before the most plausible date for the Trojan War, and into obscurity slides Schliemann's belief that he had found the remains of Agamemnon and his companions. Yet Schliemann, in pursuing his redemptive ambitions, shaped the domain of future past production by determining what was and was not of relevance: all subsequent archaeologists who work on the shaft graves are constrained to observations grounded in what he deemed worthy of observation.[121] It is from this stable and shifting ground, the ground of things, the ground of contact or lack of contact between actual entities in the present, that time arises.

Time carries with it the tenses of past, present, and future. The slow wear of the Mycenaean threshold gives one a sense of its past. Whether or not it is a matter of contemplation, one's own experience of stepping over this worn stone constitutes a present. A monumental gateway also reaches ahead of itself, predetermining future engagements, ensuring that it is something that must be contended with for those strangers yet to come. Likewise the wooden platform, now covering the great threshold, extends preservation, a non-relation with the threshold, into the future. From the angle of the projected future, streets, corridors, and terraces laid out in the thirteenth century BCE orient impending interactions. Walls and surfaces exceed the explicit expectations of designers, masons, and overlords. Citizens of the Archaic polis continued to cope with what had become of Mycenaean infrastructure; as did inhabitants of the Hellenistic *kôme*, as do visitors today. From the angle of the archaeological, Mycenaean Greece did not end in the twelfth century BCE. Even when buried, stone keeps in wait. Just as the great walls of Mycenae hindered assailants and sheltered inhabitants, they held back stratigraphy and pooled water. Whether for life or its decompositions, these walls retain their autonomy. These walls reach ahead of themselves, open to all contiguities, exchanges, and mergers, open to other potential futures. A sealed room, a collection of items in a bowl, amass, pool, and hold; they are also oriented towards prospects forthcoming. What remains is implicit, and what is implicit stretches towards what is yet to pass.

Abandoned by the wayside, what we may regard as memories of the old EO70, which followed earlier routes, themselves responsive to the lay of the land, to outcrops and ravines, to agricultural plot and settlements, transform into new things: a parking area for lorries, a driveway for a resident outside Pirgiotika, paths for farmers to their plots, or disused surfaces left to their saltational burial through communions with soil and debris, rubbish and vegetation. An empty, half-standing tholos tomb at Kazarma once sheltered the remains of two men and a woman in rock-cut cists. Excavated in 1968 and 1969, the contents of the tomb were displaced to the Archaeological Museum in Nafplion.[122] What may have been contiguous a century ago may be discontiguous today, and what may be contiguous today may have been discontiguous a century ago. Of course other things are now involved, and it is here that new things emerge and time unfurls.

At Mycenae countercurrents or eddies form within and between the room, the items, the bowl, its contents, the soil that formerly held them, and the archaeologists who worked to excavate them. Buried conditions combined with the idiosyncratic qualities of the objects themselves provided stability for ceramic bowls and their relations across millennia, which are fathomable precisely because of the significant achievement that is periodization. Excavation brought momentous metamorphoses to formerly unwavering objects and their relations. In this, something of what the bowl contains, something of its past, becomes contiguous, coextensive, with everything on the surface of Mycenae, later within the storage rooms in Nafplion, and with those who work with these materials. With the displacement of stone walls and rooms within the courtyard of the palace, the removal of a portion of the Hellenistic temple, periods more proximate in terms of their distance along a line are ripped out. Stability and metamorphosis, contiguities and folds, discontiguities and tears, yes, but also novelties and returns.

The layout of the megaron, which constrained and focused movement in the past, constrains and focuses movement today. The reality of Schliemann's delusion, manifest in the synoptic juxtaposition of the slab circle with exposed shaft graves, may yet provoke future archaeologists to rebury empty graves. And other rapports may yet recur. After being cradled for millennia in the dark, buried surfaces once again return to the stimulating radiance of the sun. The slow creep of slope, the accumulation of debris, torrential rain, the wear of goats, the growth of maquis, lay claim to a Bronze Age road terrace. A farmer and his family expand their fields, and in clearing vegetation they uncover a line of large stones. These stones hold back soils for their plot. These stones cradle their addition. A portion of an erstwhile road becomes a terrace line, only to be left on its own again, reclaimed by maquis. Prior to 2005, the bridges of Galousi and Kazarma were encountered not as mutual extensions of a Bronze Age road, but as stone crossings within their ravines, making one side of a defile contiguous with another. The obligation paid forward by Europe's oldest bridges is surely the fact that they exist, ready to hand, ready to lend support to those who require it, to those who seek to cross the ravine from one agricultural plot to another or to reach droves grazing high on the opposite maquis-covered slope.[123] After 2005 these spans are reincorporated into a path system, as was the terrace, a portion of the ancient road enrolled by the farmers. Once again, these things work together. Bridges are connected to a path of movement.

We experience time as the interplay of entropy and endurance: olive limbs bend with the weight of fragrant blossoms in May; morning poppies growing in nearby plots among the abandoned stalks of last season's grain are tilled under before the afternoon. We experience time as the mutual agitation of ephemerality and repetition: roots of kermes oak slowly rend apart blocks of stone in the buried line of a road terrace; the line of an erstwhile road persists elsewhere as a boundary between agricultural plots. Never-ending accumulation and incessant novelty, perpetual perishing and persistence, the bedfellows of time and its media are actual things and their symbioses. Things (a category inclusive of the human) and their contiguities speak to a time that does not pass everywhere in the same way.[124] Multiply these examples a thousand times, and one gets a sense of time as percolation: a time that pools in reservoirs or settles in pockets, filters and siphons off, accelerates in bursts and creeps slowly, ruptures and turns back within eddies of novelty and repetition.

F. An Archaeological Paradox

What then is archaeology? It is rarely recognized that, unlike biology, anthropology, mythology, etc., archaeology is derived from an adjective, *archaios*, rather than a proper noun, such as *bios*, *anthropos*, or *mythos*. Thus archaeology's commitment is to a quality, an attribute of being old or ancient, rather than to an actual object. Productive emphasis may be made of a common etymology derived from *ta archaia*, "things old."[125] *Ta archaia* is a neuter plural substantive built from the root *archaios*, and archaeology carries this sense etymologically, of dealing with things that are old or ancient. However, by eliding the difference between the *archaios* and *ta archaia*, archaeology misses an important distinction between things and the quality of being ancient or old: what we might gloss as that attribute of holding memory. This distinction makes it necessary to raise two fundamental questions. Where does archaeology begin? And what does it achieve?

The etymological commitment of archaeology to study things old, ancient or what has become of that which is no longer present poses a constraint, in the sense that it orients the practices of this field. However, this constraint need not (as has always been supposed) belong to the *arche*, the starting point. It may equally belong to the *telos*, the solution. Here is an archaeological paradox: in order to adequately address the *archaios*, to achieve *ta archaia*, or address historical questions of "what happened here," of "how this came to be," an archaeologist has to suspend altogether the historical imperative that something actually happened here, that what matters is absent, or that the erstwhile constitutes the reasons for why things are. For the archaeologist, what is present is not here in a resultant causal relation to the past; rather, *the things present are what make the past possible.*[126] Holding this paradox close is the only way for the archaeologist to fulfill that debt to the past, present, and future. Given this paradox, archaeology must struggle to understand things outside the refrains of human history or for us humans-among-ourselves, but this aspiration should not be seen as creating yet another taxonomic distinction between archaeology and history.[127] From archaeology's own history we learn that it is to our benefit to begin in naivety, in forced ignorance without the solution: the carrot that common history holds, which we know we must strategically avoid as an expectation that leads us astray from our objects.[128]

Archaeology is possible because objects persist, and it is with things that it begins. From these grounds the question of how to proceed is caught between what the object (which has survived in legion ways) suggests and a wider field of possibilities, a creative adventure that will eventually lead archaeologists and other things to articulate, to achieve, either *ta archaia* (old things, the material past) or *archaios* (what emerges as a quality of being old or ancient). Indeed, it would make little sense to undertake archaeological research if our objects were *a priori* entangled in their pasts, if they already pointed beyond themselves to other things. It takes substantial work to piece together what objects suggest concerning their connections, which can only provide hints as to their erstwhile rapports. Archaeology requires a trust in things to reveal something of themselves and in its own practices to disclose more than what is immediately given over in experience. Archaeology requires significant effort to apprehend something of its objects' pasts, along with creativity and imagination to form a story of what might have been, however tenuous it may be.

This paradox alone – that to articulate *an object's past*, an archaeologist must suspend any expectations about *the past* – makes archaeology a worthy companion for philosophical dialogue. Surely, part of why philosophy has hardly concerned itself with archaeology, save metaphorically, has to do with philosophy's own anthropocentrism and its corresponding neglect of things.[129] Still, such neglect is largely a problem for the archaeological tradition, a field that has (perhaps out of necessity) brought a universal model of history into the past, and in so doing willingly embraced a kind of self-estrangement from its objects.[130] While throughout the history of archaeology one may detect a deep concern with the medium of the past (that is, a concern with the nature of that which remains) in beginning with the background of separate pasts, reinforced by a linear and externalized time, the archaeological object could never have been plainly what it is.[131] Archaeology has tended to suppress what is arguably its greatest contribution, which by its nature has always offered an alternative to the very modernist historicism to which it committed itself.

When archaeologists began entering the fog of prehistory, a creationist view, with its larger loyalties to the Bible as history (or, rather, as one of the few available sources for Earth history), prevailed across Europe.[132] Famously, Archbishop James Ussher concluded that the Creation had occurred "upon the entrance of the night preceding the twenty-third day of October" in the year 4004 BC.[133] But now the Earth is 4.54 billion years old. In the space of two centuries the well of the past has expanded some 4,539,994,196 years, give or take a few million. Whereas we were formerly present for all but six days, human being now holds a minuscule share of Earth history which is, in fact, the archaeology of the Earth, for these are memories held in objects.[134] Thus, from another angle we are immersed within a bewildering polychronic multitude, and here human being holds far less than a half-share of reality. The immediate and coextensive nature of things from so many other times with so many different durations enters them into legion exchanges and rapports that can be understood in thousands of conceivable ways. Here the present is holy ground, where the living are at home in the jumble, the mixed, the variegated assemblage. Can archaeology begin yet again, along a different and no less opaque path?

Coda

Above the threshold, above the lintel, two lions paw up the platform. In contraposition their feline bodies, carved in profile, angle skyward against a central column. Did they gaze upon the column, did they gaze away from it, or did they look out to the approach? Headless, they do not answer. Their bodies, oriented to a common object, nonetheless approach from different directions. Whether or not one chooses to see them as history and archaeology, both stand firmly in the present, fashioning the past with different objects and methods, perhaps gazing on it from different directions. Better still, they look away, out to the future. No, perhaps these silent, headless bodies serve to remind us, those who pass here, that there is not only the time down the well, but also the time that upwells. One, the time of antiquity, intensely studied, meticulously scrutinized and gauged, necessary. The other, the antiquity of time, forgotten even as it continues to pile up, here, indifferent.

3

Discussion of Chapter 2

Graham Harman: In the previous chapter you gave an intricate account both of what archaeology has been and what it might become. Since each section of your argument contains multiple ideas I think it would be best to go one at a time, starting with your Section A ("Line: History, Archaeology, Time"). Here there are at least two things you seem to oppose. The first is the linear conception of time that you think was baked into early archaeological practice. Although I know you are interested in Latour, and also sense that your occasional use of "percolation" suggests an equal interest in Serres, perhaps you could clarify what is wrong with the linear conception of time and what might replace it.

The second thing you oppose is the idea that archaeology should be "the study of the human past through its material remains." You propose instead an object-oriented turn, and of course I am sympathetic to the sound of that. But what for you is the point of studying objects apart from their relation to human history? After all, you are not primarily concerned with the chemical and physical properties of the artifacts you unearth, except as indices of a human civilization that made use of these objects.

Chris Witmore: When it comes to time, lines are useful for measurement, but not for models. A two-dimensional thread connecting dots separated by quantifiable distances helps with gauging the depths of prehistory. It is of value for staking out "when," for marking out "how long," for providing a scale against which to assess continua or durations. Yet archaeology was not immune to the routine confusion of the measurement of time with the nature of time: a common misconception, which Serres underscored in his well-known conversation with Latour.[1]

The graduated line lends itself to that very peculiar historicism, as was also pointed out by Serres and Latour, where the past is posited to exist in a realm apart from the present, which in definitively breaking with the past is always located elsewhere, at another point along its homogeneous extent. The conflagrations that appear to have swept through Mycenae at the turn of the twelfth century BCE are separated by a distance of seven centuries from the Argive sack of Mycenae in 468 BCE, an event that is removed from us by nearly 2,500 years. The Late Bronze Age, understood as a five- or six-hundred-year swath from 1700 to 1200/1100 BCE, is completed and replaced by the Early Iron Age; the Early Iron Age develops into the Archaic, which gives rise to the Classical Era. With laminar and well-defined distances, these episodes are held to be successive, enclosed within their own capsules along a thread marked by terminations and replacements. Along the line one may plot a unidirectional movement from a command economy to chaos or an onward progression from a ruined citadel to a small polis, which will send a contingent of hoplites to fight at the Battle of Plataea. Along the line one may set out divisions of labor between those archaeologists who study prehistory and those who study the Classical world.

A linear conception of time that posits a close to the past cannot account for strong walls that continue to enchant those who behold them, for roadways that persist by candidly directing movement, or for stone enclosures doggedly delimiting inside from outside. A linear conception of time brutally oversimplifies what the objects of archaeology suggest. Rates of deposition in and around the citadel vary between slow accumulation over centuries and cataclysmic accretion in the wake of destructions. Objects sealed in a dark room for protection are returned to the light after millennia. Rapports between an ancient threshold stone and pedestrian traffic cease due to the burial of the former under accumulations of soil and rubble, only to be reinitiated after archaeologists unearth the full extent of the Lion Gate. Late Bronze Age walls are part of the composition of Hellenistic communities. Roman travelers are more distant from Bronze Age graves than archaeologists after the late nineteenth century. Such examples suggest a time that is far more chaotic, and we must struggle to find a model commensurate with the challenge of its portrayal.

I am fond of the concept of "percolation," which conjures a tumultuous, even weather-like image of time. Percolation allows for countercurrents and eddies in time's passage against the grounds of objects commonly situated with respect to their appearance and use. For me percolation need not imply some primordial flux somehow deeper or separate from actual objects. Rather, if we take time to be the vigor within and between things, we might understand percolation as a way of expressing the sum of these vigors.

Archaeology has always been object-oriented in what it does. However, throughout its history it kept its objects at a distance gauged along lines. The problem with archaeology's popular definition as "the study of the human past through its material remains" lies in how it relegates objects, apprehended as "material remains," to the subordinate position of means and bestows upon its ends a spurious precedence. This overly reductive, telocentric definition limits archaeological objects to the status of mere vehicles and ultimately denies those throngs of ceramic fragments, beads, conglomerate blocks, buried thresholds, or corroded coins their role as protagonists, for without them any understanding of past worlds at Mycenae would be impossible.[2] To regard objects solely as indices of human interactions not only opens archaeology to a fundamental expressive fallacy (the presumption of a human agency behind objects rendered from the angle of material memories encountered in the present), it also blinds practitioners to the long roster of objects (oak trees, goats, ox-pulled plows, flash floods laden with debris, or backhoes) that make a difference in the metamorphosis of the citadel and its surrounding milieu.[3] Above all, it relegates objects encountered in the present to a derivative position vis-à-vis specific things done in the past – *res gestae* – and these *res gestae* are set within a causal relation to other events, themselves ordered sequentially into a homogeneous and universal time.

Nonhuman objects do not need to be sidelined as protagonists or things in themselves for archaeology to be possible. That should not imply that the human element is to be ignored. If we take archaeology at its word, then it is the *logos* of *archaios*, which is research and study towards a quality or attribute of being old or ancient. Such a purview implies that archaeology yields far more than stories of the human past.[4] And while such a purview need not circumscribe our objects, it does specify our solutions. However, objects are not reducible to their qualities, their pasts, or their effects, as we both agree. They are not reducible to any particular solution. Indeed, who claims to know the solution before undertaking the analysis? By reducing that broad

hill grazed by tinkling goats to the solution – here was the citadel
of the Achaean capital – archaeologists faithful to this particular
image of the past destroyed and displaced walls, foundations,
surfaces, deposits, broken bits of ceramics, all of them objects
that held memories and suggestions of innumerable other pasts:
pasture and enclosure for animals, a ruin invested with myth,
a lure for travelers, an Argive *kôme*, an Archaic polis, and so
on. For archaeologists to begin with qualities, pasts, or effects is
to foreclose on a surplus reality which objects hold, and which
may lead us to other possibilities. For archaeologists to begin
with solutions is to destroy what becomes of Mycenae, which
emerged as legion objects. Again we are left with Plato, but
without the footnotes.[5]

Ultimately, archaeologists have a duty to resist appropriating things for whatever expectations the *archaios* places upon
the object, which means prudently dealing with residues inside
amphoras, carbonized seeds and the hearth that contains them,
or clay soils that emerged through the dissolution of mudbricks
in their own terms. Such an obligation demands a constant
struggle for ways to speak of objects, to articulate things, without subordinating them to interpretive burdens they are unfit
to carry, which includes presumptively treating them solely as
indices of other objects. One has to put in the requisite work in
order to explain one object in terms of another, without reducing one to the other. I realize that you formulated your questions
so as to begin with the specifics of the first section, but their
scope required me to pilfer examples from others, and even to
jump to the paradox posed at the end of the chapter.

GH: Feel free to jump around as you wish; it simply helps me to
organize my questions if I proceed one section at a time. But
before we move on to the next question, I have a more general one. In your response you seem skeptical of such "linear"
notions as "Bronze Age" and "Iron Age." But aren't these terms
excellent examples of a *nonlinear* and *object-oriented* sense of
time? After all, isn't the shift from bronze to iron as the dominant metal an excellent example of the subordination of human
time to the time of objects? It is humans who discovered or
invented these metals, of course. But once a new metal is introduced, it is humans who must adapt themselves to the metal
more than the reverse. And doesn't this give us an automatically
"chunky" periodization of time, just as later developments do?
It seems perfectly fair to me to think that human civilization
changed drastically once electrification lit up the nights, for

instance. I'm all in favor of percolation and of the impossibility of defining any particular artifact as "ancient" or "modern," but don't certain objects create definite thresholds that change human life as it was previously known up to that point? When I think of linear conceptions of history I think not so much of anti-percolative models of time, but of pro-gradualist ones.

CW: Your way of conceptualizing the shift from bronze to iron is an excellent example of how archaeology benefits from this conversation with OOO. It is worth recalling that the old Three Age System of stone-bronze-iron succession arises out of the typological organization of objects associated with silent pre-history.[6] By exhibiting flint spearpoints with jade axes, bronze tweezers with bronze pots, and iron swords with iron orna-ments, museum exhibitions opened a public window onto the chronological sequence of a deep past beyond the reach of talka-tive history. Such installations also suggested a trust in things brought to light through excavation over what could be gleaned from texts. Yet ultimately the time of objects was subjugated to the time of humans, for the Three Age System provided a basis for the chronometrics of a human past in moving from nomadic foragers to agrarians to configured societies for which objects were regarded as derivative.

I agree that certain objects bring about definite thresholds of change. Electric light is a wonderful example, for it more than altered circadian rhythms of light and dark. It transformed every aspect of society (labor, rest, entertainment, architec-ture) as McLuhan observed.[7] Electric light robbed the sun of its dominion over human activity. Indeed, I believe we could extend the chunky periodization of time to which you refer by involving even more lengthy continua than distinctions between stone, bronze, or iron would suggest. To be sure, it is the case that humans adapted to new metals and with them new objects proliferated. Yet bronze and iron were also enrolled in the pro-duction of agrarian implements and forms of weaponry that had long shaped human societies. And plows of wood, bronze, iron, and even stone were coextensive at various moments on the Argive plain and in the surrounding hinterlands. Greek hoplites continued to use bronze armor alongside iron swords and spear points. Many such objects and their rapports persisted up till the massive rural exoduses that occurred during the last cen-tury, or the fundamental changes in warfare associated with the Second Boer War.[8] Cities and a metabolic regime of fossil fuels, machine guns and barbed wire brought to a close the continua

within and between objects measured in millennia and even tens
of millennia.

I take your point about how thresholds of change run counter to any gradualist or processual notion of time, for these
presuppose a homogeneous flow of uniform instants of equal
consequence or an ongoing progression somehow deeper than
objects themselves. In this regard I understand your use of
"linear," since thresholds of change give shape to the passage
of time. I agree that your sense of linear history does not run
counter to a percolative model of time, which allows for such
passages without breaking definitively from the past. For me,
percolation helps to complicate the ways archaeologists have
conceptualized time and the locus of the past. It also encapsu-
lates the strange difference that archaeology makes by dredging
up objects formerly lost to Lethe and making them coextensive
within present or future circumstances. Every now and then,
whether in Greece or Texas, the electric grid goes down and
candles or oil lamps become the primary source of light. Though
this occurs against a very different background and under very
different circumstances, there is something nonetheless consistent in the style of these objects and their relations, which to me
suggests small eddies in time's passage.

GH: On that note, let's move to your Section B ("Segment(s):
From Nafplion to Kazarma 2012") where you discuss a stretch
of National Road 70 between Nafplion and Epidaurus in the
Peloponnese. By sheer coincidence this stretch of road remains
vivid in memory, since my wife Necla and I were recently there
as a spillover from our visit to the ruins of Mycenae, a site you
also discuss. Along with the obvious ancient riches along that
route, we found Nafplion itself to be an impressive town, even
though from a much more recent history. I didn't realize that the
upper portion of Nafplion is "an uplifted mass of limestone 120-
plus million years in the making," though the cliffs do make for
a dramatic sight that no visitor will soon forget. But along with
these immemorial cliffs and the Venetian fortress that crowns
them, you note the presence of such recent arrivals as "roadside soils contaminated with heavy metals, discharged with the
exhaust of automobiles burning lead gasoline prior to the 2000
EU ban, or from catalytic converters; past the former Anthos/
Kyknos canning plant turned cultural center." You stress that
along the road one finds "a polychronic composite of various
durations." This theme of the mixing of all times in a single
crucible has become familiar to philosophy through the work

of Serres and Latour, limited though their influence remains in philosophy itself. Presumably archaeology came to this insight much earlier, since it would have been under considerable internal pressure to do so.

But I also notice your two mentions of James Frazer in this part of Chapter 2. This interests me because, at first glance, Frazer might look like a linearizer of time in your bad sense of the term: magic and then religion have been replaced by scientific enlightenment. But I'm not so sure. Not so much because Frazer is just as aware of the mixing of different times in the way that we might be today, but because whatever his intentions, I as a reader of his work end up feeling even more sympathetic to magic and religion than I already was (namely, much more sympathetic than the average Western intellectual). In other words, whenever I enter Frazer's universe (and I can't claim to have finished the whole of his many-volumed *The Golden Bough*) I feel less as if religion and magic are merely primitive stages already overcome, and more as if they are like the stone and bronze that still prove useful alongside the later iron. Although Frazer wasn't exactly the focus of your chapter, I'd love to hear your thoughts on his work, as well as a report on whether anyone at all is still reading him in your archaeological circles.

CW: Alas, archaeologists have at various turns scraped away at this insight – the mixing of times – but given an obsession with the production of clocks, with organizing objects along a line of successions, with sorting them into a homogeneous time, they always fell short of a wider explication of *polychronicity*. Chronometrics is only part of the issue. Under the influence of a particular form of historicity, amplified through the division of archaeological labor into discrete eras (something reinforced by institutions, communities of practice, discursive commitments, job descriptions, etc.), the coextensive reality of the polychronic ensemble largely remained naively given within archaeological sites, landscapes, and objects. Subsumed under that expressive fallacy whereby Venetian bastions, Classical towers, or canning plants spoke to a living presence sealed off within their own time, yet again archaeologists approached their objects with the solution, ordered and circumscribed within their phases against the background of a flattened, homogeneous time. This neglect was amplified by an underlying assumption that, in paraphrasing Latour (if you will forgive my use of the term "paraphrasing," which has a precise technical sense for you), the sorting of these objects was a product of time rather than what makes time possible.[9] By distinguishing between the time of antiquity and the antiquity of time, Serres highlighted this discrepancy.[10]

No one had given the wreckage of mixed times its due, since these purified pasts were neatly sorted into their successive eras. It was as if archaeologists viewed this richness component by component, maintaining each object within its distilled and circumscribed compartment. Of course, practitioners came to focus on change "through time," diachronically, where the cross-temporal interrelation of various periods was taken up as an explicit matter of concern.[11] There remained a sense that by situating recovered artifacts by date and ordering them into an unbroken sequence, archaeologists might touch all periods to the same degree. In truth, not only did they continue to use their successive linkages as a narrative thread, one delimited within temporal compartments corresponding to areas of expertise, they also obscured emergent gaps, where the "post-history" or "after-life" of an object, as with Mycenae or the temple of Corinth, was destroyed under the weight of an idealized historical image, and presented proximities between objects dated to periods distant on a timeline. Ultimately, the succession of distinct eras in linear time continued to provide convenient frames for a synthesis; while this is understandable, it is difficult to account for the mixing of time under such scenarios. Only in recent decades have archaeologists dealt with questions of the past in the past, with memory, and ancient engagements with ruins.[12] Even then objects were treated as referents, indices, indications of something else, and thus never imparted their fair share as, among other things, coexistent media that make those pasts possible.[13] It was also as if it were only appropriate to speak of each object in terms of what it supposedly *was*, rather than what it *is*. And yet it is also appropriate to understand this mixing as fundamentally archaeological, given the routine enmeshment of objects with their diverse times, as one witnesses along the National Road 70 (EO70). For me this polychronicity, grounded in the present, is a major part of what characterizes the archaeological.

Along the route between Nafplion and the sanctuary of Asclepios at Epidaurus one also follows in the footsteps of Frazer. In taking this path in 1890 and again in 1895 (in the opposite direction), Frazer was himself following in the footsteps of the Roman traveler Pausanias, in the course of writing the multi-volume commentary to his translation of the ancient author's *Periegesis Hellados*.[14] It was in reckoning with Pausanias that I originally came to Frazer, whose commentary is still read by classicists. I immediately appreciated Frazer as a writer. I admired his smooth and balanced style, his vivid descriptions of land and scenery, his colorful depictions of flora and seasons, the care and subtlety with which he handled archaeological examples. It was only later that I read *The Golden Bough*, which among many anthropologists is still held as an object of curiosity associated with an imperialist era best to be avoided. This is unfair.[15]

By another marvelous coincidence it was in his description of the sanctuary of Asclepios that Pausanias, upon mentioning a stone tablet that recorded a dedication of twenty horses to Asclepios by Hippolytus, interjected a tale told by the people of Aricia. Hippolytus, whom Asclepios had raised from the dead, refused to forgive his father Theseus for the curse which brought about his death. Hippolytus left this land, the land of his ancestors (Theseus was a native of nearby Troezen), for Italy. There he reigned under the name of Virbius. He consecrated a sanctuary to Artemis by the sylvan lake where, down to the time of Pausanias (second century CE), the priesthood of the goddess was awarded to the victor of a single combat, open only to absconded slaves. This ritual constituted the starting point for *The Golden Bough*, and the eastern end of the valley which I discuss in the chapter is intimately linked to it.

It was in the second edition of *The Golden Bough* that Frazer introduced the tripartite scheme of evolutionary development from magic to religion to science. These phases of human thought resonate with the Three Age System of archaeology. Still, you are right to hesitate about the rigidity of their succession. Frazer "had no qualms," as Robert Ackerman put it, "about comparing items of culture from the most disparate periods and places."[16] Diverse times and locales are juxtaposed throughout *The Golden Bough*, which implies coexistence. Cutting across the three stages were what Edward Burnett Tylor called "survivals," holdovers out of kilter with the beliefs of a given phase.[17] It was to survivals that Frazer was drawn. There are also elements of recurrence between science and magic as "techniques of intervention," compared with religion which tends to abjure responsibility by surrendering to the will of God.[18] Moreover, one may point to the recurrence of iconoclasm between secondary religions (such as Christianity and Islam) and science. Against a modernist scheme of progress, which builds towards its apex of science situated at the helm of Western society, one might write off such features as anachronisms; most readers of *The Golden Bough* certainly do. This is not without reason. Frazer, however, was also more subtle. If, as you surmise, magic and religion prove useful alongside science, then it is not only because Frazer openly juxtaposes examples from these phases, but also because no system of human thought is without its gains and losses. We, those readers who embrace Western science, are none the wiser.

GH: Contemporary philosophy still works very much in an Enlightenment idiom, and in this respect there is a built-in commitment to linear historical time, and thus to the worthlessness of magic (by everyone) and religion (by most). Though I would love to spend some time defending the value of both of these Enlightenment outcasts, it's time to move on to Section C of your chapter ("Pleats and Rents: Mycenae 2014"), which is short but important. Along with your wonderful description of Mycenae, what strikes me most in this section is your reference to *topology*. Now, one hears the topological metaphor a lot these days outside its home discipline of mathematics, and perhaps some of this usage is not especially rigorous. But it raises an interesting question in the context of our discussion: namely, does topological time refer to the same kind of time as the metaphors of percolation, eddies, or countercurrents that you evoked early in your chapter? These latter terms are the sort we find in Serres and Latour, and I find myself wondering how surprising it would be if they spoke of topologies instead.

For on the one hand, both percolation and topology clearly refer to some sort of nonlinear time, and in that purely negative sense they do belong together. But the connotations could be vastly different in the two cases. Earlier, I expressed concern that the idea of time as percolation was probably too wedded to a gradualist model of incremental change. For even if time can move both backwards and forwards as percolation theorists think, the movement in both directions is fairly slow, devoid of revolutions. And though Serres is the first person I think of in connection with percolation, Latour may be an even better example for us. Why? Because Serres actually leaves room for a *topology* of time in a way that Latour might not. Latour is in many ways a thinker of unrepeatably unique events, such as Pasteur's transformation of medicine. True, Latour does not think that Pasteur is an Enlightenment genius who replaces mere "beliefs" with rigorous "knowledge," but treats him instead as an organizer of vast human and nonhuman alliances. But what we get in Serres – though not so much in Latour – is the idea of time as built of recurring patterns, and this makes me think of topology in a way that Latour never does. I remember Serres' discussion of human sacrifice in Carthage on the hollow interior of a statue of Baal. Serres argues, of course (this was after the shuttle Challenger explosion of 1986 but before the Columbia disaster in 2003), that the space shuttle can also be read as a type of human sacrifice, given that it was always statistically likely that some of those astronauts would die. As an adolescent I used to feel the same way on the final warmup laps of the Indianapolis 500 as they silently displayed the photos of all thirty-three drivers: as if a possible human sacrifice were about to occur, even though there have been no in-race fatalities since 1973.

In any case, it seems to me that percolation upsets linear time primarily by letting it move both forwards and backwards, while topological time does it in a different way, by increasing or decreasing temporal distance. To mention McLuhan again, I think he says that the automobile retrieves the knight in shining armor: whether in the highway jousts that occur between drivers, or the heraldry of fuzzy dice hanging from the mirror and provocative bumper stickers. Topology can shrink time in this way, by eliminating the calendar distance between medieval knights and two drunk teenagers in the 1950s playing a duel of "chicken." But of course, topology can also emphasize vast temporal differences between apparently coexisting elements: such as Serres' other example of the temporal heterogeneity present in a single car, with fire (1.9 million years ago), wheels (late Neolithic), glass (late Neolithic), pistons (1838), computers (1936), and airbags (early 1970s) assembled together in a single entity. My question is whether there are any cases in archaeology where the percolative and topological models of time might come into such serious conflict that irreconcilable interpretations of one and the same artifact or site would arise.

CW: Before passing on to your question it is worth taking stock of the topological examples that you raise; especially in light of the foregoing discussion of Frazer's systems of human thought and the Enlightenment idiom. Serres finds resemblances between an accident of scientific space exploration and abhorrent sacrifices in ancient religion.[19] To modern ears such comparisons sound entirely incommensurable. What recurring *topos* could possibly exist between Baal Hammon, the "Lord of the Furnaces," and exploding rockets, whether they carry astronauts or nuclear payloads?[20] We all know Serres to be playing on the same modernist scheme of progress that we discussed with Frazer. The moment that historicism is put to one side, we open up the possibility of eliminating those distances formerly held to exist between these topoi. Both the brazen Baal and Space Shuttle Challenger appear as colossal metal statues that rise upon fire and smoke; both are high technologies that require tremendous investment on the part of societies; both involve specialists who oversee the event; both fuel horrors that unfold before dumbfounded throngs of onlookers in denial. By calling them oxen, the Carthaginians deny they hear the voices of their children; by calling the Challenger disaster an accident, we refuse to acknowledge how our culture sacrifices humans and animal others to the Baal of technology, given the statistical probability you mention.[21]

Your example of the Indianapolis 500 points to another god, that of automobility. How many sacrifices are we willing to sustain in order to safeguard our ease of movement and expanded dominance of distance?[22] McLuhan's discussion of the automobile's retrieval of the medieval knight is appropriate in many respects, especially in association with the potential loss of life among the pampered aristocracy. Yet that image fails to evoke the reason why our societies are willing to endure such sacrifices, which is deeply psychological. Ease and salvation are among other psychological aspects highlighted by Peter Sloterdijk, who also points out several mechanisms of repetition.[23] Built upon a Neolithic chassis with wheels and axles, the automobile draws on a combination of mythological images and historical *topoi*. Both its speed and ease of movement were anticipated by heroes on winged horses who conquered tremendous distances. Its effects upon human psychology and safety are partially captured by McLuhan's medieval knights (or as Sloterdijk contends, centaurs, given the merger that has occurred between driver and car).[24] Its comfort and conditioned interior retrieve the litter with its cushioned seats and shaded canopy carried aloft on the shoulders of retainers.

Mycenae is not without its paradoxes. Cultures of science that claim to adhere to enlightened beacons have left their mark there; they too failed to see any resemblance between their pursuits and those of ancient cultures whose decisions were guided by religion (including myth) or magic in Frazer's sense. Nonetheless, late nineteenth-century excavations in the name of archaeology recall ancient destructions at Mycenae. Under the authority of the Archaeological Society of Athens, those labors that revealed large portions of the pre-Homeric citadel went hand in hand with the catastrophic annihilation of objects, not only those things that were held in the earth, but the very layers and deposits that encompassed them.[25] These archaeological fires, by and large, were sparked by a historical image of Mycenae under the Pelopid line, and where they burned they consumed the memories of all times subsequent to the Bronze Age abandonment. Without the non-zero-sum difference that comes with collection or documentation, one is left with nearly complete desolation, a topological rent, where legendary objects are made irrecoverably distant. Of course, new proximities are now present.

Topology has many advantages, as you have expressed so well in your question. Its appeal to archaeology is tremendous, especially when one takes into account how the field is heavily reliant upon Euclidian geometries by flattening its polychronic diversities onto two-dimensional planes.[26] Topology also brings to the fore a spatial understanding of time. Here, we may speak of those tangible proximities and distances within and between things present in the citadel. Still, for me, topology and percolation provide complementary ways of expressing or understanding the nature of time at different scales or levels of resolution.

I grasp your concern with percolation. The term comes from the Latin, *percolatio*, which means to filter or trickle through. Within archaeology, routine emphasis on consistent rates of entropy or processes of transformation reinforces a gradualist image of time, and this undermines objects. The decay of radiocarbon or the hydration of obsidian are somehow seen as more indicative of time than the charred stave of wood or the discarded blade core that linger on for millennia within their chthonic domain. In elevating a superficial sense of passing slowness, we ignore the time of objects that undergo changes saltationally: with being cut from an oak bough or worked into a portable core; with being burned in a conflagration or reduced to an unworkable portion of volcanic glass; with being buried, lodged within the soil, or uncovered by archaeologists and boxed away in artifact storage. Without these objects, processes of radioactivity or discoloration would not be possible. Were we to leave it at this, one could see how the terms topology and percolation could come into conflict: as you say, the former deals with proximities and distances between objects, while the latter is too conditioned by a gradualist image of time that undermines objects.

And yet with percolation, filtration is only half of the theme. The other side of the term evokes stimulation, the boiling or bubbling up that comes with adding the vital heat of activity, of that restlessness within and between objects. These kinetics manifest themselves in far more diverse ways than any forward or backward motion would suggest. When seen from a certain distance the time of objects leaps and dances and forms circles, eddies, and vortices. The time of objects stabilizes and festers, appearing to slow on the surface, only to burst forth into tumultuous change: which, again from the right distance, takes on the appearance of thunderous accelerations. Whereas topology allows us to speak of contact or separation between objects, percolation for me conjures a tumultuous sense of time, the verve that arises within and between legions of things. Whereas topology allows one to work through pleats and folds present within the fabric of Mycenae, which is normally flattened, percolation complicates the picture we build at the end, how we conceive of the time of the citadel or Greek lands, through the sum of changes and continua, metamorphoses and durations gauged through chronological measures. One has to remain true to these differences to avoid serious conflict between them. As with Serres, I believe topology and percolation can be used together in productive ways, but that doesn't mean that irreconcilable interpretations won't happen. Many archaeologists will continue to defend a gradualist image of time, and will probably embrace percolation in very different ways.

GH: Here I would like to ask for a point of clarification. You just said that "many archaeologists will continue to defend a gradualist image of time." This might be a good moment to ask for a brief map (which many readers will probably need as much as I do) of the various factions in contemporary archaeology. You have often told me about theoretical tensions between so-called "post-processual archaeology" and those of you who prefer to focus on objects. Could you explain this difference further, and also explain whether it is related in any way to the differing views on time we've been discussing, or whether it is an entirely unrelated dispute?

CW: By definition archaeology is omnivorous, and that means that good topographies are hard to come by. If we put to one side the world of professional field archaeology, governmental archaeology, and heritage management (of which academic archaeologists often fail to take measure), then standard atlases divide the discipline along the lines of different theoretical approaches or platforms upheld by research archaeologists often employed in universities or museums.[27] You mention post-processual archaeology. This arose in the 1980s as a reaction to a theoretical hegemony, energized by the proliferation of new techniques and methodologies in the wake of World War II, that championed archaeology as a science.[28] Those who embraced the colors of post-processualism prioritized contingencies of meaning, symbolism, and language over supposedly restrictive processes of cultural evolution conceived as an ongoing series of reactions to environmental change.[29] By embracing the "post-," archaeologists attempted to consign processualism, which had already tried to discard approaches that interpreted the spread of artifacts in terms of the movement of cultures (what was labeled "culture history"), to the rubbish pile of abandoned concepts. Here again, with such paradigmatic eliminativism, we encounter movement along an irreversible line. If anything, these older maps no longer capture archaeology's contours because the field never had the coherence that has been granted to it in retrospect.[30]

By the turn of the new millennium, archaeology under a post-processual orthodoxy, as most practitioners saw it, resembled an archipelago.[31] A pluralist diversity was seen as an indication of vitality.[32] Indiscriminate appetites meant that radically different perspectives were brought to bear in the interpretation of past remains.[33] For example, those who worked on identity and personhood found their muses in the likes of Foucault or Butler; those who elevated the observational perception of landscape over scientific modes of abstraction looked to phenomenology in its various guises; those who honed their liberating weapons in confronting inequities embraced critical theory, following the road to Frankfurt. The topography of archaeology very much reflected the theoretical landscape of the wider humanities, with its islands of Marxism, postcolonialism, indigenous archaeologies, heritage studies, and so forth. Various adherents built careers out of brandishing their theoretical insignia. Of course, reality is somewhat more nuanced than melodrama.

After the year 2000, many of us had grown uneasy with the state of archaeological theory. Bjørnar Olsen, Michael Shanks, and I shared the assessment that it had lost its bold edge. Debate had stagnated. Dominated by politics as first philosophy, incommensurable ideas proliferated and few engaged with work outside the confines of their interests.[34] We felt that such disorganized variety was not because any common delineation of the field had broken down. Instead, we knew that it had yet to be articulated.[35] Choosing to emphasize what we shared (things) rather than what separated us, we crafted a modest proposal for retuning archaeology, which was eventually published as *Archaeology: The Discipline of Things*.[36] Like you, we found intellectual kinship in the work of Latour, whose science studies we had all known for some time, and even more so in Serres, who was a professor at Stanford University where we came together in 2003. Our label – symmetrical archaeology – was both provisional and partly ironic, given the way various platforms vaunted their adjectival qualifiers. Archaeology works just fine as archaeology, but no one would hear that message, given the way the game was played.

Post-processual archaeology challenged archaeological time on the grounds of chronology, succession, and periodization by bringing new understandings to the fore: different timescales in the vein of the *Annales* School, duration, memory (specifically, a willful or "recollective" memory), or nonlinear dynamics.[37] While practitioners recognized the past here in the present and the importance of memory, they were nonetheless tied to understandings of time as an external parameter, and notions of resultant causation in which objects were merely derivative. Providing an alternative to time as it has been conceived is tied to this larger project of retuning with things at the center.

At this point, given everything we share with OOO, the reactions to our work have been similar to what you have encountered. We have now witnessed a return of authentic debate in archaeology, which takes place along a spectrum. At one end are those who have staked their careers on a game played exclusively by sentient beings, and who cannot abide object-oriented approaches.[38] Many of these critiques have taken the form of defensive posturing. Some are marred by a species of deliberate misreading and wanton misrepresentation tied to cherry-picking statements as slogans without even-handed consideration.[39] At the other end are those who take up the turn to things under different colors. Examples include: pragmatic archaeology, whose advocates embrace material semiotics;[40] process archaeologies, whether in the distinctive vein of Whitehead or from the different angle of Deleuze,[41] under the influence of the likes of Bennett's vital materialism,[42] Barad's agential realism,[43] or Ingold's work;[44] Ian Hodder's entanglement theory, which you know well;[45] and ontological alterity, which refuses to champion a unified, definitive reality as a supreme authority over the truths of other modes of existence.[46]

Having stated this, no topographer should attempt to chart contemporary archaeology without taking stock of how the discipline is shaped by its objects of study. Whether one works with Neolithic landscapes in Britain, abandoned buildings in Detroit, rock art in Scandinavia, Mayan cities in Guatemala, Cold War ruins in the Pacific, agrarian terraces in Jordan, or Late Bronze Age ceramics in the Peloponnesus, each and every object demands its own peculiar commitments. Institutions, it should be added, also exert a profound influence on the diverse configurations of the field. In the United States, for example, academic archaeologists rarely work under roofs of their own. Departments of Classics, Anthropology, and History, where most US academic archaeologists are employed, are not without their own expectations. In each case, objects are placed under the burden of significance that comes with each discipline, and this constrains archaeology in its ability to grow of its own accord.[47] Still, even in European contexts where practitioners are housed within departments of archaeology, one is not immune to such influences.[48]

GH: Indeed, philosophy has followed a similar course. Perhaps the biggest difference from what you just described in archaeology is that the "scientific" approach to philosophy and our own analogue of the "post-processual" approach did not unfold over time in one and the same disciplinary space. Instead, philosophy has been polarized for roughly a century, though arguably even since the late seventeenth century. There is analytic philosophy, dominant in the most prestigious universities of the Anglophone world, which sees itself as particularly scientific in its manner of carving out delimited research problems to be pored over with great precision by sub-communities of specialists. And there is continental philosophy, so marginalized that it is mainly found in the philosophy departments of Catholic universities, second-tier state universities, and (sometimes even more robustly) in departments other than philosophy. As you know, I'm currently working at the Southern California Institute of Architecture, and wouldn't be surprised if I am never employed by a philosophy department again, given the failure of OOO to fit under either the analytic or continental rubrics. The "scientific" approach strikes me as the wrong way to do philosophy, given my view, inspired by Socrates, that philosophy isn't about knowledge at all. At the same time, philosophy's parallel to the "post-processual" approach remains too obsessed with the purportedly almighty power of humans in shaping reality. There are numerous variants of this approach, and they all have alibis to prove that they are not outright idealisms that treat the nonhuman world as just boring rubble. What I have always shared with archaeologists like you and Bjørnar Olsen, and which made me feel an immediate kinship with those in your circle, is the sense that inanimate objects need a much larger role in our theories than they currently possess. Yes, I'm more suspicious than you are of the various New Materialisms and of the newly influential attempts to focus on "practices," but our points in common are far more important.

But now I want to turn to your Section D ("Things: Contiguities, Symbioses, Emergence"). This passage in particular interested me:

> However, one cannot divide the Late Helladic period into twelve or twenty phases in the same way as a day, which can be arbitrarily reshuffled into ten or thirty hours. The fidelity of Late Helladic phases pertains to subtle changes in ceramic typology (the technology and form of pottery, both durable and pervasive) and not to the sequential ordering of a measured, homogeneous time into which, through association with datable objects, it nonetheless translates.

In Chapter 1 we referred to Aristotle's *Physics* and *Metaphysics* and how the real difference between these two foundational works is that the first deals with continua and the second with what we might call *quanta* or irreducible chunks of reality, which for Aristotle are the primary substances: namely, individual things. In the meantime I've been writing a book called *Waves and Stones*, which discusses a number of examples of the paradox of the continuous and the discrete in numerous spheres of intellectual life.[49] And it really is a paradox: any good theory of anything needs to come up with a solution for distributing the two, and there are a finite number of possible solutions.

What you've done in the passage I just cited is to shift the problem in at least one useful way. Namely, you say that the Late Helladic period is not really a continuum: there are definite changes in ceramic typology that require this period to be split up in one way rather than another. Now, maybe there are "continuum" archaeologists, for all I know: people who really do think that the past can be divided up arbitrarily as one pleases. But somehow I doubt it. Correct me if I'm wrong, but I suspect that archaeological dissidents would say things more along the lines of "OK, the ceramic typology suggests dividing up the late

Helladic in the way you suggest, but in fact the ceramics are just epiphenomenal: if you look at farming or navigation techniques, which were far more essential to the survival of the civilization, you'll find a completely different periodization." So then, how do you go about deciding which artifacts are the key to the periodization of a given era? I doubt that it can be cut up arbitrarily as one pleases, but how exactly do you decide? And are there any notable controversies in archaeology along these lines?

CW: Broken fragments of pottery are both persistent and pervasive. Because ceramic styles change, what is left of pots can be arranged into sequences using specific characteristics: shape, decoration, and material. When these attributes are found with consistency across numerous examples, those pots (or, rather, their identifiable portions) fit within a type, which can be organized into a typological system. The ordering or phasing of types (this before that, this after that) is ideally constructed (though, at times, confirmed or modified) through correlations with deposits that are related stratigraphically. Deposits generally contain an assortment of objects, which archaeologists often refer to as "assemblages." When meticulously studied, these coextensive types generate finer gradations within the phasing, because different wares are coextensive in some deposits, but not others. With an established typological system, which often aims to encompass the broader region of ceramic distribution, archaeologists may build a "relative" chronology for a given area or site or structure. And to be sure, every area, every site, every structure is distinctive. Any well-defined sequence should be put at risk in light of what the found ceramics within stratified contexts suggest.[50] In any case, to answer your first question, because ceramic sherds are found in nearly every context (discrete layer or deposit) at Mycenae and other Bronze Age sites, and because they can be situated within a typological sequence, they have long been stressed for establishing the periodization of Bronze Age eras in Greece and elsewhere.[51]

Periodization is an achievement. It was Arne Furumark who published the first comprehensive survey of Mycenaean ceramics in 1941.[52] Elevating shape and decoration above technical features, Furumark arranged Mycenaean ceramics into a typological sequence based upon stylistic change. From Mycenaean IIIA:2 onwards, for example, "the broad conical-piriform shape" in storage jars "is transformed into a new kind of piriform shape, characterized by a fully rounded upper part, slowly tapering to a short, stem-like lower part."[53] Alan Wace,

Tsountas' successor at Mycenae, rejected Furumark's analysis
of style because, among other purported shortcomings, it lacked
confirmation through correlation with stratigraphic sequences
of deposition.[54] Wace, working in the wake of Schliemann and
Tsountas, was always at pains to establish the stratification of
ceramics at Mycenae. Nonetheless, for Wace, pottery checked
against stratified contexts rendered as evidence "was always the
safest guide" for dating other objects (structural remains, refuse
pits, tombs) in and around the citadel.[55] When revisiting the
work of Furumark and Wace one recognizes how periodization
is built upon an excruciating amount of labor directed at regis-
tering subtle changes in actual objects. From this angle, the Late
Helladic period is not a continuum. But there is more to what is
implied by your second question.

Archaeologists distinguish between relative and absolute
dating. If the former is the sequential phasing that, as I have
stated, draws on the attributes of and correlations between
actual objects, then the latter aims to situate this phasing within
calendar time; it is here that object phasing is mapped onto a
continuum, which is assumed to be in the background, even
if archaeological periods cannot be arbitrarily divided as one
pleases.[56] When Furumark published The Mycenaean Pottery,
when Wace published his Mycenae, absolute dates for Greek
prehistory could only be attained through archaeological comparisons with Egypt, where Mycenaean pots occasionally turned
up in datable contexts.[57] In Egypt, scholars had recourse to a
detailed chronology built upon the long line of Pharaonic king-
ship for which there are a number of objects – the Palermo Stone,
the Abydos King List, the Turin Canon, Manetho's History of
Egypt – that chronicle the succession of pharaohs and tie them
to some astronomical observations (solar eclipses) that could be
calculated in terms of absolute dates.[58] Late Helladic III vases
found at Tell el Amarna, the abandoned city of the monotheistic
revolutionary king, Akhenaten, for example, provided approxi-
mate dates for this phase of the Late Bronze Age in Greece.[59]

One need not stray too far from Mycenae for notable controversies. Beyond cumbersome debates over the rigidity of
organization and structure, many disputes straddle the magnificent paradox you mention: how to translate relative (local) into
absolute (universal) terms. Furumark interpreted styles in light
of the specific peoples that produced them. For him, morpho-
logical change in ceramic design was assumed to be gradual,
attenuated by "inertia" and "conservatism" within Mycenaean

societies.[60] For example, what he called Mycenaean IIIC:1*e* correlated to 1230–1200 BCE; IIIC:1*l* to 1200–1125 BCE; and IIIC:2 to 1125–1100 BCE.[61] Establishing an absolute date on stylistic grounds within the narrow space of twenty-five years, roughly the length of a generation, rests on rather shaky foundations that are never explicitly disclosed.[62] Wace took Furumark to task for this, aiming for a typology that is not solely stylistic, but also stratigraphically derived.[63] In any case, such methods cannot account for those initial phases of stylistic innovation that come in advance of standardization, because typology and seriation, arranging types into a chronological series, group together all examples bearing similar attributes.[64] As my colleague Laurent Olivier has pointed out, these methods distort the time of things in such a way that they do not correlate to the calendar time upon which chronology is based.[65]

Still, when it comes to dating methods, contemporary archaeology has considerably more options at its disposal. Natural clocks (radiocarbon and dendrochronology, among others) opened a new era of archaeological dating by providing historically independent modes of deriving absolute time (indeed, their introduction constituted a proper symbiosis within our field). While there was initial hesitation within the Aegean world over the precision of carbon-14 dating – when compared to the established and refined archaeological chronologies built upon the labors of Furumark and Wace – radiocarbon would prove fundamental in other areas of European prehistory.[66] After carbon-14, no one would suggest that Stonehenge was contemporary with Mycenae's nearly perfect double circle of standing stones.[67]

Radiocarbon dating depends on specific quanta, that is, the amount of carbon-14 present in a particular object. This too must be translated into calendar time. Physical measurements are set to a metronome that ticks at a rate based on the steady decay of ^{14}C, which reduces by half every 5,730 years.[68] The amount of ^{14}C relative to ^{12}C is a basis for translating a quantum of radiocarbon into a continuum, which is further refined for locality through various calibration techniques. In this sense, radiocarbon is also a "relative" form of dating (though it is always classified under "absolute") since it is derived from the comparative measure of quanta (amounts of ^{14}C and ^{12}C) within actual objects.[69]

As you might expect, discrepancies would arise with historically derived chronologies as radiocarbon dating methods were refined.[70] Notable today in Aegean prehistory is the controversy over the High and Low chronology of the mid-second millennium BCE.[71] New research extends the periodization of the Late Bronze Age by a century.[72] At root, this really comes down to a debate over which objects are the key to periodization. Those who embrace the High chronology favor the radiocarbon evidence; those who hold to the Low chronology back the typology-stratigraphy-derived chronology. Many major controversies have resulted from a clash between these different chronological systems, and while disputes may surface along the lines of the sciences and the humanities, this is more an issue of disparate archaeological traditions. Still, it is a good thing that archaeology didn't polarize completely, for arguably this is one of our greatest strengths.

So yes, prehistoric phases are derived from changes in objects (relative to other objects) which are capable of bearing an imprint that is generative of their own time. Yet that object memory is just as easily ignored by being co-opted, in service to a different sense of process and history. That archaeologists have long referred to the allocation of numerical coordinates to relative phases as "fixing" suggests an underlying prejudice. The "relative," which is rooted in relations between actual things, is judged *a priori* against the imagined background of continual inhabitation (a measured continuum) which is termed "absolute." By situating its objects against a continuum, a homogeneous or gradual time where every instant becomes equally relevant, archaeology displays a command over the continuity of time, which is tied to an aspiration to a total picture of the past. This ultimately obscures our actual things and their heterogeneous times.

You are correct that one could derive completely different periodizations from other objects. Archaeologists routinely establish typologies of things other than erstwhile pots. Furumark's study, for example, included chronological evidence from female terracotta figurines, spindle whorls, fibulae, swords and daggers. Stylistic change in such objects also provides archaeologists with a way to fine-tune phasing derived from ceramics. Still, a radically different sense of periodization may be drawn from relational objects associated with farming, as you point out. Whatever form plant cultivation took, it was the case that the long-lived rapports with seed and stores, cereals and pulses, seasonal variations in moisture and soil, clots of earth and hoes, eventually (in the case of Greece) olive trees and vines, traction animals and plows, fields and furrows, characterized agrarian societies from the dawn of the Neolithic to the mid-twentieth century.[73] This stretch of time – eight millennia in the plain below Mycenae – becomes conspicuous with the disruption of modes of living with land, companion species, and other objects.

GH: This might be the place to say a bit more about my book *Immaterialism*, which you have noted is where I make use of Margulis's Serial Endosymbiosis Theory. Obviously I owe a great deal to Latour and Actor–Network Theory (ANT). Yet there are several weaknesses to this theory, one of them being a relative helplessness in the case of counterfactual questions, since entities for ANT end up being defined as everything that they did along the way, which makes it surprisingly difficult to consider carefully the several possible paths that they might have followed at a given key moment. (Strangely enough, Latour does a brilliant job of proposing counterfactual lives of Serres during their famous dialogue, yet he rarely if ever does this in his solo-authored books.) But another problem with ANT that always bothered me is that it tends to treat actions as part of a continuum. Caesar crossing the Rubicon is an action for Latour, and so is a hair falling off my head, and the only reason these are different for Latour is that the crossing of the Rubicon mobilized so many other actors and had such a big impact on many other things, whereas the hair falling off my head affects very little. It's a difference of degree, and like all differences of degree it is too beholden to the model of the continuum while not incorporating any sense of quantized time. Stated differently, in my book I was looking for internal changes to the Dutch East India Company rather than external measurements of the historical noisiness of each of its battles and trade deals. And that's what led me back to Margulis, who of course has a wonderful model of what constitutes evolution: the symbiosis of previously independent organisms.

Could something like this work in archaeology as well? I recall reading somewhere the theory that it was Homer himself who invented Greek polytheism, in the sense that it was Homer who first brought a number of essentially local deities into the same theological space in the *Iliad*. Assuming that is true, then here we have a symbiosis of numerous previously separate religions, with no turning back, and here we would have something more undeniably important than any series of gradualist tweaks in ceramic styles, though of course I'm not excluding that ceramic changes might also rise to the level of symbiotic breakthrough in some cases.

CW: Your question anticipates the need for a fundamentally different theory of evolution and social change in terms of "internalization," or what we might call "anthropoiesis." This term, anthropoiesis, refers to the long making of human beings both as objects and as components within larger collectives that have emerged through symbioses of profound consequence to *Homo sapiens* as a species.[74] Homer, as you say, provides an excellent example. Polytheistic religions are deeply rooted in locality. Analogous cults appear under the names of dissimilar deities. Contrasting myths are associated with the same name, or different names with the same myths. Both Walter Burkert and Jean-Pierre Vernant made compelling arguments for the emergence of the pantheon and associated myths in their canonical forms with Homer and Hesiod.[75] Still, there are legion symbioses in agrarian societies: the merger of human groups with guided fauna in agriculture; the co-opting of surplus by a few with centralized grain stores; the amplification of production with plows pulled by yoked oxen as labor's companions; distinctive diets with the introduction of olive oil. So tenacious are many of these mergers that humans do not extract themselves until the twentieth century, after a new symbiosis with fossil-fuel metabolizing engines. With ceramics, new symbioses might occur with the development of a new clay source, the introduction of the fast wheel, or a new style of decoration derived from Minoan influences. Likewise, the examples from Chapter 2 pointed to various symbioses with objects formerly consigned to the chthonic realm.

GH: We'll be getting into symbiosis in greater detail later. But here I want to touch briefly on a topic that too often drowns out all other considerations in present-day intellectual life: politics. In *Bruno Latour: Reassembling the Political*, I tried to establish a way of looking at modern political theory different from the traditional Left/Right divide, in part because Latour is such a difficult figure to place on that spectrum. I would say that there tend to be two problems shared by the modern Left and Right. First, they are too obsessed with the question of human nature and whether it is either good or infinitely malleable over time (Left), or else either evil or largely unchanging over millennia of history (Right). Graeber and Wengrow also dislike this deadlock, but they simply replace the naturally good or naturally evil human with a naturally imaginative and experimental one, which means that they remain squarely within the debate over human nature that characterizes modern political theory, up to and including the present moment.[76] But I happen not to agree that human nature is the key political problem, since human interaction tends to be stabilized or altered by the mediation of nonhuman objects, and Latour is a theoretical pioneer on this very point. Second, both the Left and the Right seem too obsessed with politics as a kind of *knowledge* or *truth*, even if the purported truth takes the privative form of "there is no truth; the strongest will always prevail." I think that Latour has opened a possible new entry into non-modern political philosophy: a theory based on our permanent political ignorance and our reliance on inanimate things for structuring the political space.

This leads me to ask the more general question of how archaeologists interpret political situations on the basis of objects. Presumably you can venture a guess at any given site as to how hierarchical or egalitarian a given society would have been, whether slavery was present, how sharply women seem to have been segregated from political life, and so forth. Presumably ceramics remain relatively constant from one political period to another. But what sorts of object-oriented traces suggest radical political change to the archaeologist?

CW: Let's approach your question initially from a slightly different angle. Through the two-century-long history of archaeology one might be tempted to trace a curious swerve from the power politics of the Right to the truth politics of the Left. Pre-1900 European mentalities were drawn to the heroic. Captivated by the citadels of Mycenae and Tiryns, whose high walls (even if they were saturated by poetry, myth, and history) tacitly suggested the powers that built them, the first modern archaeologists, those in possession of the means to do so, dug in search of the greatness implied by what had remained. In an age of European expansion they tended to sympathize with the victor. Thus archaeologists, often Northern European themselves, were lured to the high spots. They were called to the segregated interiors that even then were protected by strong monumental walls. There, those first discoverers revealed what remained of long-buried "palaces": what one could assume to have been an elaborate enclosure of security that preserved the seat of ancient power. Indeed, the fact that these citadels with their lofty redoubts were burned and not fully reoccupied in quite the same way suggests overt political change.[77] The fact that those first archaeologists destroyed objects suggestive of other pasts (those related to the later phases of the citadel) to the advantage of a desired greatness (that which is now present) also speaks to politics.[78]

Over the course of the twentieth century, archaeological sympathies appear to shift to the other end of the spectrum that you mention. Professional positions in archaeology increased and the field opened to wider diversity. Many came from blue-collar backgrounds. Practitioners cast their nets beyond the ruined domains vacated by overlords to bring into consideration the harlequin patchwork of the countryside. New methodologies and techniques, such as surface survey and remote sensing, were crafted to address what was inscribed in the land. Brushing history against its grain, these archaeologists sifted through the wreckage, looking for what they hoped would speak to the banal memories of those who labored outside high walls, in the shadows of power, and in other eras in the shadows of history.[79] Drawn to objects that might speak to the lot of slaves, women, children, the disenfranchised, the oppressed, these archaeologists sought a form of redemption that could only come with putting a truth to that which, having never been noticed, was lost to Lethe. Of course, such a political swerve constitutes a vast over-simplification. Still, is not the past, as Nietzsche suggested, in service of the lives we learn to live?

Politics operates in the orbit of archaeological objects; that is why, when it comes to political questions, it often seems more productive to remain on the outside. In other words, many work at the interface between people and their material pasts; within a space of critical introspection, in understanding the context in which one labors.[80] And yet archaeology has long struggled to show how nonhuman objects stabilize power within a given society – as with Latour – and extend it into potential futures.[81]

Mycenae and Tiryns hold memories of an erstwhile world where exaggerated differences were sustained through monumental architectural forms. The structures established within their remote interiors maintain the forms of palatial residences with rooms staggered along corridors with restricted points of entry, which implies controlled access. These "palaces" also included large areas for guarded storage, surplus, and wealth. The quality of their materials exceeds those deployed within structures elsewhere. Monumental tholos tombs once contained burials where excessive riches, including exotic items imported from distant lands, were removed from living society in what may have been lavish spectacles that served to reinforce elite identities. The strong walls of these great citadels not only delimited those inside from those outside, they also ensured that anyone who stood before them bore witness to the manifest ability of those who lived securely within to construct such awe-inspiring edifices, which rose to the level of transcendent powers, as evidenced by later Greeks who attributed their construction to mythical beings. Likewise, one will find numerous contrasts in the city of Argos which emerged across the plain from Mycenae and Tiryns four centuries later. Open areas for assembly are established at the nexus of roads. More encompassing ramparts are erected around a much larger area allowing for a wider community to live behind shared walls. Written documents were displayed in the open for all to behold, even if literacy rates were low by twenty-first-century standards. These are just a few examples of objects that are suggestive of different political regimes.

Objects, to be sure, stabilize and extend power. Walls, rooms, corridors, open spaces, however, do not hold memories of political changes in the way of the *Histories* of Herodotus. Many attempts to narrate political change within archaeology aim to "reconstitute the past" over which history holds a monopoly.[82] In other words, the image of political oppression, of specific groups without a history, is often imposed upon non-textual objects. For example, an archaeological colleague recently chastised those of us who have stood in defense of inanimate objects for "having nothing to say about the dynamics of historical processes."[83] Attempting to generate a lot of capital out of a single sentence from the object camp ("The Hadrianic Aqueduct would be non-existent without the raw physicality of mortar, brick, and stone, combined with geometry, survey labor, and craft experience"), he plainly proclaims that "it was slaves who built the Hadrianic aqueduct that served Corinth."[84] To lead with such assurances seems always to result in disappointment for those who, to borrow your words, Graham, "truly think that objects are nothing, and human politics everything."[85]

Remnants standing on the slopes of Ntourmiza or Megalovouni (located northwest of Mycenae) suggest less than little about to whom belonged the hands that set the stones: slave, free mason, soldier, or engineer. Though expository, such memories may or may not offer suggestions as to the identity of other objects that gave rise to them, and thus more concrete instances suggestive of overt political situations. All those who existed come to share in the glorious anonymity that remains. This is not to say that archaeological objects cannot be read in historical or political terms. Rather, it is to state that archaeologists are obliged to resist appropriating calcium carbonate-encrusted, *opus incertum* arches (what has become of the Hadrianic aqueduct) as a blank canvas upon which to project expressions of "the slave economies of the classical world." What we lose from one angle, we gain in another form of memory: in the grade of an *opus signinum*-lined channel, in cutmarks left at the top of a limestone precipice, in the form of stones set within mortar, in the presence of a stone-cut tunnel, which is reused at a later date. Still, it is no loss that the memories held within and between things belong to them and are involuntary artifacts of their own past. For if the fact that the remnants of past political spaces speak to how they exceed the powers they formerly underwrote, then what has become of them is no less a source of redemption.

GH: With your beautifully written Section E ("Percolation/Time") we are back to the theme of alternatives to linear temporality. And here again I sense a difference between the two options we discussed. There is percolation, as in your title and in the closing words of the section. And then once again there is topological time, which is not explicitly named in this section but is clearly present: "What may have been contiguous a century ago may be discontiguous today and what may be contiguous today may have been discontiguous a century ago." And of course, what is contiguous or discontiguous is quite often a matter of our own work and our own contemporary standpoints. To give an example, I was recently reading the page proofs of Alain Badiou's brilliant 1986 seminar on the philosophy of Nicolas Malebranche, because Columbia University Press wanted me to provide a back cover endorsement.[86] Among other things, Badiou makes skillful use of Lacanian psychoanalysis to shed light on Malebranche's system, which otherwise might seem so odd and alien to us in its confident rationalist theology. This itself is a topological move by Badiou: the apparently outdated Malebranche as a precursor of contemporary theoretical heroes like Lacan, and even of the long dead but still fashionable German Idealist philosopher F.W.J. Schelling. But Badiou misses what would be my own topological take on Malebranche. Whereas Badiou severely downplays the occasionalism of Malebranche's philosophy, the notion that things cannot affect each other directly but only through the mediation of another (God, in this case), for me this is precisely what is most contemporary about Malebranche. In this respect, topological time is the most futuristic of them all, since there is no telling what might look contiguous in the future despite seeming utterly unrelated now. As Newton showed us with objects falling to the ground and the Moon orbiting the Earth, two things that once seemed to belong not just to different but to opposite orders of reality might one day turn out to be manifestations of one and the same force.

But of course, the lesson of topology is not just that everything is stretchable. Perhaps even more importantly, it is also that there are holes that cannot be filled or closed. After reading the proofs of Badiou's seminar I turned to another task, reading, as editor-in-chief of the journal *Open Philosophy*, an interesting article by one Michael Feichtinger about how object-oriented ontology has been an underexploited resource for postcolonial theory.[87] Now, it is easy to see why postcolonial theorists have taken very little interest in OOO so far: they have all sworn a blood oath against "essentialism," and OOO demands a certain degree of essentialism, though not in the old sense that everyone likes to demonize. The specific anti-essentialists mentioned by Feichtinger were Karen Barad and Arturo Escobar, both of them obviously quite significant. But it seems to me that these authors make a pair of important mistakes. The first is that, in preaching anti-essentialism as vehemently as they do, they draw a purportedly necessary link between a specific philosophical doctrine (anti-essentialism) and the particular political cause to which they are committed (anti-imperialism). I think this is a serious error; ontology and politics belong to different registers, and the link between them is by no means permanent. For example, if we simply go back to the period of the French Revolution (barely yesterday, for many archaeologists!) we will find that it was the conservative party that was preaching social construction and the Jacobins who were touting the essential, natural rights of human beings. Today it has flipped, and people now behave as if anti-essentialism will always be a crucial doctrine for anti-imperialists, feminists, the LGBTQ community, and so forth, when at this point it is essentialism that may actually have more to offer these causes.

But here I am more interested in the second assumption made by the likes of Barad and Escobar. They seem to assume they have made some sort of radical break with the past by simply negating the *content* of what they regard as tired old Aristotelian essentialism.[88] From here on out, they assert, we will no longer naively believe that anything has an essence. This seems like linearism at its worst, though not quite gradualism, since they seem to think we are currently living through some sort of radical event in intellectual history. My view of how history works is different. As I see it, essentialism and anti-essentialism, just like any other basic conceptual opposition, represent two permanent possibilities between which humans will repeatedly oscillate due to the tendency of each side to degenerate into clichés after a certain period of dominance. And this is where I see the generational character of human thought coming into play. The generation just ahead of mine in continental philosophy tended to be wildly enthusiastic about Derrida, presumably because he felt for them like a liberating force, whereas for me as a graduate student he was already the ruling power (and moreover, he always struck me as a uniquely awful writer). This is not to say that no one my age is interested in Derrida (of course there are many such people), but somehow their Derrida is different than the one of those born in the 1950s, for whom he seems to have been a unique revelation of some sort.

But now I'm in danger of veering into "this is more a comment than a question" territory, so let's turn it into a question. You just mentioned the shift from the "heroic" approach to Mycenae characteristic of the nineteenth century and contrasted it with the twentieth-century preference for egalitarian consideration of the humble peasants and oppressed slaves of Mycenean civilization, and we should also add women to the mix as another previously under-considered group. What always stuns me about such broad changes of fashion is that people are so quick to assume that the "heroic" approach is so rightfully dead that it can never rise again. But it probably will; most things return someday, in suitably altered form. What, if anything, do you think archaeology lost with its turn from kings and victorious heroes to humble exploited subalterns?

CW: Appearances can be deceiving, which is why we should not fully give in to the temptation to read that political swerve into the history of archaeology at a deeper level. The "heroic" approach never completely died. One could profitably understand the long shift in emphasis as an artifact of saturation. The increasing density of research taking place in one quarter implies new objects for consideration in areas of scarcity. Still, if we have learned anything from our own disciplinary history it is that archaeology cannot discriminate. Casting the net widely over all possible groups, I would add, is more than a technique of awareness. It is foolish to regard what fashion suggests to be a wrongful past by ignoring it. This is why we must, as you do, separate that impoverished logic of contradiction associated with dialectical one-upmanship from more permanent possibilities. What has become of powerful priest-kings must have a place along with what is left of everyone else. For this is the only way to anticipate the unforeseeable. You speak of the return: who is to say that future generations won't identify with the heroic in confronting the colossal challenges all around us that we must inevitably face?

GH: We inhabit an intellectual moment in which egalitarian sentiment can seemingly do no wrong. However appealing this may seem politically, in the face of growing white supremacist movements and an increasingly rigged capitalism, on another level it is purely hypocritical. We all follow the principle of merit in choosing friends, mates, opportunities, job candidates, and also in selecting what to read of the many thousands of works produced in the past, trying to avoid wasting our time with mediocrity while hitting the high points. Excellence is under-priced in intellectual life today, since our current preference is always for whomever is *excluded* by pronouncements of excellence. One result is that high culture hardly exists anymore: the Nobel Prize for Literature recently went to the folk singer Bob Dylan. Everyone in academia seems to be working on popular culture, on comic books rather than epic poetry. Fair enough. Perhaps this is the right historical moment to take a hard look at exclusion. But at the end of the day, most people are excluded in any area where we look. Only a small percentage of applicants are admitted to Harvard or Princeton, largely because they can only accommodate a finite number of students. If we consider Nietzsche's threefold schema of antiquarian, critical, and monumental histories, critical history is treated as almost the only acceptable form at the moment.[89] I am less excited about antiquarian history as the mastery of time-honored detail, though it may become a more pressing option if basic education continues to deteriorate. Monumental history seems crucial to me, however. There is no greater intellectual skill than being able to tell the difference between the more and the less important.

CW: Perhaps in striving for excellence we are obliged to craft the figure that we might aspire to be even if it is not always possible to live up to the exemplar on a daily basis? In any case, it is fitting to return to Nietzsche's three species of history with respect to the figures of the archaeologist and the philosopher. Did the archaeologist not emerge from the antiquarian? Is the philosopher not drawn to the monumental? Both species of history, the antiquarian and the monumental, are not without their gains and losses, as Nietzsche pointed out. Your point is well taken. For Nietzsche, the laws of antiquarian fidelity served to impoverish creativity.[90] At best, the antiquarian, who approaches the banal and broken, the alien and strange, with dignity and care, cultivates a "simple feeling of pleasure and contentment"; at worst, they treat every scrap of the past with equal reverence, degenerating, as you say, through their inability to determine what is important, to the detriment of the living.

The monumental inspires greatness. The exemplary achievements of the past spark new fires that, yes, rise towards the superlative. And yet, returning to a thread that we have taken up at various turns in this discussion, it emphasizes one moment of an object's history at the expense of, as you put it, the "handful" of others (some of which were devoid of human relations).[91] As you suggest, this is not entirely a bad thing. Still, the domination of the monumental over the history of archaeology, as with Mycenae, has obliterated the jumble of accumulated objects suggestive of those changes that occurred after the citadel's supposed fall from greatness, for excavation is always an act of both recovery and destruction.[92] Framed within the measured confines of historical time, the monumental held no place for the polychronic intermingling of structures and ruins that inspired those epic stories of a heroic past four to five hundred years after the Late Bronze Age destructions. It is ironic that scholars would come to see the Homeric world as bound more to what had emerged after the wreckage of Late Bronze Age citadels, for such a realization was poorly served by late-nineteenth-century excavations driven by monumental history unchecked by the antiquarian.

For Nietzsche, neither the antiquarian nor the monumental thrives without the other, nor indeed without the critical: which is necessary for us the living to divest ourselves of the fetters of the wreckage of pasts, which continues to pile up everywhere. A healthy archaeology, on some level, is informed by all three species, but it is also prepared to resist subsuming objects under the modalities of history altogether, for it deals with a thoroughly different kind of past.

GH: To return to the task at hand, we come to your chapter's closing Section F, "An Archaeological Paradox." Your simplest formulation of the paradox is as follows: "For the archaeologist, the past is not here in a resultant causal relation to what is present; rather, *the things present are what make the past possible*." The reader should note that you're not saying that it's the archaeologist's present that makes the past possible, which would be a different sort of claim; namely, that we can never step beyond our own shadow, and that to some extent the past is always in part a projection of our current concerns. Yes indeed. But the way you put the paradox leaves more of an opening to the outside, if I understand it correctly: the presence of *things* uncovered by the archaeologist is what allows the past in which *they* existed to be reconstructed. This is different, because the thing encountered by the archaeologist will already be marked by a certain strangeness for the archaeologist's present. Or perhaps even for the strangeness of an amateur's present: years ago my late father-in-law Mithat Demir happened to uncover a Hittite tablet in his garden in Ankara (which he immediately donated to the Museum of Anatolian Civilizations). I've never looked at the city the same way since hearing that story.

Let me close with the following remarks, and then a question. The first concerns your bracketing of causation when you say that the past does not have a causal relation to the present, but rather that present artifacts have an ability to reconstruct their pasts. You don't use the word "causation" for the latter, but maybe all we're rejecting here is "efficient causation," in which one thing literally produces another. Aristotle famously mentioned three other kinds of causation: formal, material, and final. It is formal cause that I want to speak about here, and that concept is absolutely central for one author we have mentioned a few times already: McLuhan. As described earlier, McLuhan actually gives individual humans quite a lot of power when it comes to changing the media in which they reside. The artist is someone who takes a cliché (i.e. an obvious piece of dead everyday content) and converts it back into an archetype (i.e. a medium that has come back to life again).[93] Sometimes media also change independently of human aims, as when a medium "heats up" and increases its content so much that it reverses into its opposite, such as when cars reverse from a convenience to an unavoidable pain in the ass.

In any case, what both processes have in common is that they involve a *cooling down*, a decrease in detail. The same thing happens in the process of canon formation in any discipline: out of all the hundreds of painters in the Italian Renaissance, the average intellectual knows about a dozen of them by name, maybe twenty at most. The reason I bring this up is to propose the following difference between archaeology and history as disciplines: archaeology tries to cool the past down, and history tries to heat it up. That is to say, the historian necessarily tries to add as much detail as possible to what we know about the past, while the archaeologist is often presented with a situation in which there simply is not that much detail to be had, and tries to reconstruct the past as a "form" rather than as an increasingly bulky set of facts.

This idea came up recently in an article I wrote about Timothy Morton entitled "Hyperobjects and Prehistory."[94] I developed the idea further in an article called "The Coldness of Forgetting," in response to a critique of *Immaterialism* by Bjørnar Olsen and Þóra Pétursdóttir; after that Tim Flohr Sørensen got involved with an article of his own, to which I then published a reply.[95] So, it turned out to be quite a voluminous debate. But in fact, this same point was already at the root of what I was trying to do in *Immaterialism* when arguing that we should reduce the amount of relevant detail about the Dutch East India Company rather than increase it.[96] A historian would try to find out as much as possible about the Company, whereas I was using the existing histories of it to try to identify five or six "symbiotic" moments, the only ones in which the Company really changed irreversibly. At the time I called this an "ontology" rather than a history of the Company. But now I realize that I might also have called it an "archaeology," if not that Foucault has already cornered the philosophical market on that term for very different theoretical purposes.[97] In any case, what am I missing if I try to read the difference between history and archaeology in terms of the different techniques required to add or subtract information?

CW: Archaeologists, as I suggested earlier, are conditioned to regard their objects as effects or consequences of a particular cause. Looking beyond the deposit, the relic wall, or the askos sherd, the questions posed of the object regard it as a result, and turn upon the *causa efficiens*, often expanding towards the other three causes: "How did this come to be?" "Of what is this fashioned?" "Where does this fall with respect to other types?" "What purposes did this serve?" And yet, if we are to look no further than the clay vat, whetstone, or inscribed stirrup jar concerning the reasons for their own existence, then efficient causation cannot take precedence over the thing itself. These objects do not gain their reality from elsewhere, for (I agree with you) it is internal to them. These objects exceed that which brought them about. For once an object emerges, it is released into its own trajectories. Upon encounter, these things bring their own idiosyncratic otherness and strangeness to the fore.[98] Whether for archaeologists or your late father-in-law, an erstwhile cause is an effect of the object that is present, not the other way round.

I find your distinction between history and archaeology, in McLuhan's terms of heating up (or adding detail) and cooling down (or suggesting form), to be novel. Here, most readers may not recognize your notion of "form" to be formulated apart from any opposition to matter, which lends nuance to this distinction.[99] In any case, this contrast suggests different aims for history and archaeology, and such a *causa finalis* holds tremendous promise. What is missing in your formulation is a recognition of how archaeology operates on several levels.

In fieldwork, archaeologists aspire to a sense of completeness in dealing with what has become of the past. Field notes, context sheets, plans, photographs, samples, labels, bagged or boxed objects, are all enrolled in an effort to capture as much detail as possible related to what is displaced through excavation or other modes of engagement with objects. We could trace this process to the fine edge of publication, which gives form to this richness, but there are other outcomes. Much now languishes on dusty shelves in the dark recesses of storage rooms, in the arcane depths of archives, and in grey literature. It requires a combination of patience, tenacity, and precisely the kind of intellectual acumen you describe to do a sufficient job of cooling down all that detail (though admittedly so much is already transformed in moving from chthonic objects in the field to such archives). So, on one level we try to retain as much specificity as possible, while on another we cool it down into a "form," as we have with numerous examples throughout this book.

I know that your use of "form" is broad enough to account for how archaeology deals with objects suggestive of pasts other than those inscribed as history. As visitors to the citadel of Mycenae, you and Necla confronted something of these pasts whether they were held in ashlar, cyclopean, and polygonal walls that did not cease with the completion of circumscribed eras in the twelfth and fifth centuries BCE or humble bits of ceramic lodged in the soil, which few ever take into explicit consideration. Both high walls and low sherds extend their past into the present, mixing with legion other objects that extend their own pasts, making the memories they hold coextensive. In a sense, are we not struggling here to understand the unique shape of time suggested by these forms?

4

Objects as the Root of Time

Graham Harman

By definition (and even by etymology) archaeology deals with a profoundly stretched-out vertical time, often viewed by the public as dealing with things that are extremely old by contrast with recent human history. In practice, however, an increasing amount of archaeology deals with recent history or even the present.[1] But while it is true that geology and astrophysics are concerned with even more ancient topics, archaeology is more than vertical enough. For this reason I should begin by saying that OOO defines time as something belonging to the uttermost surface of reality. This does not mean that OOO is unconcerned with ancient or even "ancestral" time (as Meillassoux calls time prior to the emergence of conscious beings), but only that I use different terminology to account for it.[2] Hence it will be good to begin with a brief account of OOO's fourfold structure and explain the place of time within it. This will lead to a discussion of how some other philosophers have dealt with time, and of what I see as the strengths and weaknesses of those efforts.

Fourfold structures are common in the history of human thought. They all have different motivations and highly distinct features, so we should be careful not to equate any of them too quickly. However, one nearly universal feature is that fourfolds emerge from the crossing of two distinct dualisms. If we examine Aristotle's famous four causes (formal, material, efficient, and final) we notice that the Scholastics referred to two of them as "intrinsic" causes (formal and material, which belong to any entity in its own right) and to the other two as "extrinsic" causes (efficient and final, which involve a relation to something outside the thing itself).[3] The second principle of division in Aristotle's causes initially seems harder to detect. But we can start by noting that the efficient cause is *doubly* extrinsic. Consider the case of an automobile crash, whose efficient cause may be driver inattention, or brake failure, or whatever we stipulate it to be. Now, the *final* cause of a car is already somewhat extrinsic, since final cause is the currently unfulfilled purpose of a thing: the driver is commuting to work and is not yet there. But at least the final cause is partly inscribed in the car itself, to the extent that the driver purchased it precisely because it lends itself to a certain use. But the *efficient* cause of the car is something not just located outside the car itself (like the final cause), but doubly outside it. The inattention of the driver in a crash, for instance, is not something inscribed in the car itself, but results from a human agent external to it. Working from the other direction, we can see that even the factory that produced the car is extrinsic: for while it is true that the car could not have existed without the factory, the whole point of the manufacturing process is to produce an independent entity capable of leaving the factory setting and doing something on its own.

Turning now to the form/matter pair, we find a similar duality at work. We could say that the form of the car belongs to it in a doubly intrinsic manner, since everything that exists has a form that makes it what it is. We can imagine nearly any object with different matter, a different history of efficient causation, and a different purpose while still being roughly the same thing, but with formal causation this is impossible: the thing is simply no longer itself once the form is altered. We can imagine changing the car's shape slightly at a body shop, but this is more a change in the matter than in the unified form of the car. So, just as efficient causation is the doubly extrinsic pole of the four, so too is formal causation the doubly intrinsic one. By contrast, the other two are hybrids: the material cause is an intrinsic one with extrinsic roots, while the final cause is an extrinsic cause with intrinsic roots.

A. The Quadruplicity of Time

OOO has a fourfold structure of its own, and the principles of division are as follows. On the one hand, there is an absolute difference between the non-relational and relational: any given thing is what it is, but it is also "other" in the sense that it engages in relations with other things. Philosophers sometimes call this the difference between the intrinsic and the extrinsic. Immanuel Kant is sometimes read this way, as in the work of Rae Langton, and I am basically sympathetic to her interpretation: the thing-in-itself simply is what it is regardless of its relations with anything else, while the phenomena are such only insofar as they are encountered by something else.[4] For Kant, of course, that "something else" is always a finite human being. I happen to read Heidegger in the same way: being is the non-relational, and presence is the relational. Yes, Heidegger claims that what is present is independent, but my first book explained why that is not really the case.[5] But quite differently from Heidegger, OOO generalizes the relational character of presence to cover the interaction between any two things at all, even inanimate ones, which philosophers since Kant have more or less been forbidden to discuss, simply deferring the issue to the findings of science. Whitehead is a rare and brave exception.[6] In OOO terms, this is the first axis of division: the rift between reality and relation. There is an absolute difference in status between anything in its own right and in its relations with anything else: as opposed to Actor–Network Theory, in which "to exist" always means "to be in relation" in the sense of having an effect on something else.[7] It seems to me that Aristotle already refuted this view in the *Metaphysics* when he showed, against the Megarians, how one can be a house-builder even when not currently building a house, by way of the concept of potentiality.[8] That is not to say that I accept potentiality, but we can leave this point for another time. Aristotelian potentiality at least does important work in striking down the full-blown actualism of his Megarian opponents, and Latour is in large part their descendant.[9]

The second axis of division in OOO is the rift between objects and qualities. This is somewhat harder to see, but luckily the essential work was already done for us by Edmund Husserl, founder of phenomenology.[10] Husserl thought the idea of a thing-in-itself outside thought was absurd, since in his view everything that exists must at least potentially be the correlate of some mental act. The danger that seems to worry Husserl about the thing-in-itself is skepticism. That is to say, if there is a Berlin that appears in thought, and a separate Berlin in the outside world, then there is no way my statements about Berlin could ever reach across the gap and say anything about the Berlin-in-itself that lies beyond human access.[11] I happen to think Husserl overlooked that there are *intermediate* ways to access Berlin-in-itself that don't require it to be exhaustively presentable to my mind, but that's also a topic for another time. The important point here is that Husserl collapses the first axis (real vs. relational) so that it effectively no longer exists. Everything unfolds in the world of phenomena: which is why his theory is called "phenomenology," after all. There is no Husserlian "noumenology," nor could there ever be. As he sees it, the noumena simply do not exist, and of course he is far from alone in this view.

But in taking this step, which I regard as mistaken, Husserl did open up something precious and unprecedented for philosophy. Namely, by confining himself to the phenomena, Husserl was compelled to notice more tension and nuance there than had ever been seen before. The British Empiricists (Locke, Berkeley, Hume) had denied the existence of anything like an "object."[12] What we really encounter, they held, were "bundles of qualities." There is no "apple" in my hand, but only a set of familiar qualities such as red, spherical, sweet, shiny, slippery, juicy, and the like. These qualities occur together so frequently that we assign the loose nickname "apple" to their conjunction, though no one has ever really experienced a unified thing called an apple. Hume, in certain respects the most radical of the group (Berkeley is obviously more radical in others), argued that the same is true even of our own selves: I observe a stream of perceptions and thoughts and give them the loose nickname "myself," though really none of us has ever seen a self as something apart from its various streaming perceptions and thoughts. This was still true even of Husserl's teacher, the underrated Franz Brentano, who thought that our mental life is made up of "experienced contents," which means that we never experience an apple *per se*, but only an apple in some specific perceptual setting, viewed from a specific angle and distance.[13] Husserl's silent revolution was to reverse this relationship: experience is primarily the experience *of objects*. Husserl held that we always experience differing "adumbrations" or perspectives on objects without regarding them as different objects altogether. In other words, "bundles of qualities" is a false description of what we actually experience; mental life is about objects, not contents. By contrast with his teacher Brentano, Husserl held that experience is composed not of contents, but of what he called "object-giving acts."[14]

This is the key to phenomenology. In one sense we are supposed to describe the appearances as exactly as possible. But what this ultimately means is that we ought to approach an intuition of the *essence* of any given object, which means scraping away the inessential features of any perception: it doesn't matter that I am currently seeing the back rather than the front of the Coke can, since it would be the same can either way. So, there is an absolute difference between any mental object and the specific features it displays at any given moment. Yet there are also *essential* qualities of the can, since if it did not have these then it would be no different from my hat, my watch, or the other objects now on the table in front of me. In any given case it is difficult to say exactly what these essential qualities are, though anything that comes from the senses is ruled out by Husserl in advance.

In short, there is a duality between the experienced Coke can and its surface-features, and a separate duality between the experienced Coke can and its essential ones. I take this to be one of the handful of major insights in the history of philosophy. Unfortunately, Husserl (always a mathematician at heart) went on to identify this difference with the rather different one between the senses and the intellect, as if we could somehow reach the essential features of the can by using our minds rather than our sense organs. One might think of this as a variant of seventeenth-century rationalist dogma, except that it stems from a much earlier date: for instance, the same conception is already there in Ibn Sina (Avicenna) in eleventh-century Islamic thought.[15] For OOO, the difference between the intellect and the senses simply does not run deep enough to account for the rift between the real and the relational. In fact, the intellect belongs on the relational side of the fence every bit as much as the senses do. More than this, even causal interaction belongs on the relational side, so that the essence of things is concealed from inanimate interactions no less than it is from human thought, which by no means entails the panpsychist view that Coke cans are "conscious." With this latter step OOO breaks with the whole of modern philosophy, which is dogmatically wedded to the assumption that human thought is so different in kind from the rest of the universe that it deserves to make up a full half of ontology. I have taken to calling this assumption "onto-taxonomy."[16]

We are now ready to return to our main topic: time. In OOO terminology the difference between the real and the relational becomes the difference between the real and the sensual, keeping in mind that "sensual" refers not to the senses, but to *sensuality* in the manner of immediate contact between two surfaces. Let's abbreviate real as R and sensual as S. We saw that Husserl discovered a further difference between objects and qualities, which we can abbreviate as O and Q. Husserl's initial discovery that objects of experience bear different qualities at different times can be written as a tension between SO-SQ, or sensual objects and sensual qualities. But he also discovered that the experienced sensual object has *real* qualities that it needs in order to be what it is. We can write this as SO-RQ, though as mentioned I disagree with Husserl's claim that the intellect can access it directly: nothing real can make direct contact with anything real at all. The real simply is what it is; the ways in which we might come to know it is a separate question. Turning now to Heidegger, I hold that he deployed a different tension, RO-SQ, in which the object withdraws from direct contact though its qualities remain tangibly present.[17] This is the tension dealt with in aesthetics, for reasons I have dealt with elsewhere; in Heidegger's career the best example is the analysis of the broken tool, which leaves behind broken fragments of qualities as the tool itself withdraws into mystery. That leaves us with RO-RQ, noticed no later than G.W. Leibniz, who proclaimed that his monads (ultimate individual substances) are one, while adding that each unified monad also needs a *plurality* of traits in order to distinguish it from everything else.[18] An apple is one and an orange is one, but if there were no more to it than that, we would not regard them as different things.

To summarize, we do not just have the four poles of RO, RQ, SO, and SQ, but four basic interactions between them: SO-SQ, RO-SQ, RO-RQ, and SO-RQ. These can be written in any order, and for OOO they are the building blocks of everything. For various reasons I came to identify them with what I call time, space, essence, and eidos, though at the moment we are concerned only with time. Time in OOO refers to the only sort of time any of us experiences directly: our ongoing encounter with entities that remain basically stable despite countless shifting profiles as we handle or observe them or watch their appearances shift in the fading sunlight. Kant made a similar point in his discussion of substance in his *Critique of Pure Reason*, though OOO takes substance more seriously than Kant does, given our ultimately Aristotelian roots.[19] This immediate experience of time passing is the root of our other notions of time: that of the clock, of measurable physical events, of people aging and dying, of historical circumstances changing, of the remains of dinosaurs found in primeval swamps, or of ceramic sherds unearthed from some previously forgotten site. All such discussions of time are rooted in the more primordial everyday sense we have of time flowing onward. There is at least one difference between SO-SQ phenomenological time and the other notions of time that people speak about. Whereas the latter are generally concerned with important events involving the passing away and resurgence of basic historical conditions, SO-SQ time need not have any significance at all. I can sit in a café for hours and pass through various shifting moods and rotating Coke cans without anything of significance happening. The point is not that nothing happens in time, but that things either happen or fail to happen in time. Temporality is the play of objects and qualities through which everything, something, or nothing can occur.

Here is a quick argument to that end. For OOO real objects are withheld from direct access, by me or by anything else. By definition real objects are inert: not *eternal*, mind you, but fundamentally stable unless they engage in relations in such a way that something does happen. But again, real objects cannot make direct contact. RO and RO cannot interact except through the mediation of something sensual. In the sensual realm, a real object makes contact with the accidental configurations and adumbrations of other things; sometimes this leads to nothing but a bare drifting of temporal experience. But at other times this sensual interaction leads to a momentary bridge between one real object and another, which come together and form a new object (an "event" is just another object, however transient). For this reason, even though time for OOO is entirely a creature of the surface, it is by no means unimportant, since it is the only place where change can ever be triggered. Over certain long stretches of time, nothing really happens and stability predominates; in other periods one crisis leads to the next, and revolutions might even occur. This is why time for OOO is not purely "epiphenomenal," since it is also the sole locus of causal interaction: though such interaction is usually buffered, and we cannot assume that anything will happen automatically just because "time passes." Let this serve as an initial summary of where OOO is coming from whenever we speak of "time."

B. Critiques by Wolfendale, Gratton, and Kleinherenbrink

Roughly halfway through Peter Wolfendale's long critical book on my philosophy, we find the following remark on the OOO theory of time: "[Harman's] theory of space and time is the most catastrophically inept aspect of his metaphysical system."[20] Even if we make allowance for the acerbic tone of his book as a whole, this is a remarkable accusation. While I have dealt with many of Wolfendale's claims elsewhere, some of his charges about space and time in OOO are worth recounting here to further the present discussion.[21] He begins with a competent summary of the OOO model of the four kinds of tension between objects and qualities and that which they are held to generate: SO-SQ (time), RO-SQ (space), SO-RQ (eidos), and RO-RQ (essence).[22] From there he proceeds to claim that I misportray the famous debate between Leibniz and Samuel Clarke, asserting in particular that I offer "a caricature of Leibniz's position."[23] Second, since SO-SQ is by its very nature a purely sensual account of time, Wolfendale holds that it must depend on a suppressed concept of real "deep time," since otherwise things could only change in appearance rather than reality.

We begin with the charges about my purported misreading of the Leibniz–Clarke correspondence.[24] As is well known, there was a rather violent rivalry between Leibniz and Isaac Newton as to who deserved the credit for first discovering calculus. Despite his obvious genius, Newton was also psychologically unstable and given to using surrogates and even pseudonymous work from his own hand to undercut his rivals. One of his surrogates was the theologian Samuel Clarke, who can be regarded as Newton's official representative in the debate with Leibniz on space and time. Their correspondence began in 1715 and ended prematurely with Leibniz's death the following year. Stated simply, Clarke (meaning Newton) held that time and space exist as absolute containers quite apart from the things and events that take place in them. As Newton put it in his *Principia*: "Absolute, true, and mathematical time, of itself, and from its own nature, flows equably without relation to anything external . . . Absolute space, in its own nature, without relation to anything external, remains always similar and immovable."[25] Leibniz contests these views by noting (among other things) that it would make no sense to ask whether the universe could have been created a week earlier than it was, or perhaps one hundred miles distant from where it is actually located. In other words, space and time make sense only in terms of the relations various entities have to each other, not as containers that unfold and extend independently of any content. It should already be clear that the OOO model of SO-SQ (time) and RO-SQ (space) is closer to Leibniz's position than Newton's, since for us time and space are generated by the fact that objects are out of joint with themselves.

Now, despite Wolfendale's assertion of the "catastrophically inept" OOO theory of space and time, he is never entirely clear as to how I supposedly get the Leibniz–Clarke correspondence wrong. The closest he ever comes is this: "[Harman confuses] the idea that space and time are *epiphenomenal* – spatio-temporal relations can be derived from the non-spatiotemporal properties of [Leibniz's] monads – and the idea that each monad *mirrors* every other – the non-spatiotemporal properties of *every* monad can be derived from *any* monad."[26] But I cannot recognize my argument in this formulation. We hear even less about Wolfendale's own interpretation of Leibniz and Clarke. He is content to tell us that "the debate is very complex" before mentioning his own familiarity with quantum mechanics and general relativity, which is where he seems to think the question of space and time should be settled.[27] Wolfendale reports further that "[t]he core of the debate between Leibniz and Clarke is whether we need to meta-physically distinguish between *locations* in space ... and their *occupants*."[28] This is nothing more than what I and all other read-ers of the correspondence have already said, but Wolfendale seems to make the additional, unstated assumption that time must be moving forward independently as a kind of engine or wind tunnel capable of generating change, which is apparently what he means by the "deep time" purportedly missing from my position. Given his stated interest in general relativity, we can guess he would be willing to concede that time need not move forward *uniformly* as Newton thought, but that it can be stretched or compressed depending on the acceleration of one's movement or proximity to large masses. Even so, he seems dead set in the view that change depends on time, whereas for OOO the point is that time is gener-ated by change.

The upshot of this dispute with Wolfendale is as follows. For OOO, Leibniz's arguments against the idea of space and time as pre-existent containers are decisive; individual entities are the primary topic of philosophy for us, just as for the Aristotelian tradition to which we owe so much. These entities can be analyzed into a fourfold structure that reflects the doubly loose relation between (a) an object and its relations, and (b) an object and its own qualities. Despite the Einstein-Minkowski treatment of space-time as a single four-dimensional continuum, OOO rejects this at the ontological level, since space emerges from one ten-sion (RO-SQ) and time from another (SO-SQ), making them as different from each other as the Discourse of the Master and the Discourse of the Hysteric in Lacan.[29] But contra Leibniz, space and time cannot be defined in purely relational terms. This is obvious in the case of space, since the real object (RO) pole is inherently withdrawn and non-relational. But even in the case of time, the sensual object cannot be defined by its *relation* to its sensual quali-ties; here, Leibniz is not different enough from British Empiricism. For sensual qualities are constantly shifting, with the sensual object not necessarily changing as a result: the blue shirt I am now wear-ing is not identifiable with any specific appearance it might have to anyone at any given moment. And finally, it turns out that the very term "continuum" is applicable only to time and no longer to space (as it still is for Aristotle). For insofar as space involves the disposition of real objects, which are always individualized and partly withdrawn, space for OOO is inherently quantized or chunky in a way that time is not. It is certainly true that we can speak of time in discontinuous terms, as when speaking of how Egyptian or Chinese history might be atomized into various dynasties. But OOO argues that this is merely an analogical use of the word "time," since quantization belongs inherently to space. The primary meaning of time is our experience of a flow of qualitative change, much of it leading to no alteration whatsoever in the underlying real objects.

We can deal more briefly with Gratton's critique.[30] His central claim is merely false: namely, the assertion that OOO follows a Platonic model that opposes a world of eternity to the changing world of the senses. OOO belongs instead to the Aristotelian tradition, in which primary substances (individual things) are *destructible*, not eternal. So how can Gratton bring himself to accuse me of devotion to a rock-hard "static" model of entities? He does so through a tactical maneuver, creating a needlessly high barrier that one must clear to qualify as a philosopher who takes change seriously enough: a tactic I have elsewhere termed the Game of Hurdles. "OOO holds that objects are regularly destroyed, and that it is quite likely that no object in the cosmos lasts forever? Not good enough! Harman still thinks that objects are able to endure for at least a little while, which means he is out of touch with the utterly orgasmic levels of constant tumultuous flux that any philosophy must recognize!" A milder version of this argument is made by Michael Austin, a former student of Gratton in Newfoundland, who thinks the default state of things should be flux rather than endurance.[31] This claim is not unfamiliar, since it is found not only in Heraclitus, but in the thought of Bergson and his more recent lineage. But Gratton takes a more openly partisan line, since what he is really up to is mounting a defense of Derridean *différance*.

Now, it is well known that Derrida picks up and develops Heidegger's concept of "onto-theology," their shared term for the traditional form of metaphysics which holds that the root of reality can be made directly present to the mind: hence the synonymous term "metaphysics of presence."[32] For Heidegger the metaphysics of presence can never be valid, since being itself always withdraws from all forms of presence; thus it can never adequately be captured by any representation, statement, perception, or other means of access. But Derrida puts a slightly different twist on onto-theology, claiming that even absence is a form of presence, and is therefore an inadequate means of escape. To be more specific, Derrida regards even a hidden or withdrawn self-identical thing (such as Being) as a form of presence, because he thinks that

identity counts as a form of "self-presence."[33] Yet there is no justi-
fication for rewriting "identity" as "self-presence" in this way; for
something to be itself is quite different from being *present* to itself,
which happens at most only in rare cases of self-reflexivity, though
in fact not even then, given the inherent opacity of introspection.
What this means is that Derrida has a thoroughly anti-Aristotelian,
anti-identity agenda, and Gratton is entirely on board with it.
Worse yet, Gratton follows Derrida in sloppily taking non-identity
to be the same thing as "time," as if what we call time automatically unfurled from the purported fact of nothing being the same
as itself. Additionally, Gratton tries to use Husserl's work on internal time-consciousness as a weapon on his own behalf. But any
reader who consults the relevant work will quickly see that Husserl
agrees with me rather than Gratton: the former's argument is that
there is no time without the endurance of intentional (i.e. sensual)
objects amidst their constantly shifting adumbrations. Gratton is
so opposed to the minimally durable status of even sensual entities
that he is unwilling to see that objects (even if not real ones) are
crucial to Husserl's philosophical position.[34] Like Wolfendale, he
also claims that my concept of time is merely "epiphenomenal,"
since it unfolds entirely through the sensual tension SO-SQ and
thus has no contact with the real. Yet it is worth noting that these
two critics say so for opposite reasons. Recall that for Wolfendale
there is in fact a "deep time" that he claims I am missing, a time
buried somewhere beneath the surface of things, and he thinks that
science is perfectly capable of handling it. By contrast, Gratton
is just as opposed to metaphors of depth as any other Derridean,
and thus he claims I am *too* committed to the real. In other words,
his concern is not (as with Wolfendale) that I fail to recognize the
true depth of time, but that I insult the surface character of time
by claiming there is anything deeper to be had in the first place.
Restated in different terms, Wolfendale thinks time itself is deep
but OOO time is too shallow, while Gratton thinks time is on the
surface and OOO is too falsely deep.

   That brings us to my favorite member of this trio of critics: Arjen
Kleinherenbrink, a young Dutch philosopher based in Nijmegen.
Among other achievements, he has written a marvelous book on
the relation between Deleuze and Speculative Realism.[35] Of greater
relevance to us here is his article from the same year, "The Two
Times of Objects," in which he expresses surprising agreement
with the critiques by Gratton and Wolfendale (and more briefly
with a related argument from Tristan Garcia), before arguing
that the concept of time in OOO can be salvaged nonetheless.[36]

Kleinherenbrink's attitude is more constructive and helpful than that of the others. He reminds us, among other things, that "for better or worse, it often takes decades of refinement and revision before a philosophy reaches its mature form," which is exactly what Imre Lakatos says about scientific research programs.[37]

Kleinherenbrink's strategy is to argue that there are indeed problems with my model of time, but that they can easily be remedied by linking up with a particular insight of his favorite philosopher, Deleuze. Although Deleuze's 1968 *Difference and Repetition* speaks of the deep virtual layer of reality, Kleinherenbrink notes that there is no mention of virtuality in the 1969 *The Logic of Sense*.[38] Instead, *The Logic of Sense* (an irreverent meditation on the writings of Lewis Carroll) speaks of time as something unfolding on the surface, a good match for the OOO theory of time as SO-SQ. For this reason, Kleinherenbrink recommends that OOO adopt the same twofold theory of time as both Aiôn and Chronos set forth by Deleuze in the latter work. Deleuze famously claims to draw this theory from the Stoics, though John Sellars has contested this assertion in an eye-opening article.[39] But more than this, Kleinherenbrink brilliantly notes a connection between OOO and Deleuze's 1972 second edition of his book *Proust and Signs*.[40] As Kleinherenbrink puts it, in this work Deleuze

> outlines a theory of bodies considered as "closed vessels" that "communicate only indirectly" because they only ever register each other's "signs." In a striking resemblance to Harman's ten links between the four aspects of objects [in *The Quadruple Object*], Deleuze writes that such a theory of reality entails a "galactic structure" of "ten combinations" between the various aspects of such entities.[41]

The connection is a real one, and is yet another reason (if another were needed) to be interested in Proust.

As mentioned, Kleinherenbrink begins his article by expressing agreement with the critiques of OOO time made by Gratton and Wolfendale. But as we have seen, the latter two critiques stem from entirely different philosophical motivations. Gratton ostensibly dislikes the way that OOO treats time as "epiphenomenal," though he inevitably places it on the surface as well, given that his Derridean hostility to conceptions of depth leaves him with nowhere else to put it. But what seems to bother him more is that the OOO model of time entails an enduring sensual object that withstands numerous changes in its attributes, thereby trafficking in a notion of identity that Gratton (like nearly every Derridean) regards as philosophical poison. Now, it is easy to see why some authors from a Deleuzean background would be inclined to salute this gesture by Gratton. That is to say, it is easy to imagine a Derrido-Deleuzean alliance on behalf of "difference" against the identity that OOO ascribes to both real and sensual objects. Yet there is little sign of such a strategy in Kleinherenbrink's article. Instead, he seems more interested in the point that worries Wolfendale: namely, the complaint that if time unfolds solely between sensual objects and their qualities, the real objects lying beneath them will be impermeable to change. Indeed, Kleinherenbrink quotes the following passage from Wolfendale: "Things must change within the subterranean realm of withdrawn objects, even if we only experience the ripples these changes produce in the glimmering surface world."[42]

To Kleinherenbrink's credit, he is well aware that I regard real objects as changing intermittently; he refers to the notion of symbiosis in *Immaterialism* as proof. Still, he adds that "Harman's theory of time needs to be reworked if it is to account for real objects undergoing real change."[43] While this sounds like something that Wolfendale might also say, their basic concerns are entirely different. As seen earlier, Wolfendale is primarily hostile to the idea that objects themselves might be the primary generators of change. He denies that Leibniz ever suggested such a thing, and quietly sides with Clarke's presentation of Newton's theory that "absolute, true, and mathematical time, of itself, and from its own nature, flows equably without relation to anything external." In other words, Wolfendale's "deep time" is a self-moving container inside which everything else happens, a primal flux that must be assumed if anything is to be able to change at all. For Kleinherenbrink, by contrast, time is less a container than an intertwining of two separate levels that he identifies with Aiôn and Chronos from Deleuze's *The Logic of Sense*.

We should also note the additional difference that Kleinherenbrink sees no need to get rid of the OOO fourfold structure. Although he is primarily concerned that the layer of the real has a productive force that must be identified with at least one aspect of time, he also allows the tension between sensual objects and qualities to remain in place. Indeed, he identifies it with Aiôn and renames it "manifest" time, or "the varying play of sensual objects and their qualities as apprehended by real objects."[44] This, of course, is already the OOO model of time. The additional form of time that Kleinherenbrink appends to OOO is the one he calls Chronos or "internal time," which he defines as "the temporal circuit between bodies and events ... It is the circuit between the withdrawn half of objects and the sensual half of objects."[45] Having thereby grafted Deleuze's theory of time onto OOO, he pronounces the operation successful. On this note, he proclaims that Gratton's and Wolfendale's charges have been answered, and adds that it would be even easier to address the "less damning flaws in the [OOO] theory [of time]."[46] From here, Kleinherenbrink makes an intriguing effort to demonstrate a more far-reaching compatibility between Deleuze and OOO than I have allowed for, given that I have generally placed Deleuze in the Bergsonian camp of "philosophers of becoming" to which I am opposed.[47] Kleinherenbrink's way of doing so will be familiar to readers of his *Against Continuity*: namely, he concedes my point that Deleuze's early career makes him a philosopher of becoming, while arguing that things change drastically (and for the better) with the turn to assemblages and individuals in his popular *Anti-Oedipus*, co-authored with Félix Guattari.[48] While this is not the place to argue about how best to interpret Deleuze's career, Kleinherenbrink's efforts in this direction are always stimulating and suggestive.

The heart of our disagreement is that he thinks time needs some foothold in the real, since otherwise the real would sit motionless and could never be productive. For this reason, the OOO model might sound like Platonism (as Gratton claims) and might also render change impossible (as Wolfendale claims). But it is not Platonism, for the simple reason that OOO's real objects (like Aristotle's individual primary substances) can be created and destroyed. And it does not make change impossible, because time in OOO intermittently triggers change in the real level. This idea is by no means unprecedented: Badiou finds himself making an analogous effort on behalf of retroactivity in *Logics of Worlds*, as Husserl already did in *Formal and Transcendental Logic*, and DeLanda fully allows for this possibility in his discussion of emergent assemblages.[49] But Kleinherenbrink's worry is more specific, and for this reason more useful. Here is the key passage from near the end of his article:

> OOO holds that sensual objects are translations of the real objects that lurk behind them. What any entity apprehends or experiences are therefore sensual objects that real objects *have produced*, and these can only ever be replaced by further sensual objects that real objects *then produce*. What remains present throughout this succession is the real object that registers this variation.[50]

The two key claims in this passage are as follows: (a) real objects *produce* sensual objects, with the implication that real objects must have a foothold in temporality too; (b) what remains steadfastly present throughout the dramatic flux of the sensual realm is a real object that registers this variation. How might OOO respond to these claims?

As for the first point, it is not exactly right to say that real objects produce sensual ones. When I encounter a pine tree, for instance, it is the sensual tree I encounter rather than the real withdrawn tree. But this is not because the tree is constantly producing sensual caricatures of itself and at some point I happen to run into one. Rather, what happens is that the sensual caricature is produced on the spot, just when the interaction occurs. This does not happen directly, but indirectly by way of a pre-existing sensual mediator, but that is a separate issue that can be left aside for now. The point is this: what "produces" a sensual object is not the real object cor-related with it, but rather the (indirect) interaction between the real pine tree and the real me. Neither of the real objects produces an image of itself. Real objects are not eternal or indestructible, but for OOO they are inert and unchanging, and can only be modi-fied or destroyed from the outside. Since direct contact between real objects is impossible, what Deleuze and Kleinherenbrink call "events" require a sensual mediator, which means that the tempo-ral tension between sensual objects and sensual qualities needs to be involved. Whatever the complaints about the "epiphenomenal" character of OOO's model of time, such phenomenal time is fully capable of helping carve pathways and scars back into the real. It is true that there is no sufficiently detailed account of this process in print so far, but I have often made it clear that this is how the model is supposed to work. On a related and interesting note, Kleinherenbrink worries about whether the allowance for change via symbiosis is enough to account for what we see happening in the world. Namely, he casts

> some doubt on Harman's thesis that real change . . . is rare. It seems more adequate to say that whereas *significant* real change is rare, *incremental* real change might be quite common. If a real object is open to all its sensual encounters, then it must also be possible that such an encounter leads to slight alterations of an object's real quali-ties, just as it must be possible that it simply leads to the regeneration rather than alteration of such qualities.[51]

All of this is correct. But symbiosis was only meant as an account of *significant* change that alters the identity of a social object, not a model of all possible change. I welcome further debate with Kleinherenbrink and others as to how extensive "incremental real change" might be. The topic remains open.

As for the second point made by Kleinherenbrink, about how a real object registers sensual changes, he leaves an important consideration unstated. Normally, the reader of OOO will think of the real object as the one that hides behind its sensual profile: the real pine tree behind the sensual one, for instance. It is often forgotten that the beholder of the sensual object is also a real object. The I who am experiencing the pine tree is *the real I*, not a sensual I viewed by someone or encountered by something else. But neither of these real objects produces anything in itself, since only their interaction through a sensual medium makes this possible. Real objects are outside change until they are passively affected by something sensual; even our apparent experience of "inner" flux must be accounted for in this way.

C. McTaggart on the Unreality of Time

The British Idealist philosopher J.M.E. McTaggart flourished at Cambridge in the early years of the twentieth century. Although he is almost completely ignored by the continental tradition in philosophy (during all of my continental education he was never mentioned once), among analytic philosophers his name is often the first to come up during any discussion of time. Since McTaggart is associated with the idea that time is not real, and OOO has been accused of saying much the same thing, it may be useful to give a brief comparison between the object-oriented model of time and McTaggart's own. His classic discussion of the topic is found in his 1908 article in *Mind* entitled, straightforwardly enough, "The Unreality of Time." [52] The article begins with a distinction between two importantly different aspects of time:

> Positions in time, as time appears to us *primâ facie*, are distinguished in two ways. Each position is Earlier than some, and Later than some, of the other positions. And each position is either Past, Present, or Future. The distinctions of the former class are permanent, while those of the latter are not. [53]

The Roman Empire will always be earlier than the United States, but the status of both political entities as past, present, and future has changed, and in the latter case will continue to change. The Roman Empire was present and then finally became past, though we can always debate whether that happened in 476 (Odoacer's deposition of the Western Emperor), 1453 (the fall of Constantinople to Mehmet II), or at some other point. The United States remains a present existent at the time of this writing, but at some point will surely be past, as happens to everything under the sun. McTaggart expresses the view that earlier/later and past/present/future are equally *essential* to time, but that the latter is *more fundamental*. Perhaps for this reason, his now famous terminology calls past/present/future the A Series and earlier/later the B series. He foreshadows the conclusion of his article as follows: "because the distinctions of past, present, and future seem to me to be essential for time . . . I regard time as unreal."[54] In other words, McTaggart denies the existence of past, present, and future, and that is why he denies the existence of time.

Although McTaggart's article is clear enough in its own right, I will provide a simplified account of it here, so as to re-weight its emphases in a way that bears more directly on the OOO model of time. McTaggart's first point is that the B Series is not enough to count as what we generally call "time." Yes, events fall in an order from earlier to later. But time is meaningless except in connection with *change*, and the B Series has nothing to do with change, but only with unchanging relations of earlier and later.[55] However hyper-chaotic our universe might conceivably become, however many laws of nature might one day be violated or inverted, nothing can change the fact that the Roman Empire was earlier than the United States and always will be. Any change can happen only in the A Series, where events move from future to present to past.

McTaggart pushes the point a bit further, in a way that OOO views as incorrect. Namely, he argues that changes of tense are the only qualities of a thing that can change without changing it into a different thing. In his own words: "Now what characteristics of an event are there which can change and yet leave the event the same event? . . . It seems to me that there is only one class of such characteristics – namely, the determination of the event in terms of the A Series."[56] He cites the death of Queen Anne on August 1, 1714, saying that it will always be this very death of an English queen, and that the only thing that can change is that this death slips ever further into the past. Seen from an OOO standpoint, we cannot fail to notice that McTaggart acknowledges nothing like the distinction between objects and qualities. This has the following consequence for his way of setting up the problem. First, when he claims that past, present, and future are the *only* characteristics of a thing that can change without changing the thing in its own right, he sounds a great deal like the British Empiricists with their bundles of qualities, who had not read the still unborn Husserl. For it is no exaggeration to say that the whole of Husserlian phenomenology is built on the idea that the qualities of a thing constantly change without changing that thing. I constantly experience new features of a tumbling and screeching monkey without ever imagining that it is a different monkey in each instant. And surely McTaggart would agree that the same holds for anyone who happened to be at the deathbed of Queen Anne: the qualities of the dying queen for any observer were constantly shifting and churning, but the death remained the same death nonetheless. It is worth noting that unlike OOO, McTaggart is a firm believer in what philosophers call internal relations: "the relation of X to Y involves the existence in X of a quality of relationship to Y."[57] To give an example, my relation to a pine tree in perceiving it would involve the existence in me of a relationship to the tree. But this is precisely what OOO denies. For us, this relation consists solely in a part–whole relation in which the tree and I belong to a larger entity formed from both of us. And while this larger entity might have retroactive effects on its parts, this need not always happen. Relations are inherently contingent, or external.

Now, McTaggart goes on to argue in the second half of his article that the A Series is a self-contradictory notion, and given that he thinks the existence of time is dependent upon this series, it follows that time cannot exist. Without following all the detailed twists of his attempted proof, the basic idea is that past, present, and future are contradictory determinations, yet the same moment supposedly has all three: hence the purported impossibility. If someone makes the expected rejoinder that the same moment does not have these contradictions *simultaneously* but only at different times, this response is said to be circular, since it presupposes the very notion of time that is under dispute. But in some way McTaggart considers this to be beside the point, for there is a deeper problem with the A Series: namely, "even if we ignore the contradiction which we have just discovered in the application of the A series to reality, was there ever any positive reason why we should suppose that the A series was valid of reality?"[58] The question is rhetorical; McTaggart's answer is "no." He asks another question, this time answering it directly: "Why do we believe that events are to be distinguished as past, present and future? I conceive that the belief arises from distinctions in our own experience."[59] The distinctions he means are those between perception, memory, and anticipation. All these occur in the "specious present," which refers to the "now" in our experience that has an indeterminate length: estimated by Galen Strawson to be as brief as 300 milliseconds, by Barry Dainton at around a half-second, by Michael Lockwood at

1 to 1.5 seconds, and by Ernst Pöppel to be even longer.[60] Aside from this intellectual disagreement, we are familiar with the notion of time slowing up or speeding down in different ages of life or differing situations, between distinct human individuals, and as following from biological differences in the different experience of time in various animal species.[61] McTaggart's point is that all such discussions of the variability of specious time cannot do anything to establish a time that is *real*, one in which events themselves unfold regardless of who or what may be perceiving them.

Let's turn to the final page of McTaggart's article to find something resembling a summation of his outlook: "If [my] view is adopted, the result will so far resemble those reached by Hegel rather than those of Kant. For Hegel regarded the order of the time-series as a reflexion, though a distorted reflexion, of something in the real nature of the timeless reality."[62] Here we can ignore the part about Hegel, since McTaggart subjects him to a typically British Idealist "metaphysical" interpretation that is currently out of fashion, whether deservedly or not. What we are left with is McTaggart's idea that reality itself is "timeless," and that what we call time is the experience of a subjective specious present rather than something inherently real. To what extent is this the same as the OOO model criticized by Wolfendale, Gratton, and Kleinherenbrink? There are both similarities and differences. OOO agrees with McTaggart that there is nothing like a Newtonian time driving everything forward at a uniform rate. There is no evidence for this aside from the fact that certain things in nature seem to happen uniformly, but all this means is that certain entities move through cycles far more predictably than events in the human realm. The flow of sand through an hourglass or the vibrations of an atom correlate with the revolution of the Earth far more reliably than do human moods, but this does not prove the existence of some uniform cosmic forward movement that compels them to do so. It is not change that presupposes time, but time that presupposes change, and on this point we are in accord with McTaggart. We also agree with him that evidence for past and future is confined entirely to the specious present with its various memories and anticipations. This does not imply that to refer to a past or future event means nothing more than to refer to my present memory or anticipation of it, yet it is to say that past or future events do not exist in some repository of cosmic memory, but in something closer to the mode of fiction. This is precisely why we often find ourselves in a strange sort of fiction reader's mood even when absorbing factual history, especially as concerns events that occurred prior to our own lifetimes.

To make a final point, what OOO calls "time" does not occur in the threefold A Series, but only in the specious present. There is no disagreement here with McTaggart, since he identifies the A Series with *real* time, and we agree with him that real time does not exist. But there is a crucial difference. Whereas McTaggart identifies temporal experience with the projection of "timeless" reality, OOO – contra Gratton's misportrayal – does not acknowledge anything like timeless existence, except in the minimal sense that whatever exists outside the SO-SQ tension is not time. By "timeless" McTaggart seems to mean something more like "eternal," and there is no room for eternity in OOO. Conceivably something might end up existing forever, but only because it manages to fight its way through all the successive threats to its existence. The OOO model of real objects is not of eternal and motionless things, but of things that move *intermittently*. A better analogy than timelessness would be a model of chess pieces – made of marble, bone, plastic, paper, or smoke – that remain stationary and unchanged unless moved by something that happens in the quasi-chaotic sensual world just above the chessboard. Under certain conditions the chess pieces can be moved or destroyed, and new ones even created. There is nothing "timeless" about the chess pieces in this analogy, and it is a false alternative to demand that we choose between eternity and continuous flux, as if the very *self-identity* of specific chess pieces were somehow an affront to all motion. In any case, there is no such thing as a past entity which is somehow still itself but with a "past" inflection attached to it, or a future entity with a "future" mode affixed to it; on this point we agree with McTaggart that there is a contradiction. Nonetheless, we have memories and anticipations in the present which index things that are not present. What we encounter in the specious present is an instability based on the loose relationships between sensual objects and their sensual qualities, and this is what gives us the sense of time passing. If all sensual objects had a perfectly stable set of qualities, we would not experience time at all.

In his painstaking work as a reviewer of this book for publication, Jon Cogburn noted a number of points in the OOO theory of time that he views as underdetermined. Although his remarks are both expansive and fascinating, I am forced to condense them here into three basic categories, and even then cannot do full justice to any of them. The first concerns the directionality of time, treated by McTaggart under the rubric of a "C series." The second question addresses OOO's complaint that Heidegger has no way to pass from his synchronous temporality in an instant to anything like what we call "clock time," by asking how OOO itself proposes to make this step. The third has to do with whether my earlier response to Kleinherenbrink falls into the same dilemma as Kant when he first claimed (against Hume) that causation is purely phenomenal, but then (against Berkeley) made the apparently contradictory point that the noumena must be able to cause the phenomena: a puzzle that led German Idealism to abandon the thing-in-itself in a way that OOO obviously cannot. I will take these questions in order.

McTaggart also speaks in his famous article of a "C series," which I omitted from my account above for reasons of simplicity, though Cogburn is right to ask about it.[63] The C series does not involve change (and is therefore not time in the strict sense), but only an order. The alphabetical arrangement of letters from A through Z is by definition an order, but not a temporal one, since we might just as easily read the dictionary from Z through A instead. In McTaggart's words: "the C series, while it determines the order, does not determine the direction."[64] Restated in temporal terms, the C series alone gives no reason why time should not flow from future to past, although many have deployed the laws of thermodynamics to say that this cannot happen. McTaggart argues that combining the A series with the C series is enough to give us time: we simply need to say that one point in the C series order is the present, so that the ones already passed through are the past, and the ones not yet passed through are the future. Earlier we encountered his view that the A series and B series are equally "essential" to time, but not equally "fundamental."[65] And here we see why, for "it is only when the A series, which gives change and direction, is combined with the C series, which gives permanence, that the B series [of earlier and later] can arise," and hence that we can arrive at a full picture of time.[66] However, we have already seen that McTaggart does not think it is possible to differentiate events as being either past, present, or future, and this is why he thinks time does not exist.

It is worth noting that while McTaggart treats the A series as the site of all "change," he never aligns himself explicitly with either of the two basic camps of temporality discussed in this book. Namely, if we split philosophers of time into those who are thinkers of discontinuous instants and those who deny that such instants exist, the former is the "occasionalist" cadre containing such figures as al-Ash'ari, Malebranche, Whitehead, Latour, and Heidegger himself, while the latter is the "continuist" group that includes the likes of Aristotle, Bergson, and Husserl. For the latter trio, there simply is no such thing as a punctiform instant that might be analyzed further, even if they speak of a "present" nonetheless. If anything, McTaggart seems to prefer the occasionalist model of an instantaneous present: "A position in time is called a moment," he says, which is unlike anything we might read in Aristotle, Bergson, Husserl, or even OOO.[67] This is further reinforced when McTaggart implies, on the same page, that everything happening in the present moment adds up to a single event. And quite apart from this point, by making the A series responsible for "change," he seems to identify it tacitly with a Newtonian time that drives everything forward. For OOO, by contrast, the experienced flow of the present is not connected with change at all, since the SO-SQ tension exists purely on the surface of the world. Thus it is that for OOO, no combination of the A series (change) with the C series (order) can give rise to change, since the object-oriented thinker does not accept a Newtonian version of the A series. For us, the directionality of time comes from elsewhere: namely, from two entities combining into a third, such that this third object can have irreversible retroactive effects on its components. When that happens, the landscape of reality has changed, though it involves *real* objects that exist just beyond the reach of the flux and flow of sensual experience, which is why OOO calls such change spatial rather than temporal. In terms of our earlier image, the chess pieces are sometimes moved or otherwise transformed by the gusts of wind that surround them, but do not remain in constant subjection to those gusts.

We turn now to Heidegger and the question of whether OOO can handle clock time any better than the German philosopher does. My argument is that Heidegger is a magnificent articulator of what happens in a single instant, but that he never actually guides us from the instant to the "flow" of time. It is important to note that OOO never concedes that there exists an instant of time, but always treats it as continuous. Stated differently, clock time (but let's call it "flow time" instead) is baked into OOO from the start, just as for the other positions in the continuist group. The fact that OOO thinks entities are chunky, but continua are not, is no more a contradiction than are the views found respectively in Aristotle's *Metaphysics* and *Physics*. Heidegger's problem – never resolved, and not really even formulated – is how to get from the instant to flow time. OOO's problem is very different: namely, how do we get from flow time to something that might be called "calendar time"? For OOO, that is, only the present exists; the Roman Empire is nowhere, though it has left behind numerous remnants that allow for reconstruction by historians or archaeologists in the present. Given that time for OOO is a purely sensual tension of SO-SQ in which nothing necessarily happens, how could such a mere surface-play ever result in changes to the real itself? It is, in short, a retroactivity problem.

To address it, we return to Kleinherenbrink. The heart of his Deleuze-inspired critique is that OOO only makes room for Aiôn, or "the varying play of sensual objects and their qualities as appre-hended by real objects." To this he wants to add Chronos, "the temporal circuit between bodies and events . . . the circuit between the withdrawn half of objects and the sensual half of objects." Naturally, OOO agrees that such a circuit must exist; we simply deny that it ought to be called "temporal." Or rather, it is temporal only in the sense of calendar time, which for OOO is not temporal but spatial. The OOO idea is that time passes due to composition: two separate real entities occasionally interact through a sensual mediation that sometimes allows this. A real object (such as the reader of a poem) begins by confronting a sensual object with sensual qualities, but ends up as a real object *fused* with sensual qualities that were previously just observed rather than enacted or performed as part of the reader's being. I the reader (as a real object) *become* the sea with wine-qualities, just like a method actor, and real object plus sensual qualities is exactly what OOO defines as space, including such examples as Heidegger's broken tool. Like all real entities, this one – I myself as a real wine-dark sea – has retroactive effects on both of its elements: the real me and the sensual wine-qualities. We cannot "unsee" a metaphor, though we can and do become bored with it, so that it eventually becomes literalist in character. Something like this also happens in the inani-mate realm, when a real object becomes fused with qualities that it did not previously have.

In any case, this retroactivity of a whole on its previously sep-arate components is what creates the irreversibility of time for OOO. The reader who grows bored with the wine-dark sea is not the same reader as the one who had not yet encountered it. Cogburn makes a further, ingenious technical objection to this outline of a solution. OOO's approach entails that my perception of a pine tree, for instance, occurs on the interior of a larger object that contains both the real me and the sensual tree; the example of two colliding airplanes also requires that they form a unified third object having retroactive effects on both. The OOO model requires that what happens on the interior of the third or "superordinate" object (Cogburn's term) involves the confrontation between the real me and the sensual tree (and that in cases where the tree also makes contact with me, there is a different but closely related superordinate object). But Cogburn notes a possible difficulty here. The containing object must be in some sort of relation with the two subordinate objects – one real, one sensual – on its interior. But since the containing object is by definition real, and *ex hypothesi* also makes contact with the real interior one, this flouts the OOO principle that two real objects can never be in direct relation. But if we suppose for this reason that both objects on the interior can only be sensual, this would make it impossible for them to relate at all, given that two sensual objects for OOO cannot make direct contact either, but must be mediated by a real one.

Here Cogburn arrives at the frontier between what I know and do not know; such challenges are always the most difficult, but also the most rewarding. Yet the provisional answer to his query is clear enough, especially if we change the example. In a sense we can say that water "contains" both hydrogen and oxygen. But by no means does it make contact with the *real* hydrogen or oxygen: like all wholes, it abstracts from these smaller real entities through the fact that not all aspects of these atoms are of relevance to the water. The fact that the real me confronts the sensual pine tree on the inside of the superordinate object does not mean that this object makes direct contact with the real me, even though I am there. A can "contains" the Coke in a sense, but that does mean that it contains the *real* Coke – only a fluid whose movement it restricts, which is a simplified model of the Coke rather than the thing itself. The can is not capable of anything more than this; nor is any entity. In short, containment too is a mediated relation rather than a direct one. The fact that I inhabit the interior of the superordinate object does not absolve of it dealing with me in indirect fashion, any more than water is absolved from touching hydrogen and oxygen indirectly.

D. Process, Retroaction, and the Status of the Past

Let's begin this conclusion with a point already touched upon in Chapter 1. Among many contemporary philosophers there is a sloppy tendency to speak of "process philosophies" while combining two completely different ideas under this name. When Whitehead uses the term, what he means is that the identity of a thing lasts for only the flash of an instant, and that whatever replaces it is a close successor but not exactly the same thing as what came before. Strictly speaking, an actual entity never *becomes*: instead, it can only perish and give way to a successor. But if someone now speaks of Bergson or Deleuze as "process philosophers," what they mean instead is that they are philosophers *of becoming*, which Whitehead simply never was. That is to say, it would be ridiculous to claim that Bergson thinks entities only exist for the flash of an instant before giving way to a close successor. Bergsonian *durée* is not made of instants, just as a Deleuzean "line of flight" is not made up of discrete positions. Elsewhere I have referred to Whitehead as belonging to "School X," and Bergson and Deleuze as belonging to a different group called "School Y."[68] The two schools can certainly be united by saying that "both are process philosophers *as opposed* to philosophers of substance," since it is true enough that Whitehead and Bergson are united in having no sympathy for Aristotelian *prote ousia* or enduring individuals of any other sort. But when used in this way, the phrase "process philosophy" suppresses a pivotal difference in how the two schools conceive of process. School X thinks of time as discontinuous, like the halting, jerky clay monsters that filled *Sinbad the Sailor* and other movies of my relatively low-tech childhood years. School Y thinks of it instead as an unbroken flux, so that time is continuous rather than jerky.

In what remains of this chapter, I should say something about two key issues that now confront us: (a) How exactly can non-real temporal changes (SO-SQ) lead to changes on the real level? In terms of the earlier chessboard analogy, how is it that real chess pieces are intermittently but not always moved, created, or destroyed by what happens on the surface above? (b) If only the present exists, even if it be a specious present of swirling sensual qualities and not an instantaneous flash, then what is the status of entities that are indexed by recollections in the present without actually inhabiting it? These are both difficult problems that cannot be solved in a few pages, though perhaps we can make some progress nonetheless.

For years I have made the case that the surface of reality is where everything happens. This is more or less inevitable if you accept, as does OOO, that real objects are withdrawn from direct relations with both human observers and each other: after all, this turns relations into something intermittent and difficult. In other words, only certain configurations of the surface will be able to bring depth into play. I realize, of course, that everyone in philosophy these days is suspicious of depth. After Heidegger there was a general reaction against it, and both structuralism and post-structuralism are just two of the currents that mock profundity as a false god. I happen to be reading a lot of Lacan these days, and he is rather savage in stripping Freud of anything real in the sense of hidden; Lacan's own real has no independent existence outside the direct surface of enjoyment, and otherwise simply marks the failure of the symbolic order.[69]

But while Lacan is no phenomenologist, this mimics the phenomenological regression that followed Heidegger, of which even Derrida is guilty. The reason to stick with depth is that no change is possible without a currently unexpressed surplus in the real. In other words, there is no way to account for change without RO and RQ somewhere in the picture. To posit "difference" will not do the job, since Derrida is wrong to assume that difference automatically yields temporality.

In the past I have written about the "revenge of the surface," referring to the aforementioned fact that thinkers of depth (such as Heidegger, McLuhan, and Greenberg) tend to make depth so deep that nothing can possibly happen there.[70] But rather than an abstract opposition between depth and surface, what we are looking for is a dynamic situation in which rather than just hinting at each other, content and medium can interact and transform one another. McLuhan is close to what we are looking for, though like OOO itself he has paid more attention to the formation of new real objects on top of the old ones, rather than somehow burrowing back into the old ones themselves. In OOO, for instance, the focus has been on how a beholder's relation with an aesthetic object itself becomes a new object.[71] Some have wondered if this focus on producing *new* real objects out of the sensual starting point is a way of theatrically dodging the old quest to know the initial real objects that hide behind the sensual. I do not think this is the real problem, since Heidegger and Greenberg already provide models for hinting obliquely at the old objects without their having to become directly present. The bigger concern for us is how the sensual realm is supposed to have *causal* effects on the real beneath it. McLuhan is in the same position here as OOO. He and his son/co-author Eric have developed a fine theory of how both reversal and retrieval can give rise to new media.[72] But in both cases it's about creating new media, not retroactively affecting the old ones.

This may be the right moment to introduce something that has been on my mind for several years. It is well known that OOO treats the real object as a surplus deeper than any or all of its current relational expressions, as something more than its current status in the world. That is what links us with the Aristotle of the

Metaphysics, in his famous critique of the Megarians. But there is another kind of surplus, in both OOO and the history of philosophy; and I do not mean surplus value as in Marx, which has a political, economic, or even moral sense rather than an ontological one. Along with real objects, note that sensual qualities are a different sort of surplus. Think of the apple again. I am observing it, holding it, and most of its qualities are excessive, in the sense that they can be stripped away without this apple ceasing to be this very apple. Surprisingly enough, this is the point that links us with Neo-Platonism, currently one of the least popular historical schools of philosophy.[73] We can speak here of "emanation" (ἀπορροή, *apor-rhoe*) or of the equally good translation "overflow." Instead of a deliberate creation of the visible world, each of the higher things (simply by being what it is) emanates the next layer down as if by accident. In Islamic Neo-Platonism this process involves each of the known planets, the Sun, and the Moon, to the extent that prophecy itself is often explained in this way. Of course, there is something else in emanation theory that is deeply incompatible with OOO: namely, its hierarchical structure. But OOO has a more democratic conception of objects, as readers of Levi Bryant will remember, and thus we prefer a secularized theory of emanation.[74] The apple emanates its various sensual qualities, or we could say instead that those qualities overflow the apple. Without sensual surplus of this kind, we would not be able to perceive anything. So, there are two kinds of surplus: the excess of the hidden real object, and the excess of palpable sensual qualities. A new and worthy topic for OOO would be as follows: what is the relation, if any, between these two very different kinds of surplus?

Let's recall one of the criticisms made by Kleinherenbrink. One of his major objections to the OOO theory of time is its incompatibility with the idea of real objects *producing* sensual versions of themselves. My response was that real objects themselves do not unilaterally produce anything in the first place. Instead, the sensual avatar of any real object is produced *in situ*, by which I mean that it emanates only when the real object combines with another real object to form a new compound object (and all objects are compounds), however brief its lifespan. In even the least case of perception, a new object is formed from my bond with a tree, chicken, building or whatever I perceive. The perception itself, in which the *separateness* of perceiver and perceived are stressed, despite their union in a broader object, takes place on the interior of the larger object. Here I have two observations to make. First, every object is asymmetrical. The fact that I perceive the tree does not mean that the tree perceives me in turn. It is also possible that the tree perceives me too, as when I touch the bark on its surface, but in that case there would be a separate if simultaneous object in which the tree is the dominant partner. Second observation: not all perception (and all relation is perception, even if not "consciously" so) has a retroactive effect on its elements. Most of our perceptions lead to nothing, but some do have retroactive effects on the perceiver. Consider the stories of H.P. Lovecraft, in which characters witness such abominable cosmic monstrosities that they frequently end their days as gibbering madmen in an asylum.[75] There are less disturbing examples as well. But the minimum condition for a retroactive effect on a perceiving object is that its experience must become *performative* rather than *literal*, since otherwise it is merely observing a spectacle external to itself without being fully engaged. Mere perception is usually prosaic and literal, experiencing the objects of the world as bundles of qualities. Aesthetic experience, by contrast, creates a rift between objects and their qualities. As I have often shown, this leads to a cascade of effects: the sensual object of perception is replaced by a real one; but since the real object is real, it is inaccessible.[76] If we read Homer's phrase "wine-dark sea" the wine-qualities remain accessible, but we do not know what a wine-like sea would be. This real object vanishes beyond access, but since the wine-qualities (like any others) cannot exist in detachment from any object, I myself qua perceiver am the only real object on the scene, and therefore must stand in for the missing sea. The perceiver becomes a kind of method actor performing the wine-dark qualities, because there is no alternative. This is the true sense of *mimesis* in art: not that we produce copies of things, but that we *become* copies of things.

At any rate, this is the general idea as to how the surface retroactively affects its underlying depths. My experience of the Mediterranean Sea could just be prosaic and literal, except that Homer manages to interfere with the sea's relation with its own qualities, and that's how my own being ends up disturbed by events on the temporal layer of SO-SQ. Explicit metaphor from human poets is just one way in which this can happen; a metaphorical structure is also what makes sheer physical causation possible, as Timothy Morton discusses in his book *Realist Magic*.[77] There is a lot more to be said on the topic, of course. But since our subject here is time, I simply wanted to point out that temporal surface changes leading intermittently to changes on the underlying chessboard is not unthinkable. That is why I do not think a solution of

Kleinherenbrink's sort is needed, though I thoroughly enjoyed his article.

The other issue we need to touch on is the existence of the past. Earlier I expressed rough agreement with aspects of McTaggart's position. That is to say, for me "time" is a purely sensual phenomenon and one that is confined to the "now," which I interpret as an extended or specious present and not as a single infinitesimal now-point. That being the case, what is the status of the past objects studied by archaeology? Obviously enough, these past objects exist in a present, but if we reduce them to that present then we are repeating the mistake of correlationism, by saying that we have access to nothing but their present configuration as ruins. Clearly the ruins point to something deeper than their current status, and from them we re-assemble a previously missing world. Lacan might say that we pass from the register of the real (crumbled artifacts torn loose from the symbolic order) to that of the imaginary.[78] OOO, here in polar opposition to Lacan, would say instead that the past reality of the ruins vanishes into inaccessibility and is re-enacted by the archaeologist or even the tourist, retroactively transforming their own being in this way even though the ruins themselves tend to remain ruins. The reason for the difference is that Lacan does not have a sufficiently robust sense of the real, and finds it only in direct enjoyment and unsymbolizable trauma.

5

Discussion of Chapter 4

Chris Witmore: In the previous chapter you offered a lucid and detailed account of how OOO defines time. After beginning with a concise summary of the fourfold structure of objects, you entered into a comparative assessment of how other philosophers have interpreted this structure – embracing an opportunity for further clarification – and followed with a discussion of McTaggart on "The Unreality of Time." Finally, in the last section you connected these insights with "process philosophies," occasionalisms, and some closing reflections on the existence of the past. As much as I would like to jump straight to some of the points that you raise in the conclusion, it will be to our advantage to proceed section by section, as in Chapter 3, beginning with "The Quadruplicity of Time," which provides a précis of the OOO angle on time and temporality.

  In order to understand time in OOO, one must recognize it as a tension that arises out of the fourfold structure of objects, and although you point out that fourfolds come in a number of varieties – indeed, many archaeologists will be more familiar with the semiotic square of Algirdas Greimas, which is itself a reworking of Aristotle's own square of opposition – yours involves four poles and four interactions along one rift between reality and sensation and another between objects and qualities.[1] Time, as the "tension between sensual objects and their sensual qualities," is one of the four interactions that occur between the four poles. Importantly, time is neither an external parameter nor an absolute container; rather, it is something born of, as you put it, what is "out of joint in objects themselves." Time is neither deeper than objects nor generated from within; rather, it occurs on the surface of things, fully within the realm of experience, perception, and intellect (indeed, to place the latter on the side of relations constitutes a fundamental break with modern philosophy).[2] Although apparently superficial, time is also profound, for it is the only place where "change can be triggered." I would like to return to the issue of change below; for now, let's stay with what, among other things, I find fascinating about your model, which is how it keeps time specific and local to objects, which is just as it would have been among legion past societies. This raises a fundamental question for archaeologists, anthropologists, and historians concerning how we might account for heterogeneous times. Given that our readership will be comprised of practitioners within these fields, might we begin by standing back and speculating about other possible shapes or *styles* that might accommodate these times? We have already discussed some forms at length: linear verses percolating time, topologies, and we might add cyclical conceptions of time. What possible forms might time take with OOO?

Graham Harman: The first thing that comes to mind is that the OOO model of time allows for an epochal conception of temporality. With theories of time that place it somewhere near the very center of reality, there is always a kind of hysteria to the effect that everything is fleeting and new change is constantly afoot. Greenberg has linked this conception of time to the basic principle of journalism: "Everything is changing fast!" In some ways, that really is the journalistic conception of time, with no offense intended to that profession. Greenberg was talking specifically about art world observers who frequently claim that trends in art are speeding up faster than ever. He countered this with an analysis showing that throughout the history of modern art, dominant trends have always lasted about twelve to fifteen years, with no real change in speed even in a decade as seemingly eventful as the 1960s. Twelve to fifteen years sounds about right, and I suspect that the same is true for almost any field. The reason is that there is one constant factor regulating the change of intellectual, political, or artistic trends: human generations. At some point a new idea captures the imagination of a young generation, and they invest themselves in mastering it, learning to apply it, and maybe adding their own twist on it. But every guiding idea has both its excesses and its hollow spaces, and no set of ideas deserves to dominate forever. With the advent of the following generation, the previous ruling idea is now the ruling power and thus no longer satisfying. New ideas will then arise that are to some extent at odds with the old ones.

But let's get back to the heart of your question, which concerns what new images of time the OOO model of SO-SQ might inspire. This is the first aspect: a calmer and more relaxed approach to the apparent flux and flow of everything, which OOO treats as a superficial process that need not always lead to much in the underlying configuration of objects. This entails further the somewhat scary consequence that not all work is productive. There is a very real chance that we spend years of effort on something, and it ends up not doing anything more than moving the sensual furniture around. It is actually somewhat difficult to strike a nerve in reality and move things forward. Several generations or even centuries might think they are making magnificent progress on something when really they are trapped in a long-term rut that is difficult to see from the inside. I've written about this elsewhere: two of the philosophers regarded as most "futuristic," as gateways to the ultra-advanced philosophy of the coming twenty-fourth century, are Schelling and Merleau-Ponty.[3] Both initially seem to unleash an earthquake in how we consider the modern relation between subject and object, and both of them do it by giving the "object" side more of the upper hand than is usual in modernity. Also, philosophy goes through countless Schelling Renaissances (with a new one every few decades), and the same pattern is conceivable for Merleau-Ponty, though interest in his work seems to be more constant and stable. Yet ultimately both thinkers still focus exclusively on the subject–object or thought–world dyad, even if they try to reverse it. Neither makes any real effort to escape that very duality. But what we really need to do in philosophy is go back to object–object relationships, which have become the exclusive domain of the natural sciences. I would certainly not say that Schelling and Merleau-Ponty are minor figures, but I would wager that their true position in the history of philosophy is quite a bit lower than their admirers tend to think. An intellectual career is always a risky bet on what is important and what is less important, and a lot of bets will simply end up being lost bets. We need to face the fact that there are tragic careers of this kind; the mere amassing of work over biographical time need not amount to much. Since we are in an age that is exceptionally pious about equality, this is a lesson few want to consider, but it is shockingly easy to mess up one's career by just drifting with the winds.

Along with the epochal idea that time itself is not important unless it leads to something significant, in OOO there is also the notion of time as something reversible. Latour was there first, of course. As a child in the 1970s, I never would have imagined that either slavery or piracy had much of a future. I'll also be political for a moment, and add that we also never imagined America would flirt with dictatorship in our lifetimes. We can hope that Joe Biden's victory speech put a temporary end to that, but over 47% of the American public is obviously still comfortable with the idea of a low-grade Mussolini running our country, so I doubt we are out of the woods yet. Also, in contemporary philosophy we often find the mediocre assumption that Aristotle is irretrievably dated, and that nothing quite matters unless it happened after Kant's Copernican Revolution. Against this, I would say that anything can come back if someone makes a good case for it, and we can never predict who might emerge to make such a case. This is why the future of any discipline is unpredictable, just like the future of media as described by McLuhan, in which the chance occurrence of an "artist" can lead to an old, dead medium being retrieved and changing the world.

Along with time in the sense of epochality and reversibility, OOO perhaps also offers a renewed sense of human control over time. For one thing, it is possible to create small-scale epochs in such a way that your life feels longer. For one thing, since I have never been a homeowner, I try to change residences every four years at most, since otherwise I have found that time tends to melt into an uninterrupted continuum and everything blows by too fast. With so many different apartments in my memory, it becomes easier to break past time into segments. Additionally, one of the reasons I like to write books is that the act of writing always moves us into a different mental space, and if I can write books quickly, I can undergo metamorphoses more frequently, with each one building on its predecessors. Stated differently, the act of writing books is like my personal atomic clock. Until recently I would also write a summary at the end of every month of all the good and bad things that had happened, and every new person I had met during the month, just because I dread the experience of "where did the years go?" that seems to be common among retired or elderly people. I want to have a very good idea of where those years went. Let your memory be a house of many rooms. This is somewhat under our control because there is no independent force called "time" that drives things forward automatically. What we call "time" is the product rather than the engine of change in the configuration of objects. The sense in which we do lose control over it comes from the inevitable degradation of the biological materials of which we are composed. Of course, OOO can offer no relief to the permanent human tragedy on that front.

CW: The tendency, for the modern age, was not only to regard the line as the connective tissue for its epochal models, but also to assert an image of progress which grounded its sense of directionality. So for you, one does not necessarily run afoul of OOO by construing your story of moving through apartments, writing books, and developing a philosophical perspective into maturity, as a series of improvements; one does not err by regarding tragic movement in the opposite direction as spiraling headlong into decay – falling into unhappiness with the loss of one's livelihood, as so many have done throughout the Covid-19 pandemic, and succumbing to despair in the face of fewer options. We could say that one would run afoul of OOO by rendering these episodes as attributes of a temporal flow somehow deeper than or external to the local circumstances to which it gives rise. One would err by asserting that these episodes are irreversible, lodged with an ever-increasing pace in a kinetic current beyond any human control. Thus, while the OOO model of time is epochal and can take the form of a line, it is far from modern in Latour's sense because of its reversibility: because objects, and their relationships, are generative of time.

Again, to return to the paradox you raised in Chapter 3, the epochal arises out of contact between specific objects and their mergers, so that epochs are not units within an arbitrarily divisible continuum. We might exemplify this contrast as one between the day, the month, the year and the old Babylonian cultural creation that is the seven-day week, if only to underline how the day, the month, and the year suggest another order of time: the cyclic.[4] One could bring the epochal to order in the round, as implied by your discussion of how intellectual platforms overturn every twelve to fifteen years, or the lack of productivity among so many scholars who labor at the grist mill of research: a term that holds connotations of rotation and repetition.

Before moving on to the next section, I think it important to say a bit more concerning cyclical continua as OOO opens thought in this direction. The ancient Egyptians, to take an example so effectively articulated by Jan Assmann, distinguished between cyclical and noncyclical time.[5] *Neheh* is the ancient Egyptian concept for time as the recurrence of the same: the repeated circuit of the sun through the sky and the underworld, the annual rise and fall of the Nile, the yearly preparation of the soil for planting crops, waiting out their germination, harvest, and storage of these provisions. *Djet*, by contrast, is noncyclical, but that does not imply that it is linear. *Djet* is that which lasts. It is, as Assmann puts it, "a sacred dimension of everness ... preserved in immutable permanence ... *Djet* is time at a standstill."[6] Have we arrived at a juncture when the cyclical emerges as a relevant, even necessary form for bringing the epochal to order, or at least as an essential complement to the linear? Whether with research, recycling programs, or ecological cycles, what are your thoughts on the retrieval of the ancient circle as a temporal form in our precarious times?

GH: Before responding to your question about the cyclical model of time, I'd like to share something that came up recently. I had a fine online discussion with the cognitive psychologist Donald Hoffman and the philosophy of color specialist Mazviita Chirimuuta, concerning whether evolution rewards fitness rather than truth. Hoffman's position is especially relevant to our discussion; it is covered in his widely read book *The Case Against Reality*.[7] He thinks that even space and time are just evolutionarily carved interfaces that have no pertinence to reality at all; more than this, he thinks the familiar space-time of physics is doomed. This is partly due to the "holographic principle," which suggests that a black hole is really just a two-dimensional hologram.[8] But as concerns time, Hoffman is on board with Nima Arkani-Hamed's recent lectures at Harvard, which demonstrated how much simpler many quantum-mechanical equations become if space-time is replaced by something deeper.[9] Now, although I do not agree that the evolutionary process is the primary locus for the gap between reality and human experience (this gap would exist even if Creationism were true), and though I also do not think philosophy should proceed in lockstep with the current state of science, it is suggestive to learn that the idea of time as a unidirectional continuum driving everything relentlessly forward is also suspect in recent physics.

To get back to your question about cyclical or circular time, there is some truth to this model but also some grounds for suspicion. In *Immaterialism*, for instance, I spoke about every social object first entering into a half-dozen or so symbioses before reaching a period of maturity, followed by decadence and eventual death. Insofar as I see this happening to every social subject and all its successors, in that sense there is a cyclical movement to which all such entities are condemned. However, it is not difficult to combine such movements with progressive ones. Hegelian or Marxist dialectics see recurrent processes in history without there being no progress at all. My favorite example is the periodic table of elements in chemistry: in one sense we keep coming back to alkaline earth metals or noble gases, but in another the same element is never repeated as we move through the table. In this way, periodicity is a good alternative to cyclicality, since it adds the progressive dimension that no one should wish to exclude, though conservatives do try to exclude it.

In philosophy, cyclical time is often linked with the traditionalism of *philosophia perennis*, which does not interest me. The idea that philosophy is about finding a "true content" that is repeatedly obscured and then recovered throughout the ages misses the fact that history makes irreversible advances or even retreats. For instance, one could make the case that Husserl's philosophy was misinterpreted by Heidegger, or that Freud was misunderstood by Lacan, or other such examples. But the fact remains that if you are a Husserlian who has never read Heidegger, or a Freudian who has never taken Lacan seriously, then you are probably condemned to a parochial dogmatism. Or to take a comparable example, I happen to think that Derrida did not get Heidegger right at all, but there is no question that Heidegger does look rather different after Derrida. It's not a matter of salvaging the true Heideggerian content that Derrida overlooked, but of playing the two off against each other to see what either or both may have presupposed or missed.

This brings us back to the topic of symbiosis. That is where I think the symmetry between past and future is broken: not through some modern purification movement of the sort rightly rejected by Latour, but through an unforeseen combination of two previously distinct elements. So, if we read Deleuze in the usual way as a combination of Spinoza and Bergson (as I myself do), then we not only have Deleuze himself as a new animal running loose in the history of philosophy, we also have a different Bergson and Spinoza from what we had before. The reason for studying classic figures in any field is not to learn the truth, but to come to grips with the basic elements from which new classics might be forged. I'm a defender of the notion of canonical works for the simple reason that non-canonical works are too easily reducible to content.

CW: Yes, it is the modernist (and eschatological) idea of time as a unidirectional continuum that attempts to break those ancient movements that lead back to themselves. Still, in order to observe the advantages that come with OOO's episodic and reversible model of time, where humans exert some control, it is important to see how this periodic conception may be brought to order. Mapping time's movement and lack of movement requires various shapes, whether as segmented lines, circles, or even spirals, as with productive forms of research. While the turn of the seasons is a four-part ring that accounts for qualitative and intermittent annual changes in the world, from the angle of OOO it is a symbiosis that puts a stop to the rising and falling, sediment-laden Nile (rendered as a primal cycle, the ancient Egyptian conception of *neheh*) through the great river's merger with the Aswan High Dam, which is further compounded through the Blue Nile's fusion with the new Grand Ethiopian Renaissance Dam (though this is certainly reversible, for the gift-laden Nile will return with the removal of these dams).[10] If we acknowledge, as one should, how the OOO model of time is inclusive of object–object relations of all creeds, then it would seem pertinent to consider how the manifestation of those object–object rapports behind, for example, the biogeochemical turnover of carbon, phosphorus, nitrogen, water, and oxygen, or the recycling of waste, is of cardinal importance to human observation of these dynamic cycles in the Anthropocene.[11]

In fact, this brings us to your second section, which undertakes the intellectual work of exposition by addressing three critiques of the OOO notion of time. For you such work runs to the heart of what philosophy, the love of wisdom, is about. Moreover, what allows any philosophical work to rise to the level of the canonical is *invention*. In different ways, Wolfendale, Gratton, and Kleinherenbrink take issue with your invention (which in your case always comes with the generous acknowledgment of OOO's predecessors) on the grounds that time, for OOO, plays out exclusively among superficial phenomena. Here your work is condemned or misunderstood for several reasons. The most pressing conundrum provides the backbone for the entire chapter: how can the sensual realm of time have causal effects at the deeper level of the real? Yet before we approach this crux, it will be to our benefit to connect this to an issue that we have already touched upon at various points throughout this book. To what degree are these critiques as much about the expectations that come with a *spatialized* view of time as they are about any presumed failure of the OOO model to account for time's "foothold in the real"? Do your critics expect too much from time?

GH: As discussed in the previous chapter, it is interesting that three critics with such different intellectual priorities (and such varying levels of fair play) all nonetheless agree that time should be an encompassing container that keeps everything moving along. Wolfendale's attitude is a fairly straightforward scientistic deference to what Newton and General Relativity have to say. Gratton equates time with difference, following his Derridean presumption that recognizing identity of any sort amounts to an absurd naivety; like so much of Derrida's work, this notion relies on vague background support from its never fully articulated link with a *politics* of difference. Let me be clear that I'm not dismissive of this political critique, but only of the assumption that identity is the root of the problem. Kleinherenbrink, the only one of the three who wishes me well, comes from a Deleuzean background. In an indirect sense this means that he comes from the school of Bergson, who is famously suspicious of frozen configurations of reality. This leads Kleinherenbrink, too, down the path of conceiving of time as an ever-flowing river in which all things bathe. All these critics share the idea of time as a cause, whereas in the OOO model time is not even "epiphenomenal" as Gratton claims, but a kind of residue or afterthought: the final station of the emanation train. And yet, from this unimpressive position in the backwaters of reality, time nonetheless becomes the seedbed or fertilizer for everything that happens. "So the last will be first, and the first will be last."[12]

So much contemporary thought prides itself on opposing the purported spirit of petrification that it finds in the old theories of substance, and this leads to many critiques that are two- rather than three-dimensional. When Gratton implies that because OOO accepts any notion of identity at all, it is therefore Platonism, he completely misses the point that there is nothing eternal about real objects. Although OOO's real objects are not immersed in Heraclitean flux or Bergsonian *durée* or Derridean difference, they are frequently generated and destroyed, often too quickly for anyone to notice. This is what I mean by a two-dimensional approach: "if you don't allow everything to be in a condition of utter flux, then you must be a Platonist." Nor is it necessary to single out Gratton here: the same prejudice is found in Whitehead, one of my favorite philosophers. It is so important for Whitehead that the traditional concept of substance be demolished that he makes the sweeping demand that everything be doomed to "perpetual perishing." The irony, of course, is that this perishing turns out to be so perpetual that Whitehead is left with nothing resembling time at all: just an endless series of punctiform instants cut off from one another. But since he uses the word "process" to describe this, almost everyone – again, Nail is an exception – lazily assumes that Whitehead is part of the flux gang, even though for him (as for Heidegger) it's exactly the opposite.

Levi Bryant shows some interesting ambivalence on this point in one of his many thought-provoking blog posts: one entitled "Stability and Change," from 2012. It seems at first to be written from the "everything is changing all the time" perspective, as seen in his opening words: "The important thing to understand is that it is not the possibility of change, motion, and becoming that needs explanation, but rather persistence, stability, and endurance. It is a stable entity that is improbable, not entropy."[13] But later in the post he expresses the opposite intuition: "The real question is not how it is possible for things to change, but rather why they don't just disintegrate." My reading of this second passage is not that Bryant is somehow trying to put the burden of proof on those who naively believe in stability or identity, but the opposite. Namely, if you think that everything is changing all the time, the burden is on you to explain why things are not constantly disintegrating. Bryant does immediately add that "things, patterns, stabilities, organizations, require *work* and *energy*," but elsewhere I have heard him agree that change, difference, and mutation require work and energy. As I once put it, we need something like a "stability theory" to account for the fact that sometimes nothing really happens and at other times a lot happens.[14] Paradoxically enough, what I call the Orgasmic Flux Doctrine ends up treating both boring moments and those of radical change as ontologically the same. First the Big Bang creates a universe out of nothing: "Ah, Heraclitus was right!" But then a hair falls from my head as I sit lazily and silently: "Ah, Heraclitus was right!" But we all know there is a difference between the two cases, and I see no reason to pretend there is not just because we are committed to an abstract "everything is changing all the time" hypothesis that Aristotle already bruised pretty badly in the *Physics*.[15] Put in terms of your question, yes, it is too much to expect of time that it be an all-embracing causal force. Time is not some magical elixir of motion flowing through the veins of all things. It is a surprisingly superficial tension between a sensual object and its various appearances, though I have said that this surface must not be underestimated, since it is the only place in the cosmos where direct contact of any kind can occur, or where any sort of change can be triggered.

CW: There is a strong compulsion in a lot of recent archaeological theory to jump fully into the ever-flowing river of perpetual becoming, with the buoying proviso that the "constant tumultuous flux" occurs at different rates.[16] And it is certainly the case that those who swim in the slipstream of Heraclitus, the weeping philosopher of Ephesus, are doomed to see the formation of snowflakes and the emergence of the British Neolithic in the same ontological terms. One reads, for example, in a recent book by Rachel J. Crellin, that change "always emerges from the relations within assemblages," a term defined in the style of Bennett (following Deleuze) as "living, throbbing confederations."[17] From this outlook it is "the density of relations" in the "assemblage that acts to keep things the same," and here one encounters a similar tendency to explain change and stability in almost the same terms: *almost*, as the difference comes down to an issue of varying bulk or consistency within the aggregation.[18] Not only is this merely to assert change, as you have pointed out elsewhere, it is also to neglect persistence completely. And we are left with a clear and intelligible account of neither. While we may find much to commend in Crellin's text when it renders time as heterogeneous and emergent, it nonetheless fails to hoist the burden of explanation with respect to why bronze weapon hoards are not constantly disintegrating in British soils. If one assumes the universe to be in perpetual flux, then you and Bryant are correct that one is compelled to explain situations where things actually resist change. Why, for example, did the Greek Neolithic persist for millennia, and even longer among the agrarian majority, well beyond the emergence of configured societies centered upon the favored few?[19] Of course, as soon as one accepts the axiom that stability is the norm, one is obliged to work in the opposite direction, by explaining how it is that things eventually do change, however intermittently it might be. With all due deference to Heraclitus, it seems that the path up and the path down cannot be one and the same if they wind over different mountains.

This brings us back to your critics, who by taking issue with time existing on the surface succumb, by varying degrees, to that temptation of reasserting their own understandings of time. In your own defense, you caution readers not to underestimate the surface. While you addressed this point somewhat in Chapter 4 in response to Cogburn's review of this book, I believe it would be to the benefit of readers from archaeology, anthropology, or history if you would help us understand better how time can be "generated by change" and yet also somehow postulated before-hand, as encapsulated by a statement that you make in the third section: "it is not change that presupposes time, but time that presupposes change." Though you state that it should be clear enough how the OOO model of phenomenal time is "capable of helping to carve pathways and scars back into the real," it is not necessarily easy, even for many seasoned readers of OOO, to clearly follow how this works.

GH: I'm afraid my answer will be somewhat lengthy. Let's start by introducing some provisional new terminology. There are two different ways one might go about getting at the real in philosophy, at least for those like me who do not think it is easy. The usual way would be to say that the real is submerged beneath the waves and we need to bring it to the surface where it can be seen. Let's use the adjective "submarine" to refer to the real in this sense. For many rationalists there is no problem here at all: just follow the correct epistemological, scientific, or mathematical procedures and you can easily bring the real to the surface. But obviously this cannot be a simple thing for OOO, any more than it is for Kant or Heidegger. Kant would say that what lies beneath the surface is noumenal and can only be thought, not known. Heidegger would say that it can be gradually or asymptotically brought to the surface through a process of unveiling, but never completely. OOO is somewhere between these two positions. We think there is a lot more to be said about the noumenal than Kant realizes, though he is right that it cannot be known directly. The disagreement with Heidegger is that OOO does not think any "partial" approach to being is possible either. Partial ultimately means "direct but partial," and the problem with all such models is that they cannot explain how the part of the banana that we can see relates to the part we cannot. There is a sense in which the banana is simply a single, unified banana, and though you can make some sort of cockeyed estimate that you have experienced, say, 72 percent of it while the other 28 percent is unknown, in that case you are just treating it in empiricist fashion as a "bundle of qualities." Wolfendale argues in this vein that there is only a "quantitative" unknown excess in the things, not a "qualitative" one.[20] But this means to treat the real as something that might *in principle* be translated into knowable images without being transformed, and Latour was not the first figure in the history of philosophy to grasp the impossibility of transport without transformation. We find this in some of the Scholastics as well, notably in Francisco Suárez's rejection of the Thomist *materia signata*, the model of matter stamped with form. Historically speaking, the very idea of "matter" in philosophy was created primarily as an alibi for not giving a sufficient account of how the form in the thing relates to the form we have of it in the mind. It is not a simple question of extracting a form from "matter" and bringing it into the mind while leaving the matter behind. Everywhere there is nothing but forms, and they are changed when you move them from the thing into the mind, or to anywhere else. Anyway, this is the "submarine" conception of the real; this is what your question is about, and I will get to it shortly. But first we need to talk about the opposite way of dealing with the real.

The opposite way is one that we might call "supermarine." This method amounts to saying that the reality beneath the surface is not the only kind that exists. In a normal case of perception, for instance, there are countless images and profiles that count as sensual rather than real. But the *experiencer* of this sensual reality is always real. That is to say, the "I" who looks out at the world is a real object encountering sensual ones. I am not myself a sensual object, though outside observers must see me that way, and though even in introspection I encounter myself as a sensual rather than a real object. If we capitalize on that fact, we can turn parts of the sensual realm into components of real objects simply by bringing them into a special sort of relation with an object already known to be real: I myself. So far, OOO has developed this point mostly in connection with aesthetics.[21] When Homer says "wine-dark sea," the non-literality of this phrase splits the sea-object from its wine-qualities, since their relation is vaguely compelling yet somehow also impossible. The wine-qualities remain there before us, in impossible combination with a real sea which – like all real objects – is inaccessible. Thus, I myself as a real object must stand in for the real sea, theatrically performing it in a manner analogous to Konstantin Stanislavski's acting system (which is famously called "method acting" in the United States, but Stanislavski himself called it a system).[22] But there are many other such cases aside from aesthetics. In speech-act theory, for instance, it has long been known that a promise or vow creates realities in ways that mere descriptive speech might not.[23] Lacan would say that any statement is more than what is enunciated, since it also expresses the position of the one who enunciates it. Levinas contrasts the said with the saying. These are all "supermarine" ways of building realities on top of a pre-existent sensual realm, as opposed to "submarine" methods of trying to bring pre-existent realities to the surface. OOO has dealt with the supermarine methods first, simply because they are easier to comprehend philosophically, even if *prima facie* less familiar to philosophers.

Before we return to the submarine problem, let's say a few words about the pre-history of the supermarine method. As mentioned earlier, OOO was not the first to treat of this possibility. One obvious example is Husserl's discussion of "transcendental genesis" in *Formal and Transcendental Logic*.[24] First, we should recall that there is no submarine reality in Husserl's philosophy. He finds Kant's idea of a reality that is not correlated with possible conscious access to be absurd. But of course the conscious subject has a reality of its own for Husserl, and he explores the possibility that this subject can gain new and abiding properties from its experience in the world. Derrida wrote his interesting Master's Thesis, *The Problem of Genesis in Husserl's Philosophy*, about this very problem.[25] Transcendental genesis is not quite the same thing as OOO's aesthetic theatricality, but both are supermarine approaches to establishing the real in the midst of a sensual neighborhood.

Another recent effort can be found in Badiou's philosophy, especially in his *Logics of Worlds*.[26] A "world" for Badiou is a specific phenomenal situation governed by a "transcendental," so in this respect it is a situation where everything is already "counted," and is thus the very opposite of Badiou's beloved "event" in which there is an upsurge of the uncounted from outside the situation. Nonetheless, Badiou also suggests that things happening in the situation can somehow retroactively modify something more than the situation itself. Otherwise it would be pointless to act at all: even if someone were a Badiouian super-genius able to conduct political, scientific, and aesthetic revolutions simultaneously while also falling in love, everything would dissolve into whatever banal situation they happen to occupy. For events to matter, there has to be a way to establish a link between situations and truths, which is precisely what *Logics of Worlds* is about. All right, but then the question is whether Badiouian events are of a submarine or supermarine sort. I would argue the latter, since his "inconsistent multiplicity" (that which lies outside any specific, counted situation) does not seem to have autonomous existence in the philosophically realist sense: he calls it a "void," in fact, linking this idea explicitly to the empty set as belonging to all sets in orthodox set theory.[27] In any situation, inconsistent multiplicity is there like a shadow of everything that has been counted and recognized, but it is not really there independently. In one sense, Badiou takes advantage of the fact that any given political situation excludes certain people as not really counting (the homeless, undocumented immigrants) and that such people might form the basis for a political revolution. This makes it seem like they really exist on their own, outside of any count. But Badiou's ontology does not actually allow for this; his "inconsistent multiplicity" is not an unknowable noumenon or formless *apeiron*, but simply the negative of any specific count. So as I see it, Badiou's events are also supermarine and do not bring anything hidden into the light, but simply construct a new hybrid reality built out of a subject's fidelity to a specific event. In other words, a merely sensual or situational incident – such as a few hundred people storming a prison in Paris in 1789 and releasing the inmates – becomes a real event through the fidelity of subjects who affirm that a French Revolution has begun.

We now circle back to the topic of the submarine. I am not aware of any convincing attempt to tackle this issue. On the one hand, we have those who think there is no serious problem in knowing reality: just use proper intellectual techniques and discover the true properties of things, usually in the manner of science, mathematics, or rationalist philosophy. My colleague Meillassoux belongs in this camp. On the other hand, we have philosophers who do draw a sharp distinction between something like the real and the sensual, such as Plato, Plotinus, Kant, Heidegger, and so forth. And while these thinkers offer various ways of catching a glimpse of the real, they never suggest that we can change it. Human activity may "participate" in the real in some sense, but there is no way that Plato's perfect forms or Kant's noumena can be altered, combined, or damaged by anything that happens here on Earth. Once in a while we see Heidegger scholars toying with formulations such as "God needs us," as if the actions of human being (*Dasein*) could have ramifications for Being itself.[28] But it's never clear how that would work, or whether Heidegger even held such a position consistently.

However, there is also one of my favorite passages in DeLanda, which comes in the early pages of *A New Philosophy of Society*. There he discusses the different sorts of features that belong to a real assemblage rather than to a mere collage of multiple beings without unified reality. The one that people usually speak about is emergent properties: water obviously has traits that do not belong to hydrogen or oxygen in isolation, such as the capacity to extinguish fire and quench animal thirst. DeLanda has written about this wonderfully elsewhere.[29] But it is not his primary concern in *A New Philosophy of Society*. One of his other criteria for a new assemblage is what he calls "redundant causation," which (as is often the case) is a phrase he uses differently from mainstream analytic philosophers. For DeLanda, what it means is that an assemblage is independent of any *specific* parts. At 40,000 miles we replace the tires on our car, but we would never call it a different car for that reason; within certain vague limits, any tires will do. This helps to show one major difference between DeLanda and Latour, since the latter's notion of "black boxes" implies that all the parts and history of a thing are there in the thing itself and simply hidden from view most of the time. DeLanda would object (as would I) that a black box does not just serve to hide its internal components, but also to establish its relative independence from them. Just think of how often the atoms in your body are flushed away and replaced by new ones, and now think of how little that matters. In fact, this is why DeLanda prefers chemistry to physics: in chemistry it is no longer a question of additive forces or materials, but of new levels of reality distinct from their component parts.

But the greatest interest of his discussion lies elsewhere, in two other traits of real assemblages. The first is their ability to create new parts. This is not only true for an organism, which we know produces new cells constantly. It also occurs for an assemblage as unnatural as Los Angeles, which can set up new departments and annex former suburbs, lending them all a certain vague "Los Angeles feel" in the process. Yet even when an assemblage creates no new parts, it can have retroactive effects on the parts that compose it. My and my wife's lifestyle and attitude have discernibly changed since moving to the Los Angeles area, as we adopt certain cultural norms and patterns of activity previously unknown to us in Egypt, Turkey, or Iowa. Though we are now "parts" of Los Angeles, it composes us no less than we compose it – and no doubt much more so, given our small size and limited degree of influence on the metropolis. This is where we find a hint as to how surface incidents in the sensual realm are "capable of helping to carve pathways and scars back into the real."

It has to be remembered that the OOO model of causation is not the usual one, which is diachronic and mostly attends to the fleeting collision of separate entities. Ultimately, for OOO all causation is compositional in character. There was an article a decade ago entitled "Time, Space, Essence, and Eidos" in which I gave the example of a mid-air collision between airplanes. Instead of treating this as an impact in space between two separate entities, I mentioned that any genuine relation *ipso facto* produces a new object.[30] The reason for this is that an object need not be a durable physical solid easily recognized by humans. Instead, the more basic notion of "object" is that of a new reality impenetrable to outside observers. The crash of airplanes clearly meets this expanded definition of an object: the crash is not reducible to what observers say about it, or its impact on FAA regulations and the lives of victims' families. Instead, the crash is something more than the two planes taken in isolation. It is a new object, however unstable and transient. Through their tragic meeting, the two airplanes become components of a larger third entity that contains both. It clearly has retroactive effects on its two major pieces, which are modified while both remain on the *interior* of the new third object. Yet they retain a certain independence rather than fusing permanently into the crash-object, and given the inherent instability of this object, they quickly detach in a very different form from the one they had prior to the crash.

This is my provisional answer to your question. Causal interaction takes place *not only* on the surface of reality, but also on the interior of the new third object that incorporates two previously independent terms. Incidentally, I hold that there can only be two terms in any causal relation, because it requires one real object and one sensual one, so that "three's a crowd." But the key to the problem is that causation always contains one real term along with a sensual one, though in physical reality there seems to be a symmetry at work: Real Airplane A makes contact with Sensual Airplane B, while Real Airplane B makes contact with Sensual Airplane A. Note that this is not true of all relations: I can view a long-dead star through a telescope without it being influenced by me in return, since the real star no longer exists and cannot be influenced by anything.

CW: So, phenomenal time is able to etch avenues into the real, not only because it plays out on the surface of a new third object, but also because of the indirect contact between two objects through their real and sensual counterparts; through this encounter, the two become components of the third, however fleetingly. Let us place to one side the possible difficulty raised by Cogburn of this third, real object being in contact with the real interior one. If we were to restate your answer in terms of a historical example, then the series of pyroclastic surges released by Vesuvius, and which, in meeting with the seaside town, engulfed Herculaneum over the course of a day or more in 79 CE, triggered the formation of a new object: a lethal kiln of superheated streets, insulae, temples, houses, a forum, theatre, and volcanic flows, hostile to all living things, whether those human inhabitants who sought shelter within its buildings, their companion animals, or the vegetation which formerly provided shade or sustenance to all. Given the instability of this walled volcanic inferno, the pyroclastic surge will eventually detach from the erstwhile infrastructure of the buried Roman town, leaving sintered deposits and solidified flows alongside carbonized wooden beams, furniture, and even scrolls, as with those found in the library of the Villa of Papyri.[31] Were Pliny the Younger to have observed the saltational accumulation of pyroclastic flows around the standing buildings, he would have noted time, which for you relates to the confrontation of sensual objects with their sensual qualities, while those causal relations that played out at submarine levels leave behind a well-preserved Roman town that will only start to change radically with its rediscovery in the eighteenth century.[32] So in this way, time can be generated by change while paradoxically also presupposing it.

Before advancing to your discussion of McTaggart, your response here raises two further thoughts. First, it would be advantageous to stand back and situate your answer in terms of ontography, a word that for you (notwithstanding the various ways this term has been defined by others, whether in philosophy, anthropology, or archaeology) has to do with describing and determining the pairings that emerge from the fourfold character of objects.[33] It has been over a decade since you enunciated the need for a more detailed ontographic atlas, one that maps out possible interactions in the way you have done here with time and causation.[34] How far has this endeavor moved along its path to maturity?

Second, those anthropologists who study "material culture" and those archaeologists who regard their objects as "materials" will find your point, that matter was created in philosophy "primarily as an alibi for not giving a sufficient account of how the form in the thing relates to the form we have of it in the mind," a bit perplexing. Though you state this point in passing, it would be of great importance, in my opinion, to contextualize further your angle on matter and form, especially for those readers who are unfamiliar with your rejection of materialism.[35] One of the many important attributes of your philosophy is that objects are not synonymous with materials, for they can also be ideas, fictions, figments of the imagination. Another is that objects cannot be undermined, reduced, or subjugated to matter since they come in various shapes and sizes, whether material or immaterial. Yet you go even further, for by situating discrete objects as the definitive grounds of reality, OOO comes to be at odds with materialisms in nearly all their forms, as their edifices are erected upon an image of matter as primordial ultimates, throbbing wholes, or bundles of physical properties. I take your point that what typifies an object is not its material substrate (as objects, in circumventing the privileged twofold of human and the world, may be equally immaterial) but rather that it always has a structure, that it is always formed.[36] Still, your rejection of the term "materialism" relates primarily to the primal sense of "matter" as *mater*, mother, a legacy that we may associate with the pre-Socratics who tended to associate the real with a substrate beneath the world around us.[37] But what of the physical sense of the term "matter," the one that stems from the Latin *materia* or *materies*, which means timber, lumber, construction material, or substance? If everywhere, as you say, there are "nothing but forms," then how do you respond to the archaeologist who seeks to account for the specific differences between a water jar, a hydra made of bronze, and another that is ceramic? Could one not follow Bryant and conceive of matter both in terms of this raw heft and as emergent?[38] Can materialism retain some utility if one remains open to the redefinition of the term and refuses to subjugate objects to their physical qualities?

GH: I'll start with the question about matter, then backtrack to the one about ontography. Let's begin with your point about the difference between a bronze hydra and a ceramic one. The implication seems to be that if we leave matter out of consideration, then we merely have one and the same form with no way to differentiate them. But what you're really asking about here are components, and those components are a relevant part of the form. In other words, a bronze hydra and a ceramic one actually have different *forms*, even if one can always abstract from both objects to the point where you reach a physical shape that seems to be common to both. But once that happens, you're already pretty far downstream from the object itself. For instance, Kant tries to defeat the famous ontological argument for the existence of God by saying that there is no real difference between 100 actual dollars and 100 imaginary ones, which also entails no real difference between an actual God and an imaginary one: "being is not a real predicate," as he says. Instead, he claims that the difference is only one of "position," which ultimately means the different positions between actual dollars/deities and imaginary ones with respect to us. What I would say in response is that with the actual and the imaginary object it's not as if you have two things that are identical in all respects except for the fact that one of them exists and the other does not. The existing thing actually has different qualities from the non-existent one, and that's because it has different components from the non-existent one. Returning to your example, the bronze and ceramic hydras have different forms. Yes, we can always attempt to translate something from one medium into a different one, but this entails a change in form.

As for Bryant, I'm not always sure why he wants to retain the notion of matter so badly. But he is not the only one: I wonder the same about Slavoj Žižek, among others, given the truly minuscule resemblance between his purportedly materialist position and anything that has ever been called "materialism."[39] I suspect people simply enjoy the term's ring of enlightened liberation, freedom from superstition, and so forth.[40] Materialism seems to place one in a distinguished lineage of thinkers who have boldly challenged authority: speaking the truth to power, as it is often called. Today's materialisms aren't usually Marxist or Epicurean in orientation any more, but want to call our attention to *forms* that haven't received as much attention as others: whether these be archaeological relics, women's bodies, cooking practices, the ways that animals have been buried, and the like. It is easy to see why such things look like "matter" when contrasted with words found in books, but they have every bit as much intrinsic structure, every bit as much form, as the most refined conceptual creations. Why, you might ask, am I so hostile to terms like "matter" and "materialism"? There is a purely philosophical reason, which is that I am fascinated with the movement, endurance, and translation of forms. And as soon as you introduce the notion of matter these problems are artificially amputated, because you can always just stipulate a neutral receptacle able to support whatever you put in it, even if you add the caveat that your own version of matter is "dynamic." This spoils all the philosophical questions that seem most interesting: how do multiple forms combine together to

produce a new one? Why are some forms so much more durable than others when their component pieces change? What is
the difference between a minimal shift in form and a landmark
transformation? Why do forms sometimes hide and sometimes
appear in an altered condition? This entire line of questioning
is pre-empted by conceptions of materialism; even worse, this
new materialism is itself a new orthodoxy despite its continuously repurposed air of stunning iconoclasm. These days, who
isn't calling for more "materiality" in intellectual life? And yet
we continue to recycle the same modern taxonomy that Badiou
came close to diagnosing, though not escaping: "There are only
bodies and languages."[41] I agree with this sentiment, and simply
disagree with Badiou's proposed solution that "truths" are the
golden third term excluded by this taxonomy. In my experience,
those who speak of "truth" are usually too quick to assume that
they already have it.

Just to avoid causing any needless offense, I should add that
I love it when people do actual work on small or mid-sized
physical entities in any field. I think everyone knows that I
love this, and it is probably why I've been read fairly widely in
archaeology circles. I simply don't think that "materialism" is
the right name for this kind of activity: if you're working on
things, you're working on the *forms* of those things. There has
never been any such thing as matter. The only reason to affirm
its existence is to supply a lazy substratum to explain how forms
move from one place to another without changing, thereby con-
cealing a rich vein of philosophical possibilities for accounting
for the stability and movement of forms. New Materialism has
been a useful movement in getting us past the age when texts
and power were the only things anyone wanted to talk about,
yet there is still too much overlap between these two recent
periods of intellectual history. Both hold that everything exists
primarily in relation to something else, and far too often that
relationship involves humans. Both like to undercut the notion
of identity to an implausible degree. Both are suspicious of the
real as anything other than recalcitrance or resistance to human
action (which Bennett opposes admirably, despite herself being
a New Materialist).[42] Both currents of thought have a one-sided
vision of power as something to be "transgressed" or given
the middle finger, with too little sense of the need to establish
better power and better authority. Both seem to work from the
assumption that everything is changing all the time, which has
the side effect of making it difficult to conceptualize real change

rather than the continuous flux-noise that surrounds us at all times. And of course, both assume that desire is always something to be liberated rather than sublimated, as the objections of Maurizio Ferraris have reminded us.[43] New Materialism can no longer help us at this juncture.

Your other question had to do with ontography and what progress has been made since the 2011 book *The Quadruple Object*. This is my active line of research, which means there is still a lot of sawdust in the room and it can be hard to know which steps in ontography are irrevocable, provisional, rock solid, or still questionable. Ontography refers to the fourfold diagram that depicts the various possible arrangements between the two kinds of objects and two kinds of qualities. Similar diagrams can be found in earlier authors, such as the Schema L of Jacques Lacan, the semiotic square of Greimas that you mentioned, or the tetrad of Marshall and Eric McLuhan.[44] Of course, the visual similarity of all these diagrams is simply an inevitable product of the fact that their diagrams and mine are all trying to integrate two separate dualisms, and when you do that you're automatically going to end up with a fourfold structure. What differentiates the various methods from each other are the specific character of the four poles and the mechanics of their interaction. For instance, the OOO ontography diagram is applicable to a single moment in time (though it is not punctiform), whereas the McLuhan tetrad requires actual calendar time for one medium to reverse into or retrieve another.

Years ago I began with a basically Heideggerian model in which there are real objects hiding behind their sensual qualities, though these were not the terms I was using at that early stage. Heidegger is actually somewhat reluctant to treat the realm of being or hiddenness as plural, and tends to confine the plurality of things to the derivative realm of presence found in broken tools; until that point, everything works as a seamless system. But my interpretation in *Tool-Being* already broke with Heidegger on this issue. Then for several years I struggled to differentiate between Heidegger's real tool-object and Husserl's intentional object. After all, doesn't the intentional object also "hide" behind all the various sensual adumbrations through which it appears? No! That was the sound of the first lock opening. When Husserl has us intending an apple or a blackbird, these entities are not hidden at all. They are there directly before us because we are already acknowledging their existence. Their various accidental profiles don't hide them, but are simply encrusted upon them, and only need to be scraped away if we want to find the essence of the object. To anticipate where all this was headed using later OOO terminology (which did not yet exist), a suitably reinterpreted Heidegger yields the RO-SQ axis. Importantly, this axis was already present in the work of the young Husserl's rival within the Brentano School, the brilliant Polish thinker Kasimir Twardowski.[45] He too spoke of objects outside the mind and qualities inside the mind. Husserl then had to renounce anything "outside the mind" for his phenomenology to be possible, but as compensation he found a new dualism *inside* the mind: one between objects and qualities, which allowed him to break completely with the British Empiricist reduction of objects to bundles of qualities. That gives us SO-SQ to go with the Heidegger/Twardowski RO-SQ. At some point I added RO-RQ, now known in OOO as "essence." I remember writing and lecturing as late as my Amsterdam sabbatical in 2007 only about time, space, and essence. But one of the great things about diagrams and models, even in science, is that they allow you to predict the existence of new and unknown things by looking for gaps in the current model. The left-over gap in ontography was the missing SO-RQ axis, and sure enough, it did not take long to see that Husserl had already discovered that one as well: the difference between the sensual objects we encounter and their real qualities, the ones they need in order to go on being recognized as what they are rather than changing into something else in our minds. This is what I now call "eidos." But Husserl was wrong to think these qualities were accessible to the intellect rather than the senses. Heidegger had already shown us that there is no great ontological gap between the intellect and the senses, since both give us a caricature of the things rather than the things themselves. Both the senses and the intellect traffic in the realm of presence.

So there you have it: the fourfold in complete form, comparable in some respects to Heidegger's infamous *Geviert* but different in others. The name "ontography" for the structure came about accidentally in 2009, at the wedding of the late Mark Fisher. While there I picked up a book of ghost stories by M.R. James (who ironically had been baptized in the very church where Fisher and his wife were married) and saw that "ontography" was James's comical term for the academic discipline of the pedantic professor in one of his tales.[46] I put it to immediate use in describing the fourfold structure of objects and qualities. And once you have a good name for something, it picks up speed and begins to occupy more of your attention. It did not take long to decide that ontography was important, since every possible field asks the question as to what its chief objects are and how they relate to their own qualities. Anyway, as for your question about what has happened in ontography since 2011, there are perhaps three separate topics to discuss when it comes to ontography: the poles, the tensions, and the transformations.

By the poles, I simply mean the four basic elements: real objects, real qualities, sensual objects, sensual qualities. There is unlikely to be any change to these, since I trod carefully across this bridge many times over the years, mostly in solitude, and am convinced that they are safe and solid. Most existing philosophies efface one or more of these four poles, and hence there is a good deal of critical and pedagogical work still to be done. For instance, phenomenologists never want to concede that there is any RO apart from SO, because Husserl's entire career was based on the assumption that RO (comparable to Kant's hidden thing-in-itself or Heidegger's *Sein*) does not exist. Those of a more naturalist or scientific bent are more hostile to SO, and you can also find people who are opposed to distinguishing between the two kinds of qualities: such as Wolfendale, whose book denies the very existence of hidden real qualities. That's a long critical tradition, actually: the opposition to "occult qualities," which is essentially just the scientific faith that there cannot be anything unknowable. What has really changed since 2011 is my increasing recognition of how real objects exist *above* any situation and not just beneath: as mentioned earlier, when I observe a tree, the real tree that withdraws from the situation is not alone, since I too am a real object truly deployed in acknowledging the tree. This means that in certain cases I can substitute myself for the tree, as in metaphor: the "supermarine" realm, in other words.

As for the tensions, I mean the four possible combinations: SO-SQ (time), SO-RQ (eidos), RO-SQ (space), and RO-RQ (essence). Here the critical and pedagogical work consists mostly of trying to demonstrate that terms such as time and space truly have an ontographic foundation. Obviously, time and space have a long history not only in Western philosophy, but in the common sense of everyday life and the private speculations of all humans with even a flickering of intellect. Who is not fascinated by the various paradoxes of time? Space may not be as common a theme of philosophical wonder, but it deserves to be. Anyway, time and space have long been known as the two great arenas of existence, and there is a tendency to treat them as mysterious and ultimately peerless continua. Since Einstein and Minkowski it is common to speak of a single space-time, and with the rise of string theory it is increasingly common to speculate about many more spatial dimensions than three. Yet despite these complications, space and time are always mentioned in the same breath, while it is simply assumed that nothing else deserves to be mentioned along with them. Is there any philosophy, religion, or mythological system that has attempted to add other terms to the mix? If there is, I have not yet run across it. In fact, one of the results of OOO of which I am most proud is the surprising outcome that our beloved space (RO-SQ) and time (SO-SQ) are generated by a deeper distinction between objects and their qualities, and that the ontographic model predicts the existence of two equally important terms: essence (RO-RQ) and eidos (SO-RQ). I did not go searching for this, but it popped up naturally as a result of the model and has fascinated me ever since. In short, space and time exist *because* objects have an uneasy relationship with their own qualities, something that Aristotle saw when he noted that substances can have different qualities at different times: Socrates can change from happy to sad, or from standing to sitting, while still remaining Socrates.

The real action in ontography comes in the transformations: or the "rotations," as I sometimes call them. Each of the tensions is unstable by nature, and tends to transmute into a neighboring one. The McLuhans are onto this in *Laws of Media* with their notion of media "overheating" with excess information, and reversing or flipping into their opposite. And again, Lacan is an uncanny precursor with his theory of the clockwise rotation of the four Discourses: those of the Master, the University, the Hysteric, and the Analyst.[47] How each of the four tensions of ontography destabilizes and becomes a different one, and why there are long periods of stability so that things do not transform constantly, are the areas in which most progress has been made since 2011. The emergence of Lacan as an important source for me is one index of this, since I rarely if ever discussed him in previous publications; nor did I say much if anything about Greimas. But when people see the next published version of ontography in the near future, they will be seeing fewer phenomenological references than in the past and a greater number of structuralist ones, and perhaps even others with more of a cybernetic flavor.

Simultaneously, I have been pursuing other paths that do not map immediately onto ontography, though interesting work could be done to make them so. For instance, a sharp young photographer from Iran named Erfan Ghiasi showed up in Los Angeles one day and asked how the symbioses in *Immaterialism* work in an ontographic sense. I had actually never thought of that question until he posed it, and only then did I realize that it was an interesting problem to think about. Nor do I think it's obvious how my recently completed book about architecture maps onto ontographic dynamics.[48] I think it's important in one's work not to tie everything together prematurely, because when you do that it's much too easy to force things. I have to trust that my mind, in a slow sub-verbal way, is piecing everything together, and that one day I'll see how it all connects. This has happened often enough already.

CW: Thank you for clarifying where you are with your ontography. Before moving on to my next question, it is important to emphasize for a diverse readership how many different meanings are routinely conflated under the rubric of "matter" within archaeology. As if that which is raw, tactile, weighty, in possession of mass, and exists out in the world could be summed up with a single term, the *material* is habitually deployed as an adjectival qualifier for the discipline's objects.[49] For some, this serves as a rather expedient way to distinguish archaeological things from discursive ones.[50] For others, the *material* is a convenient catch-all for the descriptive physical attributes of an artifact.[51] For still others, it is a marker of difference that relates to the identity of a given object; here your point about the hydras is well taken, for the archaeological question of difference began from the angle of typological abstraction on the basis of common vessel shapes, rather than with the thing itself. Indeed, some objects are treated as synonymous with "materials," as if the stuff of which the hydras are made is more real than the containers that hold the water.[52] For others it increasingly serves to signal, in the style of Bennett, a vital world that is something more than "a recalcitrant context for human action."[53] In any case, given how most archaeologists approach the issue from what may seem to be the opposite direction, it makes it difficult for them to understand how you are championing form.

Whereas many archaeologists regard matter, and by extension the material, as a deeper layer lying below conceptual superstructures, you like Latour see it as lodged in relations.[54] I think we can now understand how, to consider wax, linseed oil, and egg yolk as *ingredients* in paint, rather than as objects in their own right, is an attempt to "format or formulate," to borrow your words, the object that is paint because the reality of objects always lies at a greater depth than any consideration of their physical components, which are defined from without.[55] Moreover, as soon as one ties objects – whether archaeological or otherwise – to the material realm, one becomes less open to the efficacy or existence of Artemis, goddess of the hunt, the allure of the Norwegian Fossegrim, or the fear of unwholesome marsh vapors.[56] Are these not as much objects of historical concern as temples, medieval farmhouses, or the human geographies that emerge through the avoidance of marshlands?

As you put it, objects as forms "are never identical either to that of which they are made or the ways in which they are described or known."[57] So, by form, you are not alluding to the visible appearance of a thing, since the phenomenal aspect relies on its relationship to an observer. You are not conceiving of a physical shape, since the shape of an object may change without irrecoverably changing the object. Rather, by form you are evoking something autonomous, something deeply intrinsic to the thing itself, as you point out with reference to Aristotle in Chapter 4. By form, you are speaking of the idiosyncratic identity of an object without recourse to other things. Thus, the problem of differentiating the two hydras is not a matter of material: for here, to repeat, an archaeologist often begins with a common type, an achievement with a long history of archaeological research, and supplies preformatted ingredients of what a thing should be. On the contrary, to begin with different forms is to begin with the object proper. And importantly, the form of an object may be diverse.

Forgive me for drawing this out, but I want to overcome any difficulties for an archaeological readership by thinking with or alongside examples. In Chapter 1 we discussed how the Rue Saint-André des Arts in Paris follows the curve of the Neolithic path around the edge of the marshes. One might regard the modern street as an "emanation" of the form of the Neolithic path in such a way that this ancient object extends beyond the circumstances of early agrarian worlds through the orientation of Parisian streets and buildings; then again, you are leading us in a far more interesting direction. The *cardo maximus* of Lutetia, notwithstanding the fact that it seems to follow a far older route, is perhaps more itself when through burial it continues not only to uphold the iterative accumulation of new surfaces, but also condition movement through medieval Paris.[58] You might even state that the *cardo maximus* becomes something more in an aesthetic sense by continuing to support numerous resurfacings including the smooth, tarmacked roadway of the Rue Saint-Jacques. Pedestrians or carts, horses or autumn leaves need not come into contact with its original Roman paving stones for the *cardo maximus* to persist as an object into the twenty-first century. What must be emphasized, especially for an archaeological readership, is that this does not diminish the importance of each new surface as an object in its own right. One can appreciate how each surface is both its own entity and "a component as part of the form" of a Roman road.

In any event, this example provides a pertinent segue into the third section of your chapter, where you turn to McTaggart in order to compare the OOO version of time to that discussed in his famous article, "The Unreality of Time."[59] Between the A series and the B series we encounter two different ways that positions in time can be ordered, either by being rendered in terms of past, present, and future or by reckoning events in terms of earlier and later. In order to elucidate the OOO model of time as a sensual tension that unfolds in the specious present you first explain how the historical positioning of the B series is not time, for it has nothing to do with change. You then go on to point out similarities and differences with the A series, and address Cogburn's concerns about directionality with the C series. Yet given our discussions of topology, there would seem to be something missing from McTaggart's article, and thereby the comparison; that is, the possibility of temporal positions that are *anything but serial.* You mention the passing of the Roman Empire (whatever one makes of the years 476 or 1453) with respect to an historical terminus, and here McTaggart invites us to situate the Roman Empire successively as being earlier than the United States, or as simply in the past. Yet from an archaeological angle, as with OOO, the issue (as with the *cardo maximus* of Lutetia) is that the components of the Roman Empire, which are objects in themselves, linger on. Doesn't the confrontation with an *old thing*, a stable object that endures for two millennia, suggest a different temporal positionality where objects with different durations are positioned *alongside* each other? Yes, I recognize how one might think of this as "space" in OOO terms, where a 2021 BMW model X2 driving along the Rue Saint-Jacques is coextensive with the Roman road, but there seems to be more to this tension with such extended objects in terms of time, for there is a sense of persistence that provides grounds against which to recognize change in other objects, which includes me. As time is on the phenomenal surface, such a persistent object (whether in itself or as a component of modern Paris) would seem to be fundamental to detecting the intermittent movement of time. Moreover, is it wrong to hold that a sense of seemingly paradoxical *nonsequentiality* is necessary for a "time out-of-joint," which is an increasingly frequent experience in the Anthropocene, as with the strangeness of encountering the perfectly preserved corpse of a wooly rhinoceros emerging from Siberian permafrost?

GH: There are two questions here, the first about how contact with the past is not always direct (see the discussion of Cogburn in Chapter 4), and the second about the nonsequentiality of different times. In response to the first point, I have just completed an article entitled "The Shipwreck of Theseus" for Peter Campbell and Sara Rich's forthcoming anthology.[60] Archaeologists and philosophers alike seem to be generally familiar with the Ship of Theseus paradox, but just to restate it, imagine if every piece of wood on the ship were replaced with a new one. Would it still be the ship of Theseus? Even more problematically, what if the old pieces of wood removed from the ship were used to assemble a new, parallel version of it? In the latter case we would have two ships: the recognized Ship of Theseus (Ship A) which had slowly lost each and every piece of its original wood, and then a completely new ship (Ship B) which happens to be made of all the old pieces of the first one. Philosophers love puzzling over this old paradox, and I find that most of the articles about it are surprisingly insightful. However, whether one chooses Ship A or Ship B, the underlying assumption is that some sort of *detail* must be preserved for it to be the same ship, whether that detail be formal (in the visual sense) or material. Then there are interesting variants, such as that of the philosopher Peter Simons, an authority on mereology (the philosophical study of part–whole relationships). Simons argues effectively that Ship A and Ship B are both legitimate heirs to the original Ship of Theseus.[61] There are now two different ships of Theseus, placed on equal but different footing.

My approach goes in the opposite direction, since I think a thing remains most itself when it *sacrifices* detail and strips itself down to more basic features. This is why I greatly appreciate Rich's recently published book, *Shipwreck Hauntography*, since it seems to me that restorations-in-detail often miss that the ruined form of a ship can teach us things that the reconstructed form does not.[62] It is similar to my argument about how archaeology is in some ways better off dealing mostly with fragments of objects and texts rather than the reservoir of detail that is often at the disposal of the historian.[63]

To return to one of our earlier examples, the current Rue Saint-André des Arts is in some ways more illuminating than a crisp photograph of the original path along the marsh edge would be. We often think of the passage of time only as loss, in the melancholic sense. But the passage of time also has the virtue of helping us distinguish the important from the unimportant. Somewhere, Schopenhauer writes that no one should miss out on living to the age of sixty or so, since at that point all the masks of your acquaintances will have fallen away. By then, pretensions tend to vanish and we are left with a clearer vision of the life choices everyone has actually made. Although each of us will have our share of weighty biographical baggage by that age, it is probably much easier to sum up the life of a sixty-year-old than that of a forty-year-old. What, in this life of yours, have been the things that you have truly taken seriously and to which you have devoted the majority of your best energies? I'm not sure if this is a satisfactory answer to your *cardo maximus* question, and maybe I'm sounding more like Deleuze than I usually do, but there's a sense in which repetition is more effective when it's either a stripped-down version of the original or even a version augmented by contemporary concerns.[64] The best Shakespeare performance I ever attended was *King Lear* done on a geometrically abstract grid of steel girders, with the Fool spying on conversations from above while wearing noisy belled shoes. Richard Wagner's *Ring* Cycle always seems better to me without Wagner's own kitschy Nordic Viking tastes dictating the scenery. Wotan with a sombrero and an eyepatch, or the Nibelungen as oppressed steampunk factory workers, are much better than however the Bayreuth Nazis would have liked to see them costumed. Eugène Emmanuel Viollet-le-Duc, who among many other things was one of the great early architectural conservationists, said something like this as well: you don't restore the thing itself by restoring it to some actual past state of affairs. Actually, I have his exact words, since my student Jonah Klinghoffer just cited them in his final paper today.[65] As Viollet-le-Duc puts it: "To restore a building is not to preserve it, to repair, or rebuild it; it is to reinstate it in a condition of completeness which could never have existed at any given time."[66] I imagine this is the sort of question that archaeologists too have been debating for a good long while.

And of course, this leads directly to your second question about nonsequential time. In a sense, everything from the past exists only now, and the now will gain its full meaning only once its extraneous detail is stripped away and it is (over)simplified by later generations. A few months ago I had an interesting disagreement with a young academic woman on Twitter, whose name I cannot recall, in which she was arguing against the classics as belonging at the heart of education in any field, while I was arguing in favor. Her point was roughly this: "We can't read the classics for content," presumably because many of these authors are now outdated slaveholders, male chauvinists, Nazis, and the like, "so the only reason to read them is for historical importance." But the point is that we read the classics neither for content nor for historical importance. What makes a classic a classic is its irreducibility to either of these. Take the example of a mid-level philosophy classic: Malebranche in the 1600s. Of course you wouldn't read him for "content" in 2022, and for several reasons. First off, his vision of the role of the Catholic Church would strike many educated readers today as horribly reactionary. Second, he occasionally says something deeply foolish from our present vantage point, such as his bizarre claim that pregnant women who think too much about food eventually give birth to "fruits they have wanted to eat, such as apples, pears, grapes, and other similar things."[67] But it could also be boring to read Malebranche only to learn about "how much he influenced Leibniz" or "the state of French Catholic thought during the reign of Louis XIV." Instead, I read Malebranche to enjoy his deepest and most paradoxical idea: namely, his system of occasional causes. In order to see the importance of this, one of course needs to know why OOO treats occasionalism as a vitally important source for new metaphysics, even though its theological version no longer interests us. It is not easy to see things like this, however, which is why Badiou's otherwise wonderful seminar on Malebranche treats occasional causation as an embarrassing stain on his thought, rather than its living core.[68]

So, if we think of history as a beach where new treasures keep washing up, they can be added to the collection of treasures that have already washed ashore in the past. The new ones may occasionally lead us to conclude that some of the old treasures are not as valuable as we initially thought. But the idea that the value of books consists primarily in "good content" is both a literalist and a historicist idea in the bad sense of these terms. Literalism is bad because it holds that the value of anything is only what can be said about it in clear propositional prose, whereas a good deal of what is most valuable can take years if not decades to describe properly in words, and even then we never get anything quite right. Excessive historicism is bad because it relies on the notion of a more or less uniform progress within a shared framework, so that the sheer passage of time would be enough to make any random critical theorist at a university today more important than Plato and Aristotle, simply because the latter had some views that offend contemporary liberal Americans (of which I am one, despite my classicism). As I see it, the best way to live a good contemporary life is to be familiar with the greatest achievements of the human mind without lapsing into antiquarian worship that over-identifies these achievements with their specific details. To give one appalling example, I knew an American philosophy professor, a Heidegger specialist, who actually went and built himself a hut in the Black Forest. I knew another American philosophy professor, a now deceased authority in Ancient Philosophy, who used to make fun of people who claimed to understand Plato and Aristotle without knowing how to read Greek. Well, learning languages is always a fine thing, but the two greatest interpreters of Aristotle who ever lived (Averroës and St. Thomas Aquinas) were unable to read him in the original language. Everything the human mind deals with is subject to translation, in multiple senses, and it is not by mimicking the master that we ourselves become masters. We have to translate them into twenty-first-century language, while also molding our new dialect in accordance with insights we gain from the classics.

So, to wind down this response to your two questions, we live amidst discoveries and inventions from numerous times and places. But this is not historical eclecticism, because we are always under pressure to abstract from or augment the things the past has left us. Recently I made my first visit to Troy, a powerful experience, and no doubt even more powerful for archaeologists like you than for the rest of us. It was fascinating to follow the boardwalk through the ruins and see the labelling of the ten different Troys, none of them probably very knowledgeable about their predecessors on the same site – though I'll bet there was a good deal of cultural continuity in terms of what was eaten, as well as other things such as horse-breeding.

Perhaps the most amazing thing I learned in the nearby Troy Museum was what a tourist site Troy already was for people we now seek as tourists today: Alexander the Great, Julius Caesar, Mehmet II. And then just across the water from Troy is Gallipoli, where the Ottoman Empire was victorious in one of the most heart-rending battles of World War I: a place that literally brings modern Turkish citizens to tears. It was a stunning experience to see the Gallipoli Memorial at a distance while standing inside the ruins of Troy. And whatever war really put an end to Troy VI, most of us know it only in heavily translated form through Homer's *Iliad*. But the Ottomans identified with the Trojans in that conflict, and Mustafa Kemal Atatürk declared himself at Gallipoli to be partly motivated by revenge in the name of Hector! There is a tendency these days to treat such sentiments as a form of dangerous historical romanticism, but I find such repetitions and continuities to be wonderful. Sometimes they even happen within the same period: the two Civil War battles at Manassas, Virginia (Bull Run) had extensive physical overlap, but just think of how much the character of the war had changed between the first and the second.

CW: You are correct. To restore, to consolidate, to augment, to rebury, or to simply let be are longstanding and fundamental questions for all archaeologists who work with ruins.[69] Sara Rich is also correct insofar as restorations of detail, driven by a sense of ruin as loss, often neglect the positive side of ruination.[70] Did not Rainer Maria Rilke, through the example of dilapidated houses in Paris, teach his readers to view ruins as revelatory?[71] Stale, shredding paint can reveal the grain of wood used to enclose a now ruined pilothouse; gaping holes formed between broken and torn planks of decking serve as windows below deck, into the inner recesses of an abandoned fishing boat. One can certainly appreciate how the abandoned boat is a stripped down version of itself: gutted of its diesel engine, hatch cover, prop shaft, propeller, smokestack, anchor, nets, lines, and any histories of construction, use, or ownership. Yet its ruination is also akin to a form of self-excavation, where every cracked surface, every flaying strip discloses those layers beneath.[72] Thus, new details emerge in a way that was not apparent to a passerby when the boat was maintained and in use.

These observations bring us back to the questions of identity with respect to the object. Whereas you are speaking of the boat itself, an archaeologist might be caught up in its components, or even the relational object that emerges at the intersection

An abandoned fishing boat from Svaerholt, Norway

of chemical analyses and paint. It is tough for anyone who labors to squeeze fragmentary things for every ounce of empirical detail, and to extract from them new layers of information, to give more weight to the object as stripped of its extraneous minutiae.[73] Your point is that with the antiquarian celebration of detail, it can become difficult to see broader structures of history. For all the minutiae of the boat as an abandoned hulk, its small size may be what rendered it superfluous, given the changing geographies of coastal settlement in Northern Finnmark, where distances to old fishing grounds increased with the abandonment of small fishing hamlets lacking hardened ports or paved road connections.[74]

GH: When people accuse OOO of ignoring the importance of relations, they are forgetting that there are two different ways to look at them. First, any object is composed of relations, and in that sense there are relations of composition in the backstory of any object. The key is to refrain from undermining: if you explain water by saying it's just H_2O, end of story, then you have completely misunderstood water. It has properties that you will never find in hydrogen and oxygen, and also *lacks* certain properties that those two elements have in isolation, such as the capacity to fuel fire. We would no doubt find the same thing with each of the ten Troys.

CW: Among other points, you highlight a key difference that emerges with respect to *being there*, in the experience of walking through Troy or Mycenae. One has to reconcile the framing that is provided for today's visitors, which makes the bewildering jumble of old things meaningful in terms of the human story of Trojan or Mycenaean communities over millennia, with what OOO inspires us to consider – and what archaeologists must stand in defense of – namely, the strangeness that arises from within (and being alongside) objects as autonomous entities, whether ruined walls or formerly buried gateways.[75] It is here that we might open ourselves to a past other than what we associate with talkative history, a past that while unspoken is every bit as significant. What we are driving at, and continue to return to in our conversations, is the problem of different pasts held by different objects. The past conveyed by the *Iliad* is not necessarily what is suggested by the ruins of Troy VI or the citadel of Mycenae. The gate does not tell us who walked through it (or who, after the passage of centuries, was imagined to have walked there), the wall does not remember who kept watch by it in the dark of the night (or, again, who later generations envisioned upon forsaken battlements). Nonetheless, the consistent southerly orientation of the main gates of Troy I, II, and III–IV is meaningful, as are the alignment of joints between huge blocks of stone in the citadel wall of Mycenae. If gates and walls do not gain their reality from elsewhere, then the relational past that is internalized by them, as OOO recognizes, is also redefined in ways unique to stone gates and walls. Just as archaeologists are obliged to account for those pasts that emerge through the encounter with these very different objects, OOO urges us not to impose one object on the other without putting in the requisite work of explaining one in terms of the other, which always comes at a cost.

I see clearly how you are urging us to sort the wheat of important moments from the chaff of idiosyncratic detail. I also see how, whether with the Ship of Theseus or Troy, the lesson to which you are leading us has to do with "the irreducibility of larger objects to the sum total of their material components."[76] Importantly, OOO is also known for its democratic disposition for objects of all sizes and creeds. Actually, what first attracted me to your work, as an archaeologist, was its concern with entities banal, objects ordinary, things unremarkable – and here one may recall your long Latour-style litanies of objects – always acknowledging the dignity of individual stones, walls,

or gateways. To be sure, we should emphasize how OOO recognizes different levels of abstraction, which means that details
that appear extraneous or superfluous on one level are anything
but incidental or disposable on another. In fact, it is the idiosyncratic detail of burned remains and arrowheads found in
association with features from Troy VII that fuels archaeological debates about which city's destruction (VI or VIIa) served
as inspiration for Homer. This brings me around to a final
question.

Some readers may be struck by your ability to move between
Troy and the Ship of Theseus, crashing airplanes and Los
Angeles, a ball of cotton and hammers. This movement speaks
to the nature of OOO as a theory of, as you have presented
it, everything.[77] But what I appreciate about OOO is how the
question of "which picture?," "which structure?," emerges as
an artifact of the task at hand. A question arises here in terms
of how an archaeologist might engage your work to find ways
of gaining new insights. There is a difference, which you have
touched upon elsewhere, between an object-oriented philosophy
as a method, or as a "weak theory," and an object-oriented
ontology as metaphysics, or as a "strong theory."[78] With the
former, one can extract a set of light theoretical cues or guide-
lines for helping us to negotiate a given state of affairs, to detect
the relevant features of a given situation as one moves: the
avoidance of taxonomic prejudice, the irreducibility of objects
to their components or effects, or the symmetry of autonomy
and relations. With the latter, one now encounters an increasingly nuanced metaphysics that shows us how we will find those
features arranged there – the fracture between objects and qualities within things or the fourfold character of objects. Given
how many readers (as archaeologists, anthropologists, or historians) work with theory, what are your thoughts on a softer
engagement with object-oriented ontology as method, versus a
stronger understanding of object-oriented ontology as a theory
applicable to everything?

GH: The irony, I think, is that OOO is currently more developed
as a theory than it is as a method. This may be because it developed within the discipline of philosophy, rather than under the
pressure of solving a set of problems in one or more particular
disciplines as happened with Latourian Actor–Network Theory.
My sense of "method" is that of a loose set of fertile rules that,
by being applied as robotically as one wishes, can help shake
up the existing state of a situation. For instance, a university

might decide to determine professorial salaries based purely on quantity of publications, which is famously easier to measure than quality. And this might lead to gross injustice in individual cases: the prolific mediocrity earning a massive salary (these things happen) while a brilliant but less productive perfectionist is undervalued. But in a surprising number of cases, quantity will correlate with quality, so that the method is actually not a terrible one. Or again, since these days I'm reading a lot of Lacan, one good way of summarizing him is by saying that he introduces three separate registers into the psyche: the imaginary, the symbolic, and the real. The first has to do with the mirror-stage, narcissism, and rivalry; the second with language and the social order governed by the law of the Father; the third with that which is inassimilable within the symbolic order, such as trauma or enjoyment. Lacan gets a lot of mileage merely from showing how his new theory of three registers sheds light on the purported errors of his rivals. In Seminar IV, for instance, he gains powerful ammunition against Anna Freud, Melanie Klein, and Donald Winnicott, and additional ammunition for a near-total destruction of Ernest Jones by arguing that the phallus, for instance, has imaginary, symbolic, and real dimensions simultaneously. It is a powerful method that takes Lacan even beyond Freud in some respects, and also a good rule of thumb for imaging how Lacan would tackle any given psychoanalytic problem. But of course it is just a method, and as such it doesn't exhaust Lacan's entire theory.

Whenever I sit down to work, I have the painful experience of still feeling like a beginner and needing to rework the whole theory from scratch over and over again. Of course, I can also sketch the fourfold diagram for anyone who asks, and can even run through a list of implications it might have for any discipline with which I have at least a loose familiarity. That's the "method" part of OOO. And professionally, I have to keep generating methods that have some connection with philosophy. The current best example is architecture, since that is the field in which I am currently employed. A number of talented younger architects have picked up OOO and are doing interesting things with it. I began by knowing nearly nothing about the field, but by now have a reasonable command of the history and theory of the discipline, or at least enough so that my remarks are not irrelevant to an architectural audience. And though it would be absurd for someone in my position to try to legislate architectural styles, the audience always wants me to take a stab at it. Through various readings and discussions I became determined to strike at the form/function distinction, which is so central to architecture even for those who deny its continued relevance. Occasionally one hears that this distinction is passé, but it really isn't. It goes all the way back to Vitruvius (who uses a now archaic threefold distinction instead) and is absolutely central for modernist discourse. I have no idea how to design a building, but there are interesting things I can say to architects on the basis of OOO. For instance, the traditional form/function distinction needs to be rethought, because both terms are too relational. Form is generally taken to mean the visual look of a building, and function is taken to be its purpose; insofar as they are relational, both of them fall in the "sensual" realm and do not touch on the real. It's not very difficult to turn instead towards a "deep" form, which I call zero-form, and which also has something to do with the diachronic splicing together of different encounters with a building. The harder problem is zero-function, but I have come to read the career of Rem Koolhaas as paving the way for it. There is also the fact that Kant tries to save the purity of art by *excluding* function, which limits architecture to a subordinate status in the arts, whereas I think function can be retained but also "zeroed" in a way that aestheticizes function by abstracting it in the manner of the ruined shipwreck of Theseus. This allows OOO a foothold to challenge the basis of Kantian aesthetics without slipping into the unjustified relational excesses of Hegel and the Frankfurt School.

It's very rewarding to do this sort of thing anytime a new discipline calls on me to pay a visit. And it always retroactively casts my own philosophy in a new light. But I can only take it so far, since I don't have the same vast body of training in all these fields as do architects, archaeologists, or literary critics on their home terrain. But usually I've found that I can add something to the conversation, which is probably why (like Latour and even Žižek) I'm read more widely in fields outside philosophy than by philosophers themselves. I can think of a couple of reasons for this. One is that philosophy is the slowest-moving discipline. In some ways we philosophers still inhabit the Kantian universe of the 1780s, working within his basic framework and the various critical responses to it. But for architecture or archaeology to work from a 1780s standpoint would be ridiculous. You move much faster than that, and it forces me to leave my comfort zone and move much faster as well. You are under much greater pressure to innovate than philosophy ever is; yes, analytic philosophy tries to move at the faster clip of the natural sciences, but I doubt this is the right speed for philosophy. The other issue is that modern philosophy in particular is not very well equipped to enter into dialogue with other fields. It is content with a division of labor: philosophy studies the thought–world relation, while relations between objects belong to one of the other disciplines. I don't accept that division, and that's why I keep being invited to crash on couches in the academic homes of others; in fact, I often feel professionally like Dante in exile. I try my best to be a quick study and offer any help that I can, and in return am always given new terminology and a new set of previously unknown authors and case studies.

Let's conclude with a final thought. You were speaking again about how an object can have different histories. It can also have different synchronies as well, and this ties into my interest in formalism. What bothers me about anti-formalists, meaning people who want to historicize or sociologize or politicize every topic under the sun, is that they play what I earlier called the Game of Hurdles. That's the old trick of giving yourself a very low hurdle to clear and your opponents a very high one. For example, an anti-formalist can say: "formalists claim that an artwork is completely cut off from its social and historical context and the author's biography. But this is obviously ridiculous! Therefore, I will now cherry-pick my own favorite socio-political causes and historical hobbyhorses and explain the artwork in terms of them, while ignoring all the others." But the fact is that formalism does not need to exclude relations altogether; it just needs to exclude promiscuous relationality. Zaha Hadid's architecture certainly has social and biographical precursors, but the scholar has to do the difficult work of figuring out which ones matter and which ones do not. It is simply not the case that everything is important. Timothy Morton once joked that the relationist attitude amounts to a sort of "everything-is-everything-else Deleuzean Hinduism," with any resulting offense aimed at Deleuzean holists rather than at Hindus. Objects for OOO are self-contained, but that doesn't mean that nothing affects them; it just means that they absorb the energies of a finite number of other objects, and we need new methods to detect which ones those are. It does little good simply to choose one such influence (capitalism being a good example) and give it a universal and ubiquitous force, because then it just becomes a magical answer to everything. Formalism for me is not about total insularity, but about the fact that every object has gatekeepers, and only a limited number of influences pass through the gates. And when they do, they do not straightaway dominate the object (in the way that capital is supposed to stain everything it touches) but are partly transformed into the object's own terms. Timothy Mitchell, in his widely read book *Carbon Democracy*, points out that the physical properties of oil exert a force on capitalism as much as the reverse.[79] And this is how I see the relation of my philosophy to other disciplines. It's not about OOO legislating for others, but more about learning how to write *Architectural OOO* or *OOO in Troy*.

A Note on Models of Time

Objects Untimely discusses several models of time that are contrasted with the linear conception. By "linear" we mean the notion of time as moving forward in a way that leaves behind the past, whether this takes the form of potential improvement (as in most politically progressive models) or the form of either stability or decay (as in most conservative models). The alternatives discussed in this book were as follows:

- *Retroactive temporality.* In retroactive models of time, the past is still alive in the sense of constantly taking on new meaning in light of future events. Although Alexander the Great was long dead by the time of Julius Caesar, he is ratified as a predecessor by the young Caesar's tears over not yet having equaled Alexander's achievements at a comparable age. The Norman Conquest of England in 1066 retroactively becomes a signal military feat following the next millennium of failures by the Spanish Armada, Hitler, and other fantasizers who aspired to take over the island. Certain things happen later than they factually occurred. Consider the revolution in physics brought about by quantum theory. Initially it looks as if the theory first appeared in Max Planck's 1900 solution of the black-body radiation problem; only nine years later, in 1909, did Planck retroactively grasp the revolutionary character of his discovery.
- *Percolating temporality.* In Witmore's words, this is "a time that pools in reservoirs or settles in pockets, filters and siphons off, accelerates in bursts and creeps slowly, ruptures and turns back within eddies of novelty and repetition." Percolation opposes linear time by allowing for both intermittent reversals of forward movement and the isolation of static reservoirs that resist any automatic passage of time. The Iranian Revolution surprises Foucault by turning back along archaic paths; an

165

electric car in the streets of Cairo passes a donkey cart filled with bones, in front of a Nasser-era apartment complex with the Pyramids visible in the distance.

- *Countercurrents.* Sails reappear on certain cargo ships due to the rising price of oil. Maggots return once more to be placed on bullet wounds, which they clean more effectively than more expensive modern technologies. Piracy returns in force to Indonesia and the Horn of Africa. Pre-modern ethnic conflicts erupt into twenty-first-century genocides. Many riders of Uber revert to taxis, exasperated adults abandon intrusive smart phones for primitive flip phones, and Western urbanites take to raising chickens.

- *Topological time.* Points far apart on the calendar are brought close together through formal similarities. Contemporary auto races and spacecraft launches re-embody ancient human sacrifice rituals, despite the passage of thousands of years. The university students of Florida Spring Breaks and those of the *Canterbury Tales* engage in comparable mischief. Sporting event massacres strike the fans of Ahli (Port Said 2012), Juventus (Brussels 1985), and the chariot-racing fans known as the Greens (Constantinople 532). Fierce debates emerge over whether a given topology is legitimate or illegitimate. Today's Israel can claim to be the successor to an ancient people *and* be denounced as the latest European colonialist project, at the same time but from different mouths. Russia assumes the mantle of successor of the Eastern Roman Empire or Kievan Rus, while also being mocked for the first or violently resisted for the second.

- *Cyclical time.* The seasons pass each year in predictable order, as do the stages of an individual life. Perhaps democracy always decays into tyranny at some point, and perhaps the rise of a new power always triggers conflict with an established one. For centuries, Europe and the Middle East were intermittently flooded with the violent excess populations of the Great Steppe. A dominant animal species, *Homo sapiens* included, produces the seeds of its own demise.

- *Generational time.* Ibn Khaldun warns that a dynasty can only last four generations. A dominant idea bores the student generation forced to learn it; they smuggle in a new one, in some respects the opposite of the first. The most volatile and threatening segment of any population (young males) must be made to study, work, or fight wars so as not to trigger civil unrest. The wish to prolong life in one's descendants leads to stable mechanisms of inheritance and relatively permanent social classes.

- *OOO time.* What we call time is simply the surface phenomenon of a durable sensual object with varying accidental qualities. Only occasionally does this superficial drama lead to retroactive effects on the real, like stable chess pieces moved once in a while by especially strong gusts of wind.

- *Archaeology, OOO, and time.* While *Objects Untimely* explores numerous points of intersection between archaeology and philosophy with respect to time, it also invites a reflection on the possibility of a symbiosis of archaeology and OOO in terms of long-term change in human beings and societies. We call this "Anthropoiesis," mindful of the meaning of poiesis in terms of the creative making and maintenance of such human objects. This alternative theory of hominization operates on the basis not of selection and competition, but of cooperation and symbiosis.[1] Every major change in human evolution, we contend, results from a merger between two autonomous entities – human and nonhuman, from Acheulean hand-axes to architectures to guided flora to automobiles – which are absorbed into a new compound object.[2] Anthropoi emerge as autonomous entities and as components of larger compound objects. The novelty of this endeavor points to the productive potential of a symbiosis between archaeology and OOO, for it offers an inclusive biological alternative to theories of externalization, championed by André Leroi-Gourhan, McLuhan, and Serres, where tools or media were seen as outward and amplified forms of human organs: computer processors improved the human cerebral cortex, writing improved upon memory, hammerstones improved the hand, metal choppers improved the incisors. The guiding model would instead be one of the human internalization of external entities, many of them nonhuman or even inanimate.

Notes

Preface

1. Harman 2010b; 2011; Witmore 2006; 2007; 2015; 2020a: 37–57.
2. See for instance Bennett 2010; Nail 2018; Raud 2021.
3. It would not be unfair to state that an engagement with continental philosophy during the latter half of the twentieth century turned eclectic (cf. Holtorf and Karlsson 2000; see Edgeworth 2012).
4. See González-Ruibal 2013; also Webmoor 2015.
5. Of course, in many cases these philosophers were also trained as archaeologists (see Hodder 1995; Wylie 2002; Wylie et al. 2013; Kobayashi and Marion 2019).
6. This theme is already found in such works as Husserl's *Formal and Transcendental Logic* and Alain Badiou's *Logics of Worlds*, but is perhaps just as explicit in Manuel DeLanda's notion that real assemblages can have retroactive effects on their own parts (DeLanda 2006). This may be the clearest hint of a solution to the workings of retroactivity, and is developed further in Harman 2010b.

Chapter 1

1. On the notion of chronology as clock time and archaeology as clockmaking see Lucas 2005; 2021; Witmore 2007.
2. Olivier 2011: 117; Olsen et al. 2012: 6.
3. See Schnapp 1997.
4. Powell 1905: 44. The initial excavations of the temple were conducted under W. Dorpfeld in 1886; see Richardson 1897: 455.
5. On archaeology and a modernist historicism see Olivier 2011; Tamm and Olivier 2019. In the context of Ancient Corinth see Witmore 2020a: 40–8.
6. Olivier 2011: 123.

7. Olsen et al. 2012; Shanks 2012.
8. Binford 1981a.
9. See Wandsnider 2004.
10. Schiffer 1987.
11. Fowler 1932: 9.
12. Bailey 1983; 2007; McGlade and van der Leeuw 1997; McGlade 1999.
13. See for example Harris 2014; Gosden and Malafouris 2015; Cipolla 2018; Crellin 2020; Malafouris, Gosden and Bogaard 2021; Glovier and Steel 2021.
14. Heidegger 1962.
15. Harman 2002.
16. Bergson 2001; Deleuze 1990a.
17. Simondon 2020.
18. Aristotle 2018.
19. Aristotle 2016.
20. Ingold 2016: 31.
21. Barad 2007.
22. Levinas 1988; Bennett 2012.
23. Bergson 1998.
24. Harman 2016c. See also Fakhry 2007.
25. See Nadler 2011.
26. Malebranche 1997a; 1997b.
27. Descartes 1993; Spinoza 1994; Leibniz 1989; Berkeley 1982.
28. Hume 1978.
29. Kant 1965.
30. Whitehead 1978.
31. See Harman 2014e.
32. Stengers 2014.
33. Nail 2021: 11.
34. Latour 2013a; 2013b.
35. See Harman 2009a: 115; also Latour, Harman, and Erdélyi 2011: 33.
36. Latour 1999: 80–112.
37. Harman 2007a.
38. Latour 1988: 162.
39. Latour 2013a.
40. Deleuze and Guattari 2010.
41. This is true of Harman's version of OOO, though not of Levi R. Bryant's. See Bryant 2011.
42. Harman 2007a.
43. Latour 1993: 76.
44. Latour 2000: 254.
45. Latour and Hermant 1998.
46. Whitehead 1978: 39 ; on the afterlife of the acropolis, see Hamilakis and Ifantidis 2013.

47. Nietzsche 1997.
48. Serres 1982: 71–83; Serres 1995; Serres and Latour 1995: 44–70.
49. Serres 1995; Serres and Latour 1995; Witmore 2006; Prigogine and Stengers 1984.
50. Serres and Latour 1995: 60.
51. Husserl 2019.
52. Derrida 2011: 52.
53. On the "specious present" Husserl cites Stern 2007.
54. Bergson 2001: 207; Meillassoux 2008: 67.
55. Derrida 1997: 22–3.
56. Heidegger 2012.
57. Sider 1997.
58. See Harman 2011.
59. Harman 2010b.
60. Gratton 2014.
61. Deleuze 1990b: 4–10.
62. Harman 2013a; 2014c; 2020a.
63. McLuhan 1994.
64. Norden and McLuhan 1969: 56.
65. Greenberg 2003: 28.
66. McLuhan and McLuhan 1992. See also Harman 2009b.
67. Williams 2003.
68. Greenberg 1965.
69. Wittgenstein 1922: 90.
70. Harman 2013b.
71. Aristotle 1992.
72. Kripke 1981.
73. Latour 1996: 119.
74. Latour 1999: 145–73.
75. Meillassoux 2008.
76. Kuhn 1978; see also Kuhn 2000: 25–8.
77. Kuhn 2000: 27.
78. DeLanda 2006.
79. DeLanda 2011.
80. Margulis 2008.
81. Harman 2016a.
82. Leibniz 1989: 69–90.
83. Here we are paraphrasing Gardin 1980.
84. See the discussion in Olsen 2010: 10–12; Olsen et al. 2012: 17–35; Witmore 2014a.
85. See the discussion in Edgeworth 2012; see also Olsen 2007: 584–5 for a critique of Miller 2005: 14–15 as concerns the importance of philosophy.
86. Latour, Harman, and Erdélyi 2011: 46.
87. We owe this formulation to Jon Cogburn of Louisiana State University.

Chapter 2

1. The metaphor of a "thick fog" was first used to describe the enveloping atmosphere covering "a space of time which we cannot measure" by Rasmus Nyerup (see Daniel 1943: 6–7).
2. Cf. Olsen and Svestad 1994: esp. 6–10.
3. Olivier 2008. For an English translation see Olivier 2011.
4. Of course, on one level this is not so much history as it is a particular historicism, a modernist one (Gumbrecht 2014; Runia and Tamm 2019; Tamm and Olivier 2019; Witmore 2020a: 40–8). Thus, changes in archaeology happen very much in congruity with, rather than in contrast to, historiography.
5. This new relevance is tied as much to a different relationship to our objects (Olsen 2010; Witmore 2020b; see also Nativ and Lucas 2020), as it is a new "regime of historicity" (Hartog 2015; also Lorenz 2017). Yet both of these perspectives share the "abandonment of the linear, causal, and homogeneous conception of time characteristic of the previous, modern regime of historicity" (Tamm and Olivier 2019: 1).
6. Olsen et al. 2012.
7. Olsen 2003; 2010; 2012; 2013a; Witmore 2007; 2012; 2014a; 2017a; 2021a; Webmoor and Witmore 2008; Olsen et al. 2012; Hodder 2012; Lucas 2012; Pétursdóttir 2012; 2014; Nativ 2018.
8. The alternative to history includes that of historians who "focus not on the past but on the present, not on history *as what is irremediably gone*, but on history *as ongoing process*" (Runia 2006: 8, emphasis original). For examples of alternatives to historical narratives in archaeology see Olsen and Witmore 2014; Witmore 2020a; also Love and Meng 2016.
9. On the development of a different theory of time in archaeology see Olivier 2008; 2013; Witmore 2007; 2013; also Lucas 2021; Lucas and Olivier 2022. On object-oriented ontology in relation to archaeology see Harman 2014a; 2016b; 2019b; Olsen and Witmore 2015; Pétursdóttir and Olsen 2018; Sørensen 2021; Bryant 2021a; 2021b; Morton 2021; Witmore 2014a; 2020b; Rich and Campbell 2023.
10. Prior to the eighteenth century, the past had been delineated using biblical genealogies, which gave clarity to northern Europeans of the time. In the wake of this biblical certainty a new mist obscured the past, and this lack of clarity could only be addressed by using those non-textual objects that were regarded as the "material remains" of what was, both by antiquarians and those archaeologists who followed them. See Momigliano 1950; Nyerup 1806; Olsen and Svestad 1994; Schnapp 1997.
11. "Continuity is the essence of all historical study," and this is, as Eelco Runia states, "the mantra of all historians" (Runia

and Tamm 2019). Continuous history, as Foucault observed, "is the indispensable correlative of the founding function of the subject: the guarantee that everything that has eluded him may be restored to him; the certainty that time will disperse nothing without restoring it in a reconstituted unity; the promise that one day the subject – in the form of historical consciousness – will once again be able to appropriate, to bring back under his sway, all those things that are kept at a distance by difference, and find in them what might be called his abode" (Foucault 1982: 12). On the limits of history before the fog of prehistory see Lucas 2004; Olsen and Svestad 1994; also Olivier 2008 and 2013. On the contrast between talkative history and silent prehistory see Serres 1987: 209; also Olsen 2003: 88.

12. Use of the term "prehistory" should not be confused with a judgment placed on those, long dead, who once intermingled with the objects left to archaeologists as having been without "history." The problem with "prehistory" is ours, in the sense that it refers to the absence of objects that explicitly recorded history. This, however, does not free the term from its problematic temporal prefix, which suggests a unidirectional march towards written history. For a critical discussion see González-Ruibal 2013: 12; for an OOO reading of prehistory see Harman 2019a.

13. Schnapp 1997: 275–303.

14. There was, to be sure, a dissonance that set in for antiquarians between what Karen Bassi describes as "the reading of history" and "the impossibility of seeing it" (Bassi 2016: 140). Just as "looking at the historical text becomes an effect of the reader's realization that she cannot look through it" (143), antiquity's ruins were always judged in light of that which could not be seen.

15. Witmore 2020a: 150–4.

16. See Piggot 1966; Renfrew 1968.

17. Renfrew 1973; see also Lucas 2005 and 2015.

18. Olsen et al. 2012: 43–7.

19. See also Sloterdijk 2014.

20. Byzantine and Christian national collections were housed in their own museum, founded in 1914; see Mouliou 2009; on the nineteenth-century organization of the collections see Baedeker 1894: 95–104.

21. If what had persisted and accumulated from other eras was limited to them (Olsen 2010: 127), then what accumulated in their wake was destroyed to make way for that purification (Witmore 2013; González-Ruibal 2016a; see also Lucas 2021: 103–19).

22. Lowenthal 1985; Shanks 1996: 1–20; Schnapp 1997.

23. Damaskos and Plantzos 2008; Witmore 2013.
24. Klindt-Jensen 1975: 89; cf. Gräslund 1987: 101–8.
25. Olivier 2011: 156–9; see also Lucas 2001.
26. Olivier 2011: 160.
27. Marchand 1996: 75–115; Shanks 1996: 42–7; Hamilakis 2007: 57–124.
28. Schnapp 2004.
29. Olsen and Svestad 1994: 11–16.
30. This image of a rosary connects with Walter Benjamin's metaphor for historicism (Benjamin, Eiland and Jennings 2006: 397).
31. Renfrew 1980; Morris 1994; Shanks 1996; see also Kourelis 2007.
32. See Olsen et al. 2012: 47–57.
33. Renfrew 1980: 290.
34. Shanks 2012: 100
35. Snodgrass 1985; also see Hall 2014: 207–19.
36. Snodgrass 1987: 37–8.
37. Snodgrass 1985: 207; 1987: 209–10.
38. Snodgrass 1985: 194, 207; cf. Courbin 1988.
39. Olivier 2011: 182. Too often, as Hayden White (2014) has argued, the past is treated as synonymous with history. White held that while the past encompassed everything in a particular area, history dealt with that small part of it that had already been mapped in some way.
40. Witmore 2020a: 109–22.
41. Cherry 2003.
42. The path-breaking *The Minnesota Messenia Expedition*, for example, maintained a Bronze-Age focus (McDonald and Rapp 1972). On the influence of Braudel's long-term history on archaeology see Cherry et al. 1991; see also Bintliff 1991; Hodder 1987.
43. Davies and Davis 2007; Mee and Forbes 1997; Bintliff 2000.
44. Alcock and Cherry 2004; see also Knodell et al. 2022.
45. However, see Halstead 2009; Hamilakis and Anagnostopoulos 2009; also Buchli and Lucas 2001; Harrison and Schofield 2010; González-Ruibal 2019; Witmore 2020a.
46. Horden and Purcell 2000; Shryock and Smail 2011; see also Hodder 1987; Souvatzi, Baysal, and Baysal 2019.
47. Shryock and Smail 2011: 13.
48. Consider how material research in areas like prehistory, which often involved working with uncatalogued collections of miscellanea, was viewed by many nineteenth-century historians as an onerous diversion for excellent minds better served by directing their energies to other domains of historical inquiry (Langlois and Seignobos 1898: 17). For an example of the expansion of

historical research into new domains see Martin Rudwick's work in geohistory (Rudwick 2014).

49. Childe 1925; Renfrew 1972; Hodder 1990; Graeber and Wengrow 2021. See also Diamond 1998; Morris 2010; Broodbank 2013.

50. Morris 2000: 3; cf. Deetz 1996; Olsen 2010.

51. Concerning these differences see Clarke 1968; for Greece see Snodgrass 1987; Morris 2003; Hall 2013 and 2014.

52. Olsen 2010; Olivier 2011; Witmore 2013.

53. "Ethnoarchaeology" is the study of activities and their material consequences within contemporary societies, in order to develop comparative referents against which to access observations of the archaeological record. "Middle-range theory" is an attempt to build epistemic connections between what archaeologists observe in the present and the past "processes" that supposedly generated the archaeological record. On the differences between ethnoarchaeology, middle-range theory, and the archaeology of the present, compare Binford 1978 and 1981b to Rathje 1979, Rathje and Murphy 2003, or Gould and Schiffer 1981; see also González-Ruibal 2016b. In Greece, research into contemporary pasts took on a distinctive form as cultural ecology, which fell within the wider remit of anthropology – see Jameson 1976; Koster 1977; Chang 1981; also Forbes 2007; cf. Fotiatis 1995; Halstead 2009; Stroulia and Sutton 2009.

54. Buchli and Lucas 2001; Witmore 2013. The tremendous subversive potential of a field that developed to deal with times deep and distant would not be exploited till a generation later. See Graves-Brown 2000; González-Ruibal 2008; 2019; Holtorf and Piccini 2009; Harrison and Schofield 2010.

55. Binford 1983.

56. When judged in light of this untarnished past, archaeology's things are routinely seen as lacking (see the discussion in Olsen et al. 2012: 17–35).

57. A remark is necessary here with regard to Witmore's historical narrative, which greatly simplifies the matter for the sake of economy and specificity. More importantly, he uses the timeline to emphasize the temporal power of such linear narratives, as if the ball rolling downhill continued to increase in its weight and force. There is a well-known retrospective advantage that comes with writing in the present, insofar as simply by placing work at the end, that work gains in potency and even excludes earlier attempts to speak to this truth.

58. Olivier 2008; Olsen et al. 2012; Shanks 2012; also Hingley 2012. The transformative nature of the archaeological past is a central premise of formation theory (Schiffer 1987; see also Lucas 2012: 74–123). Things do reveal something of their metamorphosis

through their qualities and accidents. Still, the metamorphosis of objects can only be glossed as processes superficially, since these processes always arise through rapports between specific entities (Witmore 2014a).

59. This latency is an aspect of the pastness that these things bring to the fore. See Olsen 2010; Olivier 2011; also see Jones 2007; Lucas 2012; cf. Bergson 1991; Gumbrecht 2013: 23–4.

60. Here Witmore is connecting the notion of the past as an achievement (Olsen et al. 2012; Witmore 2013; 2015) to Harman's assertion that "any relation immediately generates a new object" (Harman 2011: 117).

61. Olsen et al. 2012; Shanks 2012; Witmore 2013; Nativ and Lucas 2020.

62. Here Witmore is building on a distinction between the time of antiquity and the antiquity of time made by Serres in *Statues* (Serres 2015b: 193). It is from Serres' distinction that this essay takes its title.

63. Despite a lawsuit brought against the farmer by the Archaeological Ephorate, the cistern still supplied water to his olive trees as of June 2012 (see Witmore 2020a: 318–20). On heavy metal exhaust from catalytic convertors see Jarvis, Parry, and Piper 2001. On the Argolid and Asini plain prior to citrus cultivation see Lehmann 1937.

64. Simpson and Hagel 2006: 158–9; Knauss 2001: 71–8.

65. Piteros 2005.

66. This bypass constitutes what Marc Augé (1995) calls a *non-lieu*. Non-lieux are non-relational: rapports are not established or maintained with farmers, crossroads, stream crossings, or carob trees. Non-lieux are non-historical: one does not confront the structures, monuments, or locales that constitute history. Non-lieux are devoid of any concern for identity: "complicities of language, local references, the unformulated rules of living know-how" are not part of this terrain.

67. See González-Ruibal 2008.

68. Witmore 2018a.

69. This is also known as the Arkadiko bridge (see Hope Simpson 1998).

70. Frazer 1898: 232.

71. On the transport of the black stone of Argos see Burford 1969: 143.

72. Pikoulas was known for the "kafeneion" method, which involved talking to local people about undocumented ancient sites in their area; see Pikoulas 1995.

73. Iakovidis et al. 2003: 2, 11.

74. This figure is given by Herodotus in *The Histories* (Herodotus 2015: 7.202).

75. Shelton 2006; see also Klein 1997.
76. Serres 1993; Serres with Latour 1995: 105. See also Witmore 2007; Shanks 2012: 112–17.
77. See Shelton 2006.
78. Klein 1997: 253.
79. Iakovidis et al. 2003.
80. Wace and Stubbings 1962: 325–6.
81. This association remained persistent until the decipherment of Linear B in 1952, when objects suggestive of a society organized unlike that portrayed by Homer returned to light (see Finley 2002 [1954]).
82. Morris 1986.
83. See Nagy 1996; see also Casey Dué and Mary Ebbott, The Homer Multitext Project: http://www.homermultitext.org.
84. Of course, this was understood from the angle of the Homeric epics' own textuality rather than their objecthood. The composite diversity of a text is a feature of late hermeneutics, reception theory, and post-structuralism (see Olsen 2006).
85. Witmore 2020a: 149–65.
86. Olsen 2010; Tamm and Olivier 2019.
87. Latour 1993.
88. See Olsen 2010; 2012: 24–7.
89. Serres and Latour 1995; Witmore 2006; 2007; 2013.
90. Karo 1915; 1930. *Altertumwissenschaft* is the science of antiquity in which all finds are accorded equal interest. Karo's efforts are celebrated for bringing the standards of professional scholarship to Schliemann's excavations; see Matz 1964: 639; Mylonas 1957: 103n1; see also Davis 2010. On the work of Stamatakis see Prag et al. 2009; also Tsountas and Manatt 1897: 83–114; Demakopoulou 1990: 101.
91. Furumark 1941a; 1941b.
92. Schliemann, it should be noted, was among the first to understand the practical utility of stratigraphy in Greece. See Wace 1949: 10.
93. Wace and Stubbings 1962: 332.
94. Cf. Ramenofsky 1998.
95. Time, as Ann Ramenofsky points out, "is not packaged, but rather infinitely divisible" (1998: 75). In extending this insight to chronologies, she argues that chronological units "cannot be discovered," but rather that they are "conceptual, defined, and imposed on the continuum of time." In making this assertion, Ramenofsky grants too much agency to the human domain without recognizing the things that make the construction of chronologies possible. How chronologies are divided up rests on the recognition of subtle changes in objects. The challenge, as Ramenofsky also recognizes, is how to measure the duration

of the intervals between those changes that allow archaeologists to translate chronologies into a continuum. On Late Helladic typology see Betancourt 2007: 156–61; also Manning 2010; Warren and Hankey 1989. On periodization in archaeology see Lucas 2018.

96. Olivier (2011: 149–77) has effectively discussed this in terms of a biology of forms.

97. This research was tied to Witmore's book, *Old Lands: A Chorography of the Eastern Peloponnese* (Witmore 2020a).

98. Here Witmore evokes an Aristotelian distinction often enrolled by Harman (2010a: 140–69) as a contrast to substances.

99. Bergson 2001; 1998; Harman 2011.

100. Lucas 2015. Of course, stating that something is contemporary suggests a wider range of possibilities than specifying something as coeval, that is, as existing in the "same age, duration, or epoch" (Fabian 2014: 31).

101. Moore and Taylour 1999: 17–21.

102. Moore and Taylour 1999: 3.

103. See Olivier 1999.

104. On the black box see Serres 1987; English translation Serres 2015b; see also Olivier 2008; English translation Olivier 2011: 1–14.

105. Extension, whose Latin root is *tendere* (to stretch), and continuum, whose Latin root is *tenere* (to hold) are linked by the Indo-European root *ten*: something that stretches, extends, endures, and continues to hold on (Watkins 2000: 90).

106. From Hume to James, contiguity has been fundamental to the association of ideas within philosophy.

107. On formational processes see Schiffer 1987. Seen from the angle of entropy as a breakdown, these processes are often regarded as corrupting a pristine order. As such, the archaeological record is a distortion of a pure temporal specificity that must be disentangled, as if these previous pasts were not already entangled with their own old things (see Lucas 2012).

108. Harman 2016a: 7.

109. See also Lucas 2018.

110. Moore and Taylour 1999; Iakovidis et al. 2003: 16–18.

111. See DeLanda 2006; 2016; in archaeology, see Witmore 2017b; cf. Fowler 2013; Robb 2013.

112. See DeLanda 2006; 2011.

113. On the importance of the chthonic to archaeology see Nativ 2018.

114. On conglomerate quarries at Mycenae see Iakovidis et al. 2003: 42, 60.

115. It is interesting that there is no contemporary Latin equivalent for the Greek term *symbiosis*. Taking its meaning from

convivium, to feast, the term conviviality has lost the connotations of the Latin root, *convivere*, to live together.

116. For an introduction to this theme see Margulis 2008.
117. Harman 2016a: 42–51.
118. Olivier 2011: 149–74.
119. Olivier 2011: 168.
120. Schliemann 1878: 332.
121. Witmore 2009.
122. Protonotariou-Deilaki 1968; 1969.
123. See also Olsen 2010.
124. For this definition of things see Olsen and Witmore 2015.
125. Olsen et al. 2012: 3.
126. Olsen 2010; 2012; Olsen et al. 2012; Witmore 2014a; 2017a; 2020a.
127. If history, as stated by Olivier (2011: 189), deals with what happens to people, then memory deals with what happens to things or places. While useful, the distinction is not taxonomic (cf. Harris 2021a).
128. Indeed, this is a better option than prejudice or vanity, pretending that we have everything at our disposal to confront what has become of the past. See also Harman 2011.
129. Though often listed among those philosophers seen as making metaphorical use of archaeology (see González-Ruibal 2013: 1), Foucault's take on the field should be considered as something more. For in opposing the historicist notion of continuity, Foucault (1970; 1982) saw archaeology as offering something distinct, a stratigraphic image of ruptures and discontinuities. On philosophy and the neglect of things see Serres 1987; 2015b; Harman 2002; 2005; also Olsen 2010.
130. There are, of course, notable exceptions. Within continental philosophy, consider Serres' *Rome* (2015a), *Statues* (2015b), and *Les origines de la géométrie* (1993). On the analytic side the engagement is more pronounced: consider the work of Wylie 2002 and Salmon 1982. See also Holtorf and Karlsson 2000; Webmoor 2015.
131. Olsen 2010.
132. See Rudwick 2014: 304.
133. Olsen and Svestad 1994: 2; also Rudwick 2005; 2014.
134. cf. Olivier 2011.

Chapter 3

1. Serres and Latour 1995; in archaeology see Ramenofsky 1998; Witmore 2007.
2. Olsen et al. 2012; Witmore 2013.

3. Witmore 2014a.
4. Pétursdóttir 2014; Pilaar Birch 2018; Farstadvoll 2019a; 2019b; Olsen et al. 2021; Rich 2021; Rich and Campbell 2023.
5. See Chapter 1 above.
6. This model was given its earliest expression in the arrangement of archaeological collections by Christian Jürgensen Thomsen in the Copenhagen museum in the 1820s.
7. McLuhan 1994.
8. Netz 2004: 56–127.
9. Latour 1993: 76.
10. Serres 2015b: 193.
11. Cherry, Davis, and Mantzourani 1991; Cherry 1994; although see Ingold 1993.
12. See for example Alcock 2002; Bradley 2002; Olivier 2004; 2011; Yoffee 2007; Rojas 2019; also Lucas and Olivier 2022.
13. Olsen et al. 2012; for further elaboration see Olsen 2010: 107–28; Olsen 2013b; Witmore 2020a: 37–57, 109–22.
14. See Witmore 2020a: 285–304.
15. See Willerslev 2011.
16. Ackerman 1987: 1.
17. On Tylor and survivals see Stocking 1995: 5–6; also Fraser 1990: 14–15; 1994: xxx.
18. This point is made by Robert Fraser (1994: xxiii) in his introduction to the Oxford University Press New Abridgement of *The Golden Bough*.
19. Serres' image of the brazen Baal draws upon Flaubert, from his novel, *Salammbô*. Flaubert, who drew upon Rabbinic accounts, also took great liberties with them. As such, this topos is more literary than historical.
20. Whereas history leaves us with questions of veracity among Greco-Roman authors who concocted such barbarous stories to defame their traditional foes – the Carthaginians – archaeology turns up, through the excavation of the tophet at Carthage, the charred bones of children and infants within urns (see Miles 2011: 68–74). Inscriptions on stelae found in association with these burials suggest sacrifice; they speak of children vowed to Baal Hammon in rites necessary for the sustained security of the whole community.
21. Just as humans and other living beings were sacrificed to Baal Hammon, dozens of other living creatures were sacrificed along with humans in the course of numerous space programs: from the Alberts to Laika and even to the insects and microbes that shared the fate of the astronauts in the later Columbia disaster.
22. In 2017 there were over 65,000 human automobile fatalities in the US and EU alone.
23. Sloterdijk presents four mechanisms of repetition: "(1) the

recurrence of the nomadic in the settled, (2) the recurrence of the fetal in the world outside the womb, (3) the recurrence of the maritime on dry land, and (4) the recurrence of Pangaea in the breaking up of the continents" (2011: 21).

24. Sloterdijk 2011.
25. Christos Tsountas, director of these excavations, wrote few words. Apart from all too brief excavation reports, only two of possibly four original notebooks survive (see Shelton 2006: 159–60).
26. Witmore 2007.
27. While these constitute the largest sectors of the field, where most professional archaeologists find employment, standard maps of archaeology leave large swathes of these territories uncharted. On the question of intradisciplinary divisions see Trigger 2010; Rathje, Shanks, and Witmore 2013; Harris and Cipolla 2017.
28. Examples include new techniques of site location and remote sensing, radiocarbon dating, X-ray fluorescence, and new methods of computation (see Clarke 1973).
29. Shanks and Tilley 1992.
30. See Witmore and Shanks 2013: 383–7; also Harris and Cipolla 2017.
31. Rathje, Shanks, and Witmore 2013.
32. Hodder 2003; see also Hegmon 2003.
33. See discussion in Edgeworth 2012 with comments.
34. Olsen, Shanks, and Witmore 2003; see also Olsen 2012: 17; Witmore and Shanks 2013.
35. We have tried to enroll Stengers' notion of an "ecology of practices" to map the discipline in a novel way – and Witmore is aware of Harman's reservations about this concept (Harman 2014b) – around institutions, affiliates, gaining and perpetuating competence, manifesting material pasts, knowledge design, memory practices, politics, the commons, and what we all share, things. – CW (Witmore and Shanks 2013; also see Olsen et al. 2012: 36–57).
36. Olsen et al. 2012.
37. See Lucas 2005; 2014; also Bailey 2007; Karlsson 2001; Murray 1999; Robb and Pauketat 2008; on recollective memory see Olsen 2010: 109–10.
38. See, for example, Barrett 2014; 2016; Pollock et al. 2014; Van Dyke 2015; 2021; Cipolla 2017; Ion 2018; McGuire 2021a; 2021b.
39. See the discussion in Olsen and Witmore 2021.
40. Preucel 2016; also Crossland and Bauer 2017.
41. Gosden and Malafouris 2015; Malafouris, Gosden and Bogaard 2021; also Fowler 2013; Jervis 2019.
42. Cipolla 2018; Harris 2014.

43. Govier and Steel 2021.
44. Ingold 2012; 2013; see also Witmore 2014a.
45. Hodder 2012; Harman 2014a.
46. Alberti 2016; Alberti, Jones, and Pollard 2013.
47. Hodder et al. 2013.
48. Olsen 2012.
49. Harman 2023b.
50. See Lucas 2018 for a concise discussion of "periodization from the ground up."
51. Ceramics are key objects for periodization from the start of the Neolithic (ca. 7000 BCE in Greece) till the "Age of Plastics." Prior to the Neolithic, archaeologists build typologies out of lithics (see Bintliff 2012).
52. *The Mycenaean Pottery* was divided into two volumes, *Analysis and Classification* (Volume 1) and *Chronology* (Volume 2).
53. Furumark 1941b: 25.
54. Furumark 1941b: 28–31; Wace 1956: 89; also see Siapkas 2018.
55. Wace 1949: 11. There is, to be sure, a significant disjuncture, as pointed out by Gavin Lucas (2018), between the kind of site-wide periodization that follows ceramic change and the piecemeal changes found in individual structures, deposits, surfaces, etc. around a given site.
56. See Furumark 1941b: 36.
57. The first radiocarbon dates were published by Willard Libby in 1949, the same year as Wace's *Mycenae*.
58. See Assmann 2003: 18–24. In Greece, there are few historical sources for dates in the Heroic Age. The Marmor Parium or "Parian Chronicle" and Eratosthenes were widely referenced prior to radiometric clocks (Wace and Stubbings 1962: 358).
59. The Amarna period dates from 1352 to 1338 BCE. However, in the 1940s it was calculated as c. 1370–50 BCE (see Wace and Stubbings 1962: 359).
60. Furumark 1941a: 3–4.
61. Furumark 1941b: 115.
62. Furumark 1941b: 110–15.
63. Wace 1956: 89.
64. Lucas and Olivier 2022: 12–14.
65. Lucas and Olivier 2022: 13.
66. See Kohler and Ralph 1961.
67. See Piggot 1966; Renfrew 1968.
68. While there are many nuances, carbon-14 dates derived from short-lived samples are preferred to long-lived tree species, which can generate ages, decades, or centuries older than the context.
69. Witmore takes this in a different sense from Gavin Lucas (2005: 4) who also states that ^{14}C is a relative chronology, given the

calibration of ^{14}C with dendrochronology. Indeed, all scientific dating methods termed absolute involve the translation of measurable quanta into continua: dendrochronology, amino acid racemization, obsidian hydration, thermoluminescence, etc.

70. Also see Olivier 2011: 33.
71. Manning 2010: 22.
72. Manning et al. 2006.
73. See Witmore 2018a.
74. Witmore 2022.
75. Burkert 1977; Vernant 1965; 1976.
76. Graeber and Wengrow 2021.
77. Morris 2000: 195–256.
78. Elsewhere, Witmore has described this in terms of "chronopolitics" (Witmore 2013; 2020c).
79. See for example Alcock 1993; Woolf 1998.
80. González-Ruibal 2018.
81. For a recent example, see Olsen and Vinogradova 2020.
82. See also Olivier 2011; 2017.
83. Barrett 2016: 1685.
84. Olsen et al. 2012: 120. For the critique of the sentence see Barrett 2016: 1685; for other examples of this debate see Ion 2018 and the reply by Pétursdóttir 2018.
85. Harman 2016b: 44.
86. Badiou 2019.
87. Feichtinger 2019.
88. Barad 2007; Escobar 2015.
89. Nietzsche 1997.
90. See also Foucault 1984.
91. See Chapter 1, p. 14.
92. Excavating Mycenae is not like translating Shakespeare, for once archaeological translation occurs, such translation – various modes of documentation, archives of things, and the site at the close of archaeological labor – is all we have, whether it is good or bad (see the discussion in DeLanda and Harman 2017: 94).
93. McLuhan and Watson 1970.
94. Harman 2019a; Morton 2013a.
95. Pétursdóttir and Olsen 2018; Harman 2019b; 2023a; Sørensen 2021.
96. Harman 2016a.
97. Foucault 1982.
98. Olsen 2010; Pétursdóttir 2014; see also Edgeworth 2012 with comments.
99. See DeLanda and Harman 2017: 20–1; Harman 2016b.

Chapter 4

1. Rathje 1979; Deetz 1996; Olsen and Pétursdóttir 2014; González-Ruibal 2019; Olsen et al. 2021.
2. Meillassoux 2008.
3. Suárez 1994.
4. Kant 1965; Langton 2001.
5. Harman 2002.
6. Whitehead 1978.
7. Latour 2007a.
8. Aristotle 2016.
9. See Harman 2009a: 28–9.
10. Husserl 1970.
11. Husserl 1993.
12. Locke 1959; Berkeley 1982; Hume 1978.
13. Brentano 1995.
14. Husserl 1970, vol. 1: 276.
15. Ibn Sina 2007: 153ff.
16. Harman 2020b; see also Young 2021.
17. Heidegger 2002.
18. Leibniz 1989: 214.
19. Kant 1965.
20. Wolfendale 2014: 188.
21. For a more detailed response to Wolfendale see Harman 2020c: 195–295.
22. Wolfendale 2014: 189.
23. Wolfendale 2014: 193.
24. Leibniz and Clarke 2000.
25. Newton 1934: 6.
26. Wolfendale 2014: 193.
27. Wolfendale 2014: 194. In this respect he simply echoes the scientistic views of Ladyman and Ross 2009. For a critique of the latter authors see Harman 2010b.
28. Wolfendale 2014: 193.
29. Lacan 2007b.
30. Gratton 2014.
31. Austin 2010. For a counterargument contending that no "primal flux" should be presupposed see Harman 2014d, though Aristotle already made such an argument in 2016: VIII.3.
32. Heidegger 1969.
33. Derrida 1997. For a critical response see Harman 2012: 195–9.
34. Husserl 2019. Harman's response to Gratton on this point can be found in Harman 2020c, Chapter 3.
35. Kleinherenbrink 2019a.
36. Kleinherenbrink 2019b. His reference to Tristan Garcia at 543n30 is to Garcia 2013.

37. Kleinherenbrink 2019b: 539; Lakatos 1978. For a discussion of this aspect of Lakatos see Harman 2019c.
38. Deleuze 1990b; 1994.
39. Sellars 2007.
40. Deleuze 2000.
41. Kleinherenbrink 2019b: 546.
42. Wolfendale 2014: 199.
43. Kleinherenbrink 2019b: 544.
44. Kleinherenbrink 2019b: 548.
45. Kleinherenbrink 2019b: 548.
46. Kleinherenbrink 2019b: 551.
47. He refers above all to Harman 2014e.
48. Deleuze and Guattari 2010.
49. Badiou 2009; Husserl 1977; DeLanda 2006.
50. Kleinherenbrink 2019b: 548.
51. Kleinherenbrink 2019b: 549.
52. McTaggart 1908.
53. McTaggart 1908: 458.
54. McTaggart 1908: 458.
55. McTaggart 1908: 458.
56. McTaggart 1908: 460.
57. McTaggart 1908: 461.
58. McTaggart 1908: 471.
59. McTaggart 1908: 471.
60. McTaggart 1908: 472; Strawson 2009: 5.9; Dainton 2000: 171; Lockwood 2005: 381; Pöppel 2004: 298. The individual figures come from Dainton 2018.
61. See for instance Uexküll 2010.
62. McTaggart 1908: 474.
63. McTaggart 1908: 461–4.
64. McTaggart 1908: 462.
65. McTaggart 1908: 463.
66. McTaggart 1908: 464.
67. McTaggart 1908: 458.
68. Harman 2014e.
69. The main collection of writings is Lacan 2007a. Anyone already somewhat familiar with Freud is advised to work through Lacan's multi-volume Seminar beginning with the first, Lacan 2013.
70. Harman 2013a.
71. Harman 2020a.
72. McLuhan and McLuhan 1992.
73. Plotinus 1975.
74. Bryant 2011.
75. Lovecraft 2005.
76. Harman 2014f; 2019d.
77. Morton 2013b.
78. Lacan 1991.

Chapter 5

1. See Domanska 2006; Shanks 2012: 132–44.
2. See Harman 2020b.
3. See Harman 2020b: 142.
4. It should be noted how the latter may have been an artifact of seeking order among heavenly bodies; that is, it may have emerged through the observation of celestial sevenhoods, whether those actual entities that traveled the zodiac (Sun, Moon, and the five planets visible to the naked eye) or the brightest stars in the northern skies. See Copeland 1939.
5. Assmann 2003: 18–19.
6. Assmann 2003: 18–19.
7. Hoffman 2019; Chirimuuta 2017.
8. See Susskind and Lindesay 2004.
9. Arkani-Hamed 2019.
10. In the ancient world, the beautiful and the cyclic were one and same: *horaios*, the turn of the season, seasonality, cyclical, the rightness of time, the prime of life, youth, what is beautiful.
11. See Arènes, Latour, and Gaillardet 2018.
12. Matthew 20:16.
13. Bryant 2012.
14. Harman 2014d.
15. Aristotle 2018.
16. Cipolla 2018; Crellin 2020; Glovier and Steel 2021; Harris 2014.
17. Crellin 2020: 165; Bennett 2010: 23.
18. Crellin 2020: 69–74, 170–1, 173.
19. Witmore 2018a.
20. Wolfendale 2014: 70.
21. Harman 2019d.
22. Stanislavski 2010.
23. Austin 1975.
24. Husserl 1977.
25. Derrida 2003.
26. Badiou 2009.
27. Badiou 2006.
28. See for instance Wolfson 2017.
29. DeLanda 2015.
30. Harman 2010b.
31. Wallace-Hadrill 2011.
32. For a description of the eruption and Pliny the Younger's observations see Sigurdsson, Cashdollar, and Sparks 1982.
33. Compare Bogost 2012; Holbraad 2009; within archaeology see Harris 2021b: 199–221. On the fourfold object see Harman 2011: 124–35.
34. Harman 2011: 135.

35. Harman 2010c; 2014f; 2016a; 2016b.
36. Harman 2014f: 96.
37. Harman 2011: 8–10; Witmore 2021b.
38. Bryant 2014.
39. Žižek 2009; Harman 2021.
40. For a contrary view see Sbriglia 2021.
41. Badiou 2009: 1.
42. Bennett 2010: 61.
43. Ferraris 2014.
44. Lacan 1991; Greimas 1983; McLuhan and McLuhan 1992. For a discussion of the McLuhan version of the diagram see Harman 2007b.
45. Twardowski 1977.
46. James 1987: 57.
47. Lacan 2007b.
48. Harman 2022.
49. This tendency is so pervasive that it hardly warrants citation. But just to offer an important example, consider how Olivier deploys the term "material" in order to qualify the difference between aspects of archaeology and history in his highly influential book, *Le sombre abîme du temps: mémoire et archéologie* (2008; English translation, 2011).
50. See the discussion in Sørensen 2021; see also Witmore 2018b: 517–18.
51. See Witmore 2021b.
52. Ingold 2007; consider for example Boivin 2008; Conneller 2011.
53. Bennett 2010: 111; Glovier and Steel 2021.
54. Latour 2007b; Harman 2009a: 139–44.
55. Ingold 2007: 7; Witmore 2014b: 241; Harman 2009a: 142.
56. Witmore 2020a: 455–69; 2020b: 59–60.
57. Harman 2014f: 97.
58. Deutsch 2013: 24.
59. McTaggart 1908; for a discussion of McTaggart in the context of archaeology see Lucas 2005: 21–2; 2015: 10.
60. Harman 2023a; Rich and Campbell 2023.
61. Simons 2000.
62. Rich 2021.
63. Harman 2019b.
64. Deleuze 1994.
65. Klinghoffer 2021.
66. Viollet-le-Duc 1854.
67. Malebranche 1997b: 117.
68. Badiou 2019.
69. See DeSilvey 2017; Pétursdóttir 2012; 2014.
70. Concerning the positive side of ruination see DeSilvey 2006; Olsen and Pétursdóttir 2014; also Shanks 2012.

71. Rilke 1949: 46–8.
72. Olsen and Pétursdóttir 2014: 11–12.
73. Sørensen 2021.
74. Olsen and Witmore 2014.
75. Olsen 2010.
76. Harman 2018: 28.
77. Harman 2018.
78. Latour, Harman, and Erdélyi 2011: 58–9. On the distinction between weak and strong theory see Sedgwick 1997; Stewart 2008; Pétursdóttir and Olsen 2018; Olsen and Witmore 2021; also see Lucas and Witmore 2022.
79. Mitchell 2013.

A Note on Models of Time

1. Margulis 2008.
2. Witmore 2022.

References

Ackerman, R. 1987. *J.G. Frazer: His Life and Work.* Cambridge: Cambridge University Press.

Alberti, B. 2016. Archaeologies of ontology. *Annual Review of Anthropology* 45: 163–214.

— A.M. Jones, and J. Pollard (eds.) 2013. *Archaeology After Interpretation: Returning Materials to Archaeological Theory.* Walnut Creek, CA: Left Coast Press.

Alcock, S.E. 1993. *Graecia Capta: The Landscapes of Roman Greece.* Cambridge: Cambridge University Press.

— 2002. *Archaeologies of the Greek Past: Landscape, Monuments, and Memories.* Cambridge: Cambridge University Press.

— and J.F. Cherry. 2004. *Side-by-Side Survey: Comparative Regional Studies in the Mediterranean World.* Oxford: Oxbow.

Arènes, A., B. Latour and J. Gaillardet. 2018. Giving depth to the surface: An exercise in the Gaia-graphy of critical zones. *The Anthropocene Review* 5.2: 120–35.

Aristotle. 1992. *The Art of Rhetoric*, trans. H. Lawson-Tancred. London: Penguin.

— 2016. *Metaphysics*, trans. C.D.C. Reeve. Indianapolis: Hackett. Kindle edition.

— 2018. *Physics*, trans. C.D.C. Reeve. Indianapolis: Hackett. Kindle edition.

Arkani-Hamed, N. 2019. Spacetime & quantum mechanics: Total positivity and motives. YouTube lecture, September 6, at <https://www.youtube.com/watch?v=Sn0W_mwA7Q0>.

Assmann, J. 2003. *The Mind of Egypt: History and Meaning in the Time of the Pharaohs.* Cambridge, MA: Harvard University Press.

Augé, M. 1995. *Non-places: Introduction to an Anthropology of Supermodernity.* London: Verso.

Austin, J. 1975. *How to Do Things with Words*, Second Edition. Cambridge, MA: Harvard University Press.

Austin, M. 2010. To exist is to change: A friendly disagreement with

Graham Harman about why things happen. *Speculations* 1(1): 66–83.

Badiou, A. 2006. *Being and Event*, trans. O. Feltham. London: Continuum.

— 2009. *Logics of Worlds: Being and Event* II, trans. A. Toscano. London: Continuum.

— 2019. *Malebranche: Theological Figure, Being 2*, trans. J. Smith with S. Spitzer. New York: Columbia University Press.

Baedeker, K. 1894. *Greece: A Handbook for Travellers*, 2nd rev. ed. Leipzig: Karl Baedeker.

Bailey, G. 1983. Concepts of time in Quaternary prehistory. *Annual Review of Anthropology* 12: 165–92.

— 2007. Time perspectives, palimpsests and the archaeology of time. *Journal of Anthropological Archaeology* 26: 198–223.

Barad, K. 2007. *Meeting the Universe Halfway: Quantum Physics and the Entanglement of Matter and Meaning*. Durham, NC: Duke University Press.

Barrett, J.C. 2014. The material constitution of humanness. *Archaeological Dialogues* 21.1: 65–74.

— 2016. The new antiquarianism? *Antiquity* 90.354: 1681–6.

Bassi, K. 2016. *Traces of the Past: Classics Between History and Archaeology*. Ann Arbor: University of Michigan Press.

Benjamin, W., H. Eiland, and M.W. Jennings. 2006. *Selected Writings, Volume 4: 1938–1940*. Cambridge, MA: Belknap Press.

Bennett, J. 2010. *Vibrant Matter: A Political Ecology of Things*. Durham, NC: Duke University Press.

— 2012. Systems and things: A response to Graham Harman and Timothy Morton. *New Literary History* 43: 225–33.

Bergson, H. 1991. *Matter and Memory*, trans N.M. Paul and W.S. Palmer. New York: Zone Books.

— 1998. *Creative Evolution*, trans. A. Mitchell. Mineola, NY: Dover.

— 2001. *Time and Free Will: An Essay on the Immediate Data of Consciousness*. Mineola, NY: Dover.

Berkeley, G. 1982. *Treatise Concerning the Principles of Human Knowledge*. Indianapolis: Hackett.

Betancourt, P.P. 2007. *Introduction to Aegean Art*. Philadelphia, PA: Institute for Aegean Prehistory Academic Press.

Binford, L.R. 1978. *Nunamiut Ethnoarchaeology*. New York: Academic Press.

— 1981a. Behavioural archaeology and the Pompeii premise. *Journal of Anthropological Research* 37: 195–208.

— 1981b. *Bones: Ancient Men and Modern Myths*. New York: Academic Press.

— 1983. *In Pursuit of the Past: Decoding the Archaeological Record*. New York: Thames and Hudson.

Bintliff, J.L. 1991. *The Annales School and Archaeology*. Leicester: Leicester University Press.

— 2000. Reconstructing the Byzantine countryside: New approaches from landscape archaeology. In K. Blelke et al. (eds.) *Byzanz als Raum*. Vienna: Österreichische Akademie der Wissenschaften, 37–63.

— 2012. *The Complete Archaeology of Greece: From Hunter-Gatherers to the 20th Century AD*. Chichester: Wiley-Blackwell.

Bogost, I. 2012. *Alien Phenomenology: Or What Is It Like to Be a Thing?* Minneapolis: University of Minnesota Press.

Boivin, N. 2008. *Material Cultures, Material Minds: The Impact of Things on Human Thought, Society, and Evolution*. Cambridge: Cambridge University Press.

Bradley, R. 2002. *The Past in Prehistoric Societies*. London: Routledge.

Brentano, F. 1995. *Psychology from an Empirical Standpoint*, trans. A. Rancurello, D.B. Terrell and L. McAlister. New York: Routledge.

Broodbank, C. 2013. *The Making of the Middle Sea: A History of the Mediterranean from the Beginning to the Emergence of the Classical World*. Oxford: Oxford University Press.

Bryant, L. 2011. *The Democracy of Objects*. Ann Arbor, MI: Open Humanities Press.

— 2012. Stability and change. *Larval Subjects* blog post. December 10, at <https://larvalsubjects.wordpress.com/2012/12/10/stability-and-change/>.

— 2014. *Onto-Cartography: An Ontology of Machines and Media*. Edinburgh: Edinburgh University Press.

— 2021a. Wilderness heritage: For an ontology of the Anthropocene. In T.R. Bangstad and Þ. Pétursdóttir (eds.) *Heritage Ecologies*. Abingdon: Routledge, 66–80.

— 2021b. Wild things. In B. Olsen, M. Burström, C. Desilvey, and Þ. Péturdóttir (eds.) *After Discourse: Things, Affects, Ethics*. Abingdon: Routledge, 42–58.

— N. Srnicek, and G. Harman. 2011. *The Speculative Turn: Continental Materialism and Realism*. Melbourne: re.press.

Buchli, V. and G. Lucas (eds.) 2001. *Archaeologies of the Contemporary Past*. London: Routledge.

Burford, A. 1969. *The Greek Temple Builders at Epidauros: A Social and Economic Study of Building in the Asklepian Sanctuary*. Toronto: University of Toronto Press.

Burkert, W. 1977. *Griechische Religion der archaischen und klassischen Epoche*. Stuttgart: Kohlhammer.

Chang, C. 1981. *The Archaeology of Contemporary Herding Sites in Greece*. Doctoral Dissertation, State University of New York at Binghamton.

Cherry, J.F. 1994. Regional survey in the Aegean: The "New Wave" (and after). In P.N. Kardulias (ed.) *Beyond the Site: Regional Studies in the Aegean Area.* Lanham, MD: University Press of America, 91–112.

— 2003. Archaeology beyond the site: Regional survey and its future. In R.M. Leventhal and J.K. Papadopoulos (eds.) *Theory and Practice in Mediterranean Archaeology: Old World and New World perspectives.* Los Angeles: Cotsen Institute of Archaeology, University of California, 137–60.

— J.L. Davis and H. Mantzourani. 1991. *Landscape Archaeology as Long-term History: Northern Keos in the Cycladic Islands from Earliest Settlement to Modern Times.* (Monumenta Archaeologica 16). Los Angeles: UCLA Institute of Archaeology.

Childe, V.G. 1925. *The Dawn of European Civilization.* London: Paul, Trench, Trubner & Co.

Chirimuuta, M. 2017. *Outside Color: Perceptual Science and the Puzzle of Color in Philosophy.* Cambridge, MA: MIT Press.

Cipolla, C.N. 2017. Postscript. Postcolonial archaeology in the age of things. In C.N. Cipolla (ed.) *Foreign Objects: Rethinking Indigenous Consumption in American Archaeology.* Tucson: University of Arizona Press, 222–9.

— 2018. Earth flows and lively stone. What differences does "vibrant" matter make? *Archaeological Dialogues* 25.1: 49–70.

Clarke, D.L. 1968. *Analytical Archaeology.* London: Methuen.

— 1973. Archaeology: The loss of innocence. *Antiquity* 47: 6–18.

Conneller, C. 2011. *An Archaeology of Materials: Substantial Transformations in Early Prehistoric Europe.* Abingdon: Routledge.

Copeland, L.S. 1939. Sources of the seven-day week. *Popular Astronomy* 47.4: 175–82.

Courbin, P. 1988. *What is Archaeology? An Essay on the Nature of Archaeological Research,* trans. P.G. Bahn. Chicago: University of Chicago Press.

Crellin, R.J. 2020. *Change and Archaeology.* Abingdon: Routledge.

Crossland, Z. and A. Bauer. 2017. Im/materialities. *Semiotic Review,* 4, at <https://semioticreview.com/ojs/index.php/sr/article/view/9>.

Dainton, B. 2000. *Stream of Consciousness.* London: Routledge.

— 2018. Temporal consciousness. *The Stanford Encyclopedia of Philosophy* (Winter 2018 Edition), ed. Edward N. Zalta, at <https://plato.stanford.edu/archives/win2018/entries/consciousness-temporal/>.

Damaskos, D. and D. Plantzos (eds.) 2008. *A Singular Antiquity: Archaeology and Hellenic Identity in Twentieth-Century Greece.* Athens: The Benaki Museum.

Daniel, G.E. 1943. *The Three Ages: An Essay on Archaeological Method.* Cambridge: Cambridge University Press.

Davies, S. and J.L. Davis. 2007. *Between Venice and Istanbul: Colonial Landscapes in Early Modern Greece.* Princeton, NJ: American School of Classical Studies at Athens.

Davis, J.L. 2010. "That special atmosphere outside of national boundaries": Three Jewish directors and the American School of Classical Studies at Athens. *Annuario della Scuola Archeologica Italiana di Atene* 87: 119–31.

Deetz, J. 1996. *In Small Things Forgotten: An Archaeology of Early American Life*, exp. and rev. ed. New York: Doubleday.

DeLanda, M. 2006. *A New Philosophy of Society: Assemblage Theory and Social Complexity*. New York: Continuum.

— 2011. Emergence, causality and realism. In L. Bryant, N. Srnicek, and G. Harman (eds.) *The Speculative Turn: Continental Materialism and Realism*. Melbourne: re.press, 381–92.

— 2015. *Philosophical Chemistry: Genealogy of a Scientific Field*. London: Bloomsbury.

— 2016. *Assemblage Theory*. Edinburgh: Edinburgh University Press.

— and G. Harman. 2017. *The Rise of Realism*. Cambridge: Polity.

Deleuze, G. 1990a. *Bergsonism*, trans. H. Tomlinson and B. Habberjam. New York: Zone Books.

— 1990b. *The Logic of Sense*, trans. M. Lester and C. Stivale. New York: Columbia University Press.

— 1994. *Difference and Repetition*, trans. P. Patton. New York: Columbia University Press.

— 2000. *Proust and Signs. The Complete Text*, trans. R. Howard. Minneapolis: University of Minnesota Press.

— and F. Guattari. 2010. *Anti-Oedipus: Capitalism and Schizophrenia*, trans. R. Hurley, M. Seem, and H. Lane. Minneapolis: University of Minnesota Press.

Demakopoulou, K. (ed.) 1990. *Troy, Mycenae, Tiryns, Orchomenos: Heinrich Schliemann, the 100th Anniversary of his Death*. Athens: Ministry of Culture of Greece.

Derrida, J. 1997. *Of Grammatology*, trans. G.C. Spivak. Baltimore: Johns Hopkins University Press.

— 2003. *The Problem of Genesis in Husserl's Philosophy*, trans. M. Hobson. Chicago: University of Chicago Press.

— 2011. *Voice and Phenomenon: Introduction to the Problem of the Sign in Husserl's Phenomenology*, trans. L. Lawlor. Evanston, IL: Northwestern University Press.

Descartes, R. 1993. *Meditations on First Philosophy*, trans. D. Cress. Indianapolis: Hackett.

DeSilvey, C. 2006. Observed decay: Telling stories with mutable things. *Journal of Material Culture* 11.3: 318–38.

— 2017. *Curated Decay: Heritage Beyond Saving*. Minneapolis: University of Minnesota Press.

Deutsch, L. 2013. *Metronome: A History of Paris from the Underground Up*. New York: St. Martin's Griffin.

Diamond, J.M. 1998. *Guns, Germs, and Steel: The Fates of Human Societies*. New York: W.W. Norton.

Domanska, E. 2006. The material presence of the past. *History and Theory* 45.3: 337–48.

Edgeworth, M. 2012. Follow the cut, follow the rhythm, follow the material. With comments and reply. *Norwegian Archaeological Review* 45.1: 76–114.

Escobar, A. 2015. Thinking-feeling with the earth: Territorial struggles and the ontological dimension of the epistemologies of the south. *Revista de Antropología Iberoamericana* 11.1: 11–32.

Fabian, J. 2014. *Time and the Other: How Anthropology Makes Its Object*. New York: Columbia University Press.

Fakhry, M. 2007. *Islamic Occasionalism: And its Critique by Averroes and Aquinas*. New York: Routledge.

Farstadvoll, S. 2019a. *A Speculative Archaeology of Excess: Exploring the Afterlife of a Derelict Landscape Garden*. Doctoral Dissertation, UiT The Arctic University of Norway.

— 2019b. Growing concerns: Plants and their roots in the past. *Journal of Contemporary Archaeology* 5.2: 174–93.

Feichtinger, M. 2019. The obstinate real: Barad, Escobar, and object-oriented ontology. *Open Philosophy* 2: 86–97.

Ferraris, M. 2014. *Manifesto of New Realism*, trans. S. De Sanctis. Albany, NY: SUNY Press.

Finley, M.I. 2002 [1954]. *The World of Odysseus*. New York: The New York Review of Books.

Forbes, H. 2007. *Meaning and Identity in a Greek Landscape: An Archaeological Ethnography*. Cambridge: Cambridge University Press.

Fotiatis, M. 1995. Modernity and the past-still-present: Politics in the birth of regional archaeological projects in Greece. *American Journal of Archaeology* 99: 59–78.

Foucault, M. 1970. *The Order of Things: An Archaeology of the Human Sciences*. New York: Pantheon Books.

— 1982. *The Archaeology of Knowledge*. New York: Vintage.

— 1984. Nietzsche, genealogy, history. In P. Rabinow (ed.) *The Foucault Reader*. New York: Pantheon Books, 76–100.

Fowler, C. 2013. *The Emergent Past: A Relational Realist Archaeology of Early Bronze Age Mortuary Practices*. Oxford: Oxford University Press.

Fowler, H.N. 1932. Corinth and the Corinthia. In H.N. Fowler and R. Stillwell (eds.) *Corinth I.i: Introduction, Topography, Architecture*. Cambridge, MA: Harvard University Press, 18–114.

Fraser, R. 1990. *The Making of the Golden Bough: The Origins and Growth of an Argument*. New York: St. Martin's Press.

— 1994. Introduction. In J.G. Frazer, *The Golden Bough. A New Abridgement*. Oxford: Oxford University Press.

Frazer, J.G. 1898. *Pausanias's Description of Greece*, vol. 3. London: Macmillan.

Furumark, A. 1941a. *The Mycenaean Pottery: Analysis and Classification*. Stockholm: K. Vitterhets Historie och Antikvitets Akademien.

— 1941b. *The Mycenaean Pottery: The Chronology*. Stockholm: K. Vitterhets Historie och Antikvitets Akademien.

Garcia, T. 2013. Crossing ways of thinking: On Graham Harman's system and my own. Trans. M.A. Ohm. *Parrhesia* 16: 14–25.

Gardin, J.C. 1980. *Archaeological Constructs: An Aspect of Theoretical Archaeology*. Cambridge: Cambridge University Press.

Glovier, E. and L. Steel. 2021. Beyond the "thingification" of worlds: Archaeology and the new materialisms. *Journal of Material Culture* 26.3: 298–317.

González-Ruibal, A. 2008. Time to destroy: An archaeology of supermodernity. *Current Anthropology* 49: 247–79.

— (ed.) 2013. *Reclaiming Archaeology: Beyond the Tropes of Modernity*. London: Routledge.

— 2016a. Archaeology and the time of modernity. *Historical Archaeology* 50: 144–64.

— 2016b. Ethnoarchaeology or simply archaeology? *World Archaeology* 48.5: 687–92.

— 2018. Ethics of archaeology. *Annual Review of Anthropology* 47: 345–60.

— 2019. *An Archaeology of the Contemporary Era*. London: Routledge.

Gosden, C. and L. Malafouris. 2015. Process archaeology (P-Arch). *World Archaeology* 47.5: 701–17.

Gould, R.A. and M.B. Schiffer. 1981. *Modern Material Culture: The Archaeology of Us*. New York: Academic Press.

Govier, E. and L. Steel. 2021. Beyond the "thingification" of worlds: Archaeology and the new materialisms. *Journal of Material Culture* 26.3: 298–317.

Graeber, D. and D. Wengrow. 2021. *The Dawn of Everything: A New History of Humanity*. New York: Penguin.

Gräslund, B. 1987. *The Birth of Prehistoric Chronology: Dating Methods and Dating Systems in Nineteenth-Century Scandinavian Archaeology*. Cambridge: Cambridge University Press.

Gratton, P. 2014. *Speculative Realism: Problems and Prospects*. London: Bloomsbury.

Graves-Brown, P. (ed.) 2000. *Matter, Materiality, and Modern Culture*. London: Routledge.

Greenberg, C. 1965. *Art and Culture: Critical Essays*. Boston: Beacon Press.

— 2003. *Late Writings*. Minneapolis: University of Minnesota Press.

Greimas, A.J. 1983. *Structural Semantics: An Attempt at a Method*, trans. D. McDowell, R. Schleifer, and A. Velie. Lincoln, NE: University of Nebraska Press.

Gumbrecht, H.U. 2013. *After 1945: Latency as Origin of the Present.* Stanford, CA: Stanford University Press.

— 2014. The future of reading? Memories and thoughts toward a genealogical approach. *boundary 2* 41.2: 99–111.

Hall, J.M. 2013. *A History of the Archaic Greek World, ca. 1200–479 BCE,* 2nd ed. Malden, MA: John Wiley.

— 2014. *Artifact and Artifice: Classical Archaeology and the Ancient Historian.* Chicago: University of Chicago Press.

Halstead, P. 2009. Studying the past in the present: Archaeological engagement with modern Greece. *British School at Athens Studies* 17: 201–15.

Hamilakis, Y. 2007. *The Nation and Its Ruins: Antiquity, Archaeology, and National Imagination in Greece.* Oxford: Oxford University Press.

— and A. Anagnostopoulos. 2009. What is archaeological ethnography? *Public Archaeology: Archaeological Ethnographies* 8: 65–87.

— and F. Ifantidis. 2013. The other Acropolises: Multi-temporality and the persistence of the past. In P. Graves-Brown, R. Harrison, and A. Piccini (eds.) *The Oxford Handbook of the Contemporary World.* Oxford: Oxford University Press, 758–81.

Harman, G. 2002. *Tool-Being: Heidegger and the Metaphysics of Objects.* Chicago: Open Court.

— 2005. *Guerrilla Metaphysics: Phenomenology and the Carpentry of Things.* Chicago: Open Court.

— 2007a. On vicarious causation. *Collapse* II: 171–205.

— 2007b. The tetrad and phenomenology. *Explorations in Media Ecology* 6.3: 189–96.

— 2009a. *Prince of Networks: Bruno Latour and Metaphysics.* Melbourne: re.press.

— 2009b. The McLuhans and metaphysics. In J.-K. Berg Olsen, E. Selinger, and S. Riis (eds.) *New Waves in Philosophy of Technology.* London: Palgrave, 100–22.

— 2010a. *Towards Speculative Realism: Essays and Lectures.* Winchester: Zero Books.

— 2010b. Time, space, essence, and eidos: A new theory of causation. *Cosmos and History: The Journal of Natural and Social Philosophy* 6.1: 1–17.

— 2010c. I am also of the opinion that materialism must be destroyed. *Environment and Planning D: Society and Space* 28.5: 772–90.

— 2011. *The Quadruple Object.* Winchester: Zero Books.

— 2012. The well-wrought broken hammer: Object-oriented literary criticism. *New Literary History* 43: 183–203.

— 2013a. The revenge of the surface: Heidegger, McLuhan, Greenberg. *Paletten* 291/292: 66–73.

— 2013b. Undermining, overmining, and duomining: A critique.

In J. Sutela (ed.) *Metaphysics*. Aalto: Aalto Design Research Laboratory, 40–51.

— 2014a. Entanglement and relation: A response to Bruno Latour and Ian Hodder. *New Literary History* 45.1: 37–49.

— 2014b. Stengers on emergence. *BioSocieties* 9.1: 99–104.

— 2014c. Greenberg, Duchamp, and the next avant-garde. *Speculations* V: 251–74.

— 2014d. Conclusions: Assemblage theory and its future. In M. Acuto and S. Curtis (eds.) *Reassembling International Theory: Assemblage Thinking and International Relations*. London: Palgrave Macmillan, 118–31.

— 2014e. Whitehead and schools X, Y, and Z. In N. Gaskill and A.J. Nocek (eds.) *The Lure of Whitehead*. Minneapolis: University of Minnesota Press, 231–48.

— 2014f. Materialism is not the solution: On matter, form, and mimesis. *Nordic Journal of Aesthetics* 47: 94–110.

— 2016a. *Immaterialism: Objects and Social Theory*. Cambridge: Polity.

— 2016b. On behalf of form: The view from archaeology and architecture. In M. Bille and T.F. Sørensen (eds.) *Elements of Architecture: Assembling Archaeology, Atmosphere, and the Performance of Building Space*. London: Routledge, 30–46.

– 2016c. A new occasionalism? In Bruno Latour and Peter Weibel (eds.) *Reset Modernity!* Cambridge, MA: MIT Press, 129–38.

— 2017. Buildings are not processes: A disagreement with Latour and Yaneva. *Ardeth* 01: 113–22.

— 2018. *Object-Oriented Ontology: A New Theory of Everything*. London: Penguin.

— 2019a. Hyperobjects and prehistory. In S. Souvatzi, A. Baysal, and E. Baysal (eds.) *Time and History in Prehistory*. London: Routledge, 195–209.

— 2019b. The coldness of forgetting: OOO in philosophy, archaeology, and history. *Open Philosophy* 2: 270–9.

— 2019c. On progressive and degenerating research programs with respect to philosophy. *Revista Portuguesa de Filosofia* 75.4: 2067–102.

— 2019d. A new sense of mimesis. In M.F. Gage (ed.) *Aesthetics Equals Politics: New Discourses Across Art, Architecture, and Philosophy*. Cambridge, MA: MIT Press, 49–63.

— 2020a. *Art and Objects*. Cambridge: Polity.

— 2020b. The only exit from modern philosophy. *Open Philosophy* 3: 132–46.

— 2020c. *Skirmishes: With Friends, Enemies, and Neutrals*. Brooklyn, NY: punctum.

— 2021. Žižek's parallax, or the inherent stupidity of all philosophical positions. In D. Finkelde, C. Menke, and S. Žižek (eds.)

Parallax: The Dialectics of Mind and World. London: Bloomsbury, 27–38.

— 2022. *Architecture and Objects.* Minneapolis: University of Minnesota Press.

— 2023a. The shipwreck of Theseus. In P. Campbell and S. Rich (eds.) *Contemporary Philosophy for Maritime Archaeology: Flat Ontologies, Oceanic Thought, and the Anthropocene.* Leiden: Sidestone Press.

— 2023b. *Waves and Stones: The Continuous and the Discontinuous in Human Thought.* London: Allen Lane.

Harris, O.J.T. 2014. (Re-)assembling communities. *Journal of Archaeological Method and Theory* 21: 76–97.

— 2021a. Archaeology, process and time: Beyond history versus memory. *World Archaeology* 53.1: 104–21.

— 2021b. *Assembling Past Worlds: Materials, Bodies, and Architecture in Neolithic Britain.* London: Routledge.

— and C.N. Cipolla. 2017. *Archaeological Theory in the New Millennium: Introducing Current Perspectives.* London: Routledge.

Harrison, R. and A.J. Schofield. 2010. *After Modernity: Archaeological Approaches to the Contemporary Past.* Oxford: Oxford University Press.

Hartog, F. 2015. *Regimes of Historicity: Presentism and Experiences of Time*, trans. S. Brown. New York: Columbia University Press.

Hegmon, M. 2003. Setting theoretical egos aside: Issues and theory in North American archaeology. *American Antiquity* 68.2: 213–43.

Heidegger, M. 1962. *Being and Time*, trans. J. Macquarrie and E. Robinson. New York: Harper.

— 1969. *Identity and Difference*, trans. J. Stambaugh. New York: Harper & Row.

— 2002. The origin of the work of art. In *Off the Beaten Track*, trans. J. Young and K. Haynes. Cambridge: Cambridge University Press, 1–55.

— 2012. The Thing. In *Bremen and Freiburg Lectures: Insight Into That Which Is and Basic Principles of Thinking*, trans. A. Mitchell. Bloomington: Indiana University Press, 5–22.

Herodotus. 2015. *The Histories*, trans. T. Holland. London: Penguin.

Hingley, R. 2012. Living landscape: Reading Hadrian's Wall. *Landscapes* 12.2: 41–62.

Hodder, I. 1987. *Archaeology as Long-term History.* Cambridge: Cambridge University Press.

— 1990. *The Domestication of Europe: Structure and Contingency of Neolithic Societies.* Oxford: Basil Blackwell.

— 1995. Of mice and men: Collingwood and the development of archaeological thought. In D. Boucher, J. Connelly, and T. Modood (eds.) *Philosophy, History and Civilization: Interdisciplinary*

Perspectives on R.G. Collingwood. Cardiff: University of Wales Press, 364–83.

— 2003. Archaeology as a discontinuous domain. In C.S. VanPool and T.L. VanPool (eds.) *Essential Tensions in Archaeological Method and Theory*. Salt Lake City: University of Utah Press.

— 2012. *Entangled: An Archaeology of the Relationships between Humans and Things*. Malden, MA: John Wiley.

— with W.L. Rathje, M. Shanks, and C. Witmore. 2013. Ian Hodder. In W.L. Rathje, M. Shanks, and C. Witmore (eds.) *Archaeology in the Making: Conversations through a Discipline*. London: Routledge, 122–38.

Hoffman, D. 2019. *The Case Against Reality: Why Evolution Hid the Truth from Our Eyes*. New York: W.W. Norton.

Holbraad, M. 2009. Ontology, ethnography, archaeology: An afterword on the ontography of things. *Cambridge Archaeological Journal* 19: 431–41.

Holtorf, C. and A. Piccini (eds.) 2009. *Contemporary Archaeologies: Excavating Now*. Frankfurt: Peter Lang.

Holtorf, C. and H. Karlsson (eds.) 2000. *Philosophy and Archaeological Practice: Perspectives for the 21st Century*. Goteborg: Bricoleur Press.

Hope Simpson, R. 1998. The Mycenaean highways. *Échos du monde classique: Classical Views* 42.2: 239–60.

Horden, P. and N. Purcell. 2000. *The Corrupting Sea: A Study of Mediterranean History*. Oxford: Blackwell.

Hume, D. 1978. *A Treatise of Human Nature*. Oxford: Oxford University Press.

Husserl, E. 1970. *Logical Investigations*, 2 vols., trans. J. N. Findlay. London: Routledge and Kegan Paul.

— 1977. *Formal and Transcendental Logic*, trans. D. Cairns. The Hague: Martinus Nijhoff.

— 1993. Intentional objects. In *Early Writings in the Philosophy of Logic and Mathematics*, trans. and ed. D. Willard. Dordrecht: Kluwer, 345–87.

— 2019. *The Phenomenology of Internal Time-Consciousness*, trans. J. Churchill. Bloomington: Indiana University Press.

Iakovidis, S.E., E.B. French, K. Shelton, C. Ioannides, A. Jansen, and J. Lavery (eds.) 2003. *Archaeological Atlas of Mycenae*. Athens: Archaiologikē Hētaireia.

Ibn Sina. 2007. Ibn Sina. In J. McGinnis and D. Reisman (eds.) *Classical Arabic Philosophy: An Anthology of Sources*. Indianapolis: Hackett, 146–237.

Ingold, T. 1993. The temporality of the landscape. *World Archaeology* 25.2: 152–74.

— 2007. Materials against materiality. *Archaeological Dialogues* 14(1): 1–16.

— 2012. Toward an ecology of materials. *Annual Review of Anthropology* 41: 427–42.

— 2013. *Making: Anthropology, Archaeology, Art and Architecture.* London: Routledge.

— 2016. Archaeology with Its Back to the World. *Norwegian Archaeological Review* 49.1: 30–2.

Ion, A. 2018. A taphonomy of a dark Anthropocene: A response to Þóra Pétursdóttir's OOO- inspired "Archaeology and Anthropocene." *Archaeological Dialogues* 25.2: 191–203.

James, M.R. 1987. *Casting the Runes and Other Ghost Stories.* Oxford: Oxford University Press.

Jameson, M.H. 1976. A Greek countryside. *Expedition Magazine* 19.1: 2–4.

Jarvis, K.E., S.J. Parry, and J.M. Piper. 2001. Temporal and spatial studies of autocatalyst-derived platinum, rhodium, and palladium and selected vehicle derived traces in the environment. *Environmental Science and Technology* 35: 1031–6.

Jervis, B. 2019. *Assemblage Thought and Archaeology.* London: Routledge.

Jones, A. 2007. *Memory and Material Culture.* Cambridge: Cambridge University Press.

Kant, I. 1965. *Critique of Pure Reason*, trans. N.K. Smith. New York: St. Martin's Press.

Karlsson, H. (ed.) 2001. *It's About Time: The Concept of Time in Archaeology.* Goteborg: Bricoleur Press.

Karo, G. 1915. Die Schachtgräber von Mykenai. *Mitteilungen des Deutschen Archäologischen Instituts, Athenische Abteilung* 40: 113–230.

— 1930. *Die Schachtgräber von Mykenai.* Munich: F. Bruckmann.

Klein, N.L. 1997. Excavation of the Greek temples at Mycenae by the British School at Athens. *The Annual of the British School at Athens* 92: 247–322.

Kleinherenbrink, A. 2019a. *Against Continuity: Gilles Deleuze's Speculative Realism.* Edinburgh: Edinburgh University Press.

— 2019b. The two times of objects: A solution to the problem of time in object-oriented ontology. *Open Philosophy* 2: 539–51.

Klindt-Jensen, O. 1975. *A History of Scandinavian Archaeology.* London: Thames and Hudson.

Klinghoffer, J. 2021. A hybrid methodology of thinking in architectural restoration. Final paper submitted to HT 2735 (Ecological theories of Bruno Latour), Summer 2021, Southern California Institute of Architecture. Instructor: Graham Harman.

Knauss, J. 2001. *Spåthelladische Wasserbauten: Erkundungen zu wasserwirtschaftlichen Infrastrukturen der mykenischen Welt: Zusammenfassung aller bisherigen Untersuchungsergebnisse.*

Munich: Lehrstuhl und Versuchsanst für Wasserbau und Wasserwirtschaft der Technischen Univ. München.

Knodell, A.R., T.C. Wilkinson, T.P. Leppard, and H.A. Orengo. 2022. Survey archaeology in the Mediterranean world: Regional traditions and contributions to long-term history. *Journal of Archaeological Research*, DOI: 10.1007/s10814-022-09175-7.

Kobayashi, C. and M. Marion. 2019. Collingwood as an archaeologist and the Gabbay-Woods schema for abductive reasoning. In D. Gabbay, L. Magnany, W. Park, and A.-V. Pietarinen (eds.) *Natural Arguments: A Tribute to John Woods. Tributes 40*. London: College Publications, 481–96.

Kohler, E.L. and E.K. Ralph. 1961. C-14 dates for sites in the Mediterranean area. *American Journal of Archaeology* 65: 357–67.

Koster, H. 1977. *The Ecology of Pastoralism in Relation to Changing Patterns of Land Use in the Northeast Peloponnese*. Doctoral Dissertation, Department of Anthropology, University of Pennsylvania.

Kourelis, K. 2007. Byzantium and the avant-garde: Excavations at Corinth, 1920s–1930s. *Hesperia* 76.2: 391–442.

Kripke, S. 1981. *Naming and Necessity*. Hoboken, NJ: Wiley-Blackwell.

Kuhn, T. 1978. *Black-Body Theory and the Quantum Discontinuity, 1894–2012*. Chicago: University of Chicago Press.

— 2000. *The Road Since Structure: Philosophical Essays, 1970–1993, With an Autobiographical Interview*. Chicago: University of Chicago Press.

Lacan, J. 1991. *The Seminar of Jacques Lacan, Book II: The Ego in Freud's Theory and in the Technique of Psychoanalysis, 1954–1955*, trans. S. Tomaselli. New York: W.W. Norton.

— 2007a. *Écrits: The First Complete Edition in English*, trans. B. Fink. New York: W.W. Norton.

— 2007b. *The Seminar of Jacques Lacan, Book XVII: The Other Side of Psychoanalysis, 1969–1970*, trans. R. Grigg. New York: W.W. Norton.

— 2013. *The Seminar of Jacques Lacan, Book 1: Freud's Papers on Technique, 1953–1954*, trans. J. Forrester. New York: W.W. Norton.

Ladyman, J. and D. Ross, with D. Spurrett and J. Collier. 2009. *Every Thing Must Go: Metaphysics Naturalized*. Oxford: Oxford University Press.

Lakatos, I. 1978. *The Methodology of Scientific Research Programs: Collected Philosophical Papers*, vol. 1. Cambridge: Cambridge University Press.

Langlois, C.V. and C. Seignobos. 1898. *Introduction aux études historiques*. Paris: Hachette.

Langton, R. 2001. *Kantian Humility: Our Ignorance of Things in Themselves*. Oxford: Clarendon Press.

Latour, B. 1988. Irreductions. Trans. J. Law. In *The Pasteurization of France*, trans. A. Sheridan and J. Law. Cambridge, MA: Harvard University Press, 153–238.

— 1993. *We Have Never Been Modern*. trans. C. Porter. Cambridge, MA: Harvard University Press.

— 1996. *Aramis, or The Love of Technology*, trans. C. Porter. Cambridge, MA: Harvard University Press.

— 1999. *Pandora's Hope: Essays on the Reality of Science Studies*. Cambridge, MA: Harvard University Press.

— 2000. On the partial existence of existing *and* non-existing objects. In L. Daston (ed.) *Biographies of Scientific Objects*. Chicago: University of Chicago Press, 247–69.

— 2004. *Politics of Nature: How to Bring the Sciences Into Democracy*, trans. C. Porter. Cambridge, MA: Harvard University Press.

— 2007a. *Reassembling the Social: An Introduction to Actor-Network Theory*. Oxford: Oxford University Press.

— 2007b. Can we get our materialism back, please? *Isis* 98.1: 138–42.

— 2013a. *An Inquiry Into Modes of Existence: An Anthropology of the Moderns*. Cambridge, MA: Harvard University Press.

— 2013b. *Rejoicing: Or the Torments of Religious Speech*, trans. J. Rose. Cambridge: Polity.

— and A. Yaneva. 2008. "Give me a gun and I will make all buildings move": An ant's view of architecture. In R. Geiser (ed.) *Explorations in Architecture: Teaching, Design, Research*. Basel: Birkhäuser Verlag, 80–9.

— and E. Hermant. 1998. *Paris Invisible City*, trans. L. Carey-Libbrecht, corrected by V. Pihet, at <http://www.bruno-latour.fr/virtual/index.html>.

— G. Harman, and P. Erdélyi. 2011. *The Prince and the Wolf: Latour and Harman at the LSE*. Winchester: Zero Books.

Lehmann, H. 1937. *Argolis: Landeskunde der Ebene von Argos und ihrer Randgebiete*. Athens: Deutsches Archäologisches Institut.

Leibniz, G.W. 1989. *Philosophical Essays*, trans. R. Ariew and D. Garber. Indianapolis: Hackett.

— and S. Clarke. 2000. *Correspondence*. Indianapolis: Hackett.

Levinas, E. 1988. *Existence and Existents*, trans. A. Lingis. The Hague: Martinus Nijhoff.

— 1998. *Otherwise Than Being, or Beyond Essence*, trans. A. Lingis. The Hague: Martinus Nijhoff.

Locke, J. 1959. *An Essay Concerning Human Understanding*, 2 vols. Mineola, NY: Dover.

Lockwood, M. 2005. *The Labyrinth of Time*. Oxford: Oxford University Press.

Lorenz, C. 2017. "The times they are a-changin'": On time, space and periodization in history. In M. Carretero, S. Berger, and M. Grever (eds.) *Palgrave Handbook of Research in Historical Culture and Education*. London: Palgrave Macmillan, 109–31.

Love, G. and M. Meng. 2016. Histories of the dead? *Time and Mind* 9.3: 223–44.

Lovecraft, H.P. 2005. *Tales*. New York: Library of America.

Lowenthal, D. 1985. *The Past is a Foreign Country*. Cambridge: Cambridge University Press.

Lucas, G. 2001. *Critical Approaches to Fieldwork: Contemporary and Historical Archaeological Practice*. London: Routledge.

— 2004. Modern disturbances: On the ambiguities of archaeology. *Modernism/Modernity* 11: 109–20.

— 2005. *The Archaeology of Time*. London: Routledge.

— 2012. *Understanding the Archaeological Record*. Cambridge: Cambridge University Press.

— 2014. Time. In Gardner, A., M. Lake, and U. Sommer (eds.) *The Oxford Handbook of Archaeological Theory*. Oxford: Oxford University Press.

— 2015. Archaeology and contemporaneity. *Archaeological Dialogues* 22: 1–15.

— 2018. Periodization in archaeology: Starting in the ground. In S.G. Souvatzi, A. Baysal, and E.L. Baysal (eds.) *Time and History in Prehistory*. New York: Routledge, 77–94.

— 2021. *Making Time: The Archaeology of Time Revisited*. London: Routledge.

— and C. Witmore. 2022. Paradigm lost: What is a commitment to theory in contemporary archaeology? *Norwegian Archaeological Review* 55.1: 1–14.

— and L. Olivier. 2022. *Conversations About Time*. Abingdon: Routledge.

McDonald, W.A. and G.R. Rapp. 1972. *The Minnesota Messenia Expedition: Reconstructing a Bronze Age Regional Environment*. Minneapolis: University of Minnesota Press.

McGlade, J. 1999. The times of history: Archaeology, narrative and non-linear causality. In T. Murray (ed.), *Time and Archaeology*. London: Routledge, 139–63.

— and S.E. van der Leeuw (eds.) 1997. *Time, Process and Structured Transformation in Archaeology*. London: Routledge.

McGuire, R.H. 2021a. A Relational Marxist critique of posthumanism in archaeology. *Cambridge Archaeological Journal* 31.3: 495–501.

— 2021b. Writing the deep history of human economy. In S. Gimatzidis and R. Jung (eds.) *The Critique of Archaeological Economy*. Cham: Springer, 19–33.

References203

McLuhan, M. 1994. *Understanding Media: The Extensions of Man.* Cambridge, MA: MIT Press.
— and E. McLuhan. 1992. *Laws of Media: The New Science.* Toronto: University of Toronto Press.
— and W. Watson. 1970. *From Cliché to Archetype.* New York: Viking.
McTaggart, J.M.E. 1908. The unreality of time. *Mind* 17: 456–73.
Malafouris, L., C. Gosden, and A. Bogaard (eds.) 2021. Process Archaeology. *World Archaeology,* 53.1.
Malebranche, N. 1997a. *Dialogues on Metaphysics and Religion,* ed. N. Jolley and D. Scott. Cambridge: Cambridge University Press.
— 1997b. *The Search After Truth: With Elucidations of the Search After Truth,* ed. T. Lennon and P. Olscamp. Cambridge: Cambridge University Press.
Manning, S. 2010. Chronology and terminology. In E.H. Cline (ed.) *The Oxford Handbook of the Bronze Age Aegean (ca. 3000–1000 BC).* Oxford: Oxford University Press, 11–28.
— C. Bronk Ramsey, W. Kutschera, T. Higham, B. Kromer, P. Steier, and E.M. Wild. 2006. Chronology for the Aegean Late Bronze Age 1700–1400 B.C. *Science* 312.5773: 565–69.
Marchand, S.L. 1996. *Down from Olympus: Archaeology and Philhellenism in Germany, 1750–1970.* Princeton, NJ: Princeton University Press.
Margulis, L. 2008. *Symbiotic Planet: A New Look at Evolution.* New York: Basic Books.
Matz, F. 1964. Georg Karo. *Gnomon* 36.6: 637–40.
Mee, C. and H. Forbes. 1997. *A Rough and Rocky Place: The Landscape and Settlement History of the Methana Peninsula, Greece. Results of the Methana Survey Project, Sponsored by the British School at Athens and the University of Liverpool.* Liverpool: Liverpool University Press.
Meillassoux, Q. 2008. *After Finitude: An Essay on the Necessity of Contingency,* trans. R. Brassier. London: Continuum.
Miles, R. 2011. *Carthage Must Be Destroyed: The Rise and Fall of an Ancient Civilization.* New York: Viking.
Miller, D. 2005. Materiality: An introduction. In D. Miller (ed.) *Materiality.* Durham, NC: Duke University Press.
Mitchell, T. 2013. *Carbon Democracy: Political Power in the Age of Oil.* London: Verso.
Momigliano, A. 1950. Ancient history and the antiquarian. *Journal of the Warburg and Courtauld Institutes* 13.3–4: 285–315.
Moore, A.D. and W.D. Taylour. 1999. *Well-Built Mycenae, fascicule 10, The Temple Complex.* Oxford: Oxbow.
Morris, I. 1986. The use and abuse of Homer. *Classical Antiquity* 5.1: 81–138.

— 1994. *Classical Greece: Ancient Histories and Modern Archaeologies*. Cambridge: Cambridge University Press.

— 2000. *Archaeology as Culture History*. Oxford: Blackwell.

— 2003. Archaeology, standards of living, and Greek economic history. In I. Morris and J.G. Manning (eds.) *The Ancient Economy: Evidence and Models*. Stanford, CA: Stanford University Press, 91–126.

— 2010. *Why the West Rules – For Now: The Patterns of History, and What They Reveal About the Future*. New York: Farrar, Straus and Giroux.

Morton, T. 2013a. *Hyperobjects: Philosophy and Ecology After the End of the World*. Minneapolis: University of Minnesota Press.

— 2013b. *Realist Magic: Objects, Ontology, Causality*. Ann Arbor, MI: Open Humanities Press.

— 2021. Inheritance. In T.R. Bangstad and Þ. Pétursdóttir (eds.) *Heritage Ecologies*. Abingdon: Routledge, 383–90.

Mouliou, M. 2009. The concept of diachronia in the Greek archaeological museum: reflections on current challenges. In J.L. Binliff and H. Stöger (eds.) *Medieval and Post-Medieval Greece: The Corfu Papers*. Oxford: Archaeopress, 233–41.

Murray, T. (ed.) 1999. *Time and Archaeology*. London: Routledge.

Mylonas, G.E. 1957. *Ancient Mycenae: The Capital City of Agamemnon*. Princeton, NJ: Princeton University Press.

Nadler, S. 2011. *Occasionalism: Causation among the Cartesians*. Oxford: Oxford University Press.

Nagy, G. 1996. *Homeric Questions*. Austin: University of Texas Press.

Nail, T. 2018. *Being and Motion*. Oxford: Oxford University Press.

— 2021. *Theory of the Object*. Edinburgh: Edinburgh University Press, 2021.

Nativ, A. 2018. On the object of archaeology. *Archaeological Dialogues* 25.1: 1–21.

— and G. Lucas. 2020. Archaeology without antiquity. *Antiquity* 94.376: 852–63.

Netz, R. 2004. *Barbed Wire: An Ecology of Modernity*. Middletown, CT: Wesleyan University Press.

Newton, I. 1934. *Philosophiae Naturalis Principia Mathematica*, Bk. 1; trans. A. Motte, rev. F. Cajori. Berkeley: University of California Press.

Nietzsche, F. 1997. On the uses and disadvantages of history for life. In *Untimely Meditations*, trans. R.J. Hollingdale. Cambridge: Cambridge University Press, 57–124.

Norden, E. and M. McLuhan. 1969. Marshall McLuhan: A candid conversation with the high priest of the popcult and metaphysician of media. *Playboy* 16.3: 53–74, 158.

Nyerup, R. 1806. Oversyn over Fædernelandets Mindesmærker fra

Oldtiden, saaledes som samme kan tænkes opstillede i et tilkom-
mende National-Museum. Et Forsøg. *Historisk-statistisk Skildring
af Tilstanden i Danmark og Norge i ældre og nyere Tider*, vol. 4.
Copenhagen: Soldin.

Olivier, L. 1999. The Hochdorf princely grave and the question of the
nature of archaeological funerary assemblages. In T. Murray (ed.)
Time and Archaeology. London: Routledge, 123–52.

— 2004. The past of the present: Archaeological memory and time.
Archaeological Dialogues 10.2: 204–13.

— 2008. *Le sombre abîme du temps: mémoire et archéologie*. Paris:
Seuil.

— 2011. *The Dark Abyss of Time: Archaeology and Memory*, trans.
A. Greenspan. Lanham, MD: AltaMira Press.

— 2013. The business of archaeology is the present. In A. González-
Ruibal (ed.) *Reclaiming Archaeology: Beyond the Tropes of
Modernity*. London: Routledge, 117–29.

— 2017. I can't get no satisfaction: For an archaeology of the contemporary past. In J.-M. Blaising, J. Driessen, J.-P. Legendre, and
L. Olivier (eds.) *Clashes of Time: The Contemporary Past as a
Challenge for Archaeology*. Louvain-la-Neuve: UCL Presses univer-
sitaires de Louvain, 11–22.

Olsen, B. 2003. Material culture after text. Re-membering things.
Norwegian Archaeological Review 36: 87–104.

— 2006. Scenes from a troubled engagement: Post-structuralism
and material culture studies. In C. Tilley, W. Keane, S. Kuechler,
M. Rowlands, and P. Spyer (eds.) *Handbook of Material Culture*.
London: SAGE, 85–103.

— 2007. Keeping things at arm's length: A genealogy of asymmetry.
World Archaeology 39.4: 579–88.

— 2010. *In Defense of Things: Archaeology and the Ontology of
Objects*. Lanham, MD: AltaMira Press.

— 2012. After interpretation: Remembering archaeology. *Current
Swedish Archaeology* 20: 11–34.

— 2013a. Reclaiming things: An archaeology of matter. In P.L. Carlile,
D. Nicolini, A. Langley, and H. Tsoukas (eds.) *How Matter Matters:
Objects, Artifacts and Materiality in Organization Studies*. Oxford:
Oxford University Press, 171–96.

— 2013b. Memory. In P. Graves-Brown, R. Harrison, and
A. Piccini (eds.) *The Oxford Handbook of the Archaeology of the
Contemporary World*. Oxford: Oxford University Press, 204–18.

— and A. Svestad. 1994. Creating prehistory: Archaeology museums
and the discourse of modernism. *Nordisk Museologi* 1: 3–20.

— and C. Witmore. 2014. Sværholt: Re-covered memories from a
POW camp in the far north. In B. Olsen and Þ. Pétursdóttir (eds.)
*Ruin Memories: Materialities, Aesthetics and the Archaeology of
the Recent Past*. London: Routledge, 162–90.

— and C. Witmore. 2015. Archaeology, symmetry, and the ontology of things: A response to critics. *Archaeological Dialogues* 22.2: 187–97.

— and C. Witmore. 2021. When defense is not enough: On things, archaeological theory, and the politics of misrepresentation. *Forum Kritische Archäologie* 10: 67–88.

— and S. Vinogradova 2020. (In)significantly Soviet: The heritage of Teriberka. *International Journal of Heritage Studies* 26.9: 901–18.

— and Þ. Pétursdóttir (eds.) 2014. *Ruin Memories: Materiality, Aesthetics, and the Archaeology of the Recent Past.* London: Routledge.

— M. Shanks, and C. Witmore. 2003: Innocence regained? Or is there a new consensus in archaeology. Paper given in the Stanford Archaeology Lecture Series, November 20.

— M. Shanks, T. Webmoor, and C. Witmore. 2012. *Archaeology: The Discipline of Things.* Berkeley: University of California Press.

— M. Burström, C. DeSilvey, and Þ. Pétursdóttir (eds.) 2021. *After Discourse: Things, Affects, Ethics.* Abingdon: Routledge.

Pétursdóttir, Þ. 2012. Small things forgotten now included, or what else do things deserve? *International Journal of Historical Archaeology* 16.3: 577–603.

— 2014. Things out-of-hand: The aesthetics of abandonment. In B. Olsen and Þ. Pétursdóttir (eds.) *Ruin Memories: Materiality, Aesthetics, and the Archaeology of the Recent Past.* London: Routledge, 335–64.

— 2018. Lyrics for a duskier Enlightenment: In response to Alexandra Ion. *Archaeological Dialogues* 25.2: 205–13.

— and B. Olsen. 2018. Theory adrift: The matter of archaeological theorizing. *Journal of Social Archaeology* 18.1: 97–117.

Piggot, S. 1966. Mycenae and barbarian Europe. *Sbornik Narodniho Muzea v Praza* 20: 117.

Pikoulas, Y. 1995. *Odikó díktyo kaí ámyna. Apo tín Kórintho stó Árgos kaí tín Arkadías.* Athens: Horos.

Pilaar Birch, S.E. (ed.) 2018. *Multispecies Archaeology.* Abingdon: Routledge.

Piteros, C. 2005. Ergasies Diamorphosis – Anadeixes: Arkadiko. *Archaiologikon deltion* 60, B1 (Chronika): 267.

Plotinus. 1975. *The Essential Plotinus.* Indianapolis: Hackett.

Pollock, S., R. Bernbeck, C. Jauß, J. Greger, C. von Rüden, and S. Schreiber. 2014. Entangled discussions: Talking with Ian Hodder about his book *Entangled. Forum Kritische Archäologie* 3: 151–61.

Pöppel, E. 2004. Lost in time: A historical frame, elementary processing units and the 3-second window. *Acta Neurobiologie Experimentalis* 64: 295–301.

Powell, B. 1905. The Temple of Apollo at Corinth. *American Journal of Archaeology* 9.1: 44–63.

Prag, A.J.N.W., L. Papazoglou-Manioudaki, R.A.H. Neave, D. Smith, J.H. Musgrave, and A. Nafplioti. 2009. Mycenae revisited Part 1: The human remains from Grave Circle A: Stamatakis, Schliemann and two new faces from Shaft Grave VI. *Annual of the British School at Athens* 104: 233–77.

Preucel, R.W. 2016. Pragmatic archaeology and semiotic mediation. *Semiotic Review*, 4, at <https://semioticreview.com/ojs/index.php/sr/article/view/11>.

Prigogine, I. and I. Stengers. 1984. *Order Out of Chaos: Man's New Dialogue with Nature*. Toronto: Bantam Books.

Protonotariou-Deilaki, E. 1968. Tholotos taphos Kazarma. *Archaiologika Analekta ex Athinon/Athens Annals of Archaeology* 1: 236–8.

— 1969. Tholotos taphos Kazarma. *Archaiologika Analekta ex Athinon/Athens Annals of Archaeology* 2: 3–6.

Ramenofsky, A. 1998. The illusion of time. In A. Ramenofsky and A. Steffen (eds.) *Unit Issues in Archaeology: Measuring Time, Space, and Material*. Salt Lake City: University of Utah Press, 74–84.

Rathje, W.L. 1979. Modern material culture studies. *Advances in Archaeological Method and Theory* 2: 1–27.

— and C. Murphy. 2003. *Rubbish! The Archaeology of Garbage*. Tucson: University of Arizona Press.

— M. Shanks, and C. Witmore (eds.) 2013. *Archaeology in the Making: Conversations through a Discipline*. London: Routledge.

Raud, R. 2021. *Being in Flux: A Post-Anthropocentric Ontology of the Self*. Cambridge: Polity.

Renfrew, C. 1968. Wessex without Mycenae. *Annual of the British School at Athens* 63: 277–85.

— 1972. *The Emergence of Civilisation: The Cyclades and the Aegean in the Third Millennium B.C.* London: Methuen.

— 1973. *Before Civilization: The Radiocarbon Revolution and Prehistoric Europe*. New York: Knopf.

— 1980. The great tradition versus the great divide: Archaeology as anthropology? *American Journal of Archaeology* 84: 287–98.

Rich, S.A. 2021. *Shipwreck Hauntography: Underwater Ruins and the Uncanny*. Amsterdam: University of Amsterdam Press.

— and P.B. Campbell (eds.) 2023. *Contemporary Philosophy for Maritime Archaeology: Flat Ontologies, Oceanic Thought, and the Anthropocene*. Leiden: Sidestone Press.

Richardson, R.B. 1897. The excavations at Corinth in 1896. *American Journal of Archaeology* 1.6: 455–80.

Rilke, R.M. 1949. *The Notebooks of Malte Laurids Brigge*, trans. M.D. Herter Norton. New York: W.W. Norton.

Robb, J. 2013. Material culture, landscapes of action, and emergent causation: A new model for the origins of the European Neolithic. *Current Anthropology* 54.6: 657–83.

— and T. Pauketat (eds.) 2008. Time and change in archaeological interpretation. Special Section of *Cambridge Archaeological Journal* 18.1: 57–99.

Rojas, F. 2019. *The Pasts of Roman Anatolia: Interpreters, Traces, Horizons*. Cambridge: Cambridge University Press.

Rudwick, M.J.S. 2005. *Bursting the Limits of Time: The Reconstruction of Geohistory in the Age of Revolution*. Chicago: University of Chicago Press.

— 2014. *Earth's Deep History: How it Was Discovered and Why it Matters*. Chicago: University of Chicago Press.

Runia, E. 2006. Presence. *History and Theory* 45.1: 1–29.

— and M. Tamm. 2019. The past is not a foreign country: A conversation. *Rethinking History* 23.3: 403–33.

Salmon, M. 1982. *Explanation and Archaeology*. New York: Academic Press.

Sbriglia, R. 2021. Notes toward an extimate materialism: A reply to Graham Harman. *Open Philosophy* 4.1: 106–23.

Schiffer, M.B. 1987. *Formation Processes of the Archaeological Record*. Albuquerque: University of New Mexico Press.

Schliemann, H. 1878. *Mycenae: A Narrative of Researches and Discoveries at Mycenae and Tiryns*. London: John Murray.

Schnapp, A. 1997. *The Discovery of the Past: The Origins of Archaeology*, trans. I. Kinnes and G. Varndell. London: British Museum Press.

— 2004. Eduard Gerhard: Founder of classical archaeology? *Modernism/Modernity* 11.1: 169–71.

Sedgwick, E.K. 1997. Paranoid reading and reparative reading: Or, you're so paranoid, you probably think this introduction is about you. In E. Sedgwick (ed.) *Novel Gazing: Queer Readings in Fiction*. Durham, NC: Duke University Press, 1–40.

Sellars, J. 2007. Aiôn and chronos: Deleuze and the Stoic theory of time. *Collapse* 3: 177–205.

Serres, M. 1982. *Hermes: Literature, Science, Philosophy*. Baltimore: The Johns Hopkins University Press.

— 1987. *Statues: le second livre des fondations*. Paris: Editions Julliard.

— 1993. *Les origines de la géométrie: Tiers livre des fondations*. Paris: Flammarion.

— 1995. *Genesis*, trans. G. James and J. Nielson. Ann Arbor: University of Michigan Press.

— 2015a. *Rome: The First Book of Foundations*, trans. R. Burks. London: Bloomsbury

— 2015b. *Statues: The Second Book of Foundations*, trans. R. Burks. London: Bloomsbury.

— and B. Latour. 1995. *Conversations on Science, Culture, and Time*, trans. R. Lapidus. Ann Arbor: University of Michigan Press.

Shanks, M. 1996. *Classical Archaeology of Greece: Experiences of the Discipline*. London: Routledge.

— 2012. *The Archaeological Imagination*. Walnut Creek, CA: Left Coast Press.

— and C. Tilley. 1992. *Re-constructing Archaeology*. London: Routledge.

Shelton, K. 2006. The long lasting effect of Tsountas on the study of Mycenae. *Mythos: La préhistoire égéenne du XIXe au XXIe siècle après J.-C. BCH* suppl. 46: 159–64.

Shryock, A. and D.L. Smail. 2011. *Deep History: The Architecture of Past and Present*. Berkeley: University of California Press.

Siapkas, J. 2018. Negotiated positivism: The disregarded epistemology of Arne Furumark. *Journal of Archaeology and Ancient History* 22: 1–21.

Sider, T. 1997. Four dimensionalism. *Philosophical Review* 106: 197–231.

Sigurdsson, H., S. Cashdollar, and S.R.J. Sparks. 1982. The Eruption of Vesuvius in A.D. 79: Reconstruction from historical and volcanological evidence. *American Journal of Archaeology* 86.1: 39–51.

Simondon, G. 2020. *Individuation in Light of Notions of Form and Information*, trans. T. Adkins. Minneapolis: University of Minnesota Press.

Simons, P. 2000. *Parts: A Study in Ontology*. Oxford: Clarendon Press.

Simpson, R.H. and D.K. Hagel. 2006. *Mycenaean Fortifications, Highways, Dams and Canals*. Sävedalen: Paul Åströms Förlag.

Sloterdijk, P. 2009. Spheres theory: Talking to myself about the poetics of space. *Harvard Design Magazine* 30: 1–8.

— 2011. Society of centaurs: Philosophical remarks on automobility. Trans. K. Ritson. *Transfers* 1.1: 14–24.

— 2014. Museum – School of alienation. Trans. I.B. Whyte. *Art in Translation* 6: 437–48.

Snodgrass, A.M. 1985. Greek archaeology and Greek history. *Classical Antiquity* 4.2: 193–207.

— 1987. *An Archaeology of Greece: The Present State and Future Scope of a Discipline*. Berkeley: University of California Press.

Sørensen, T.F. 2021. That raw and ancient cold: On Graham Harman's recasting of archaeology. *Open Philosophy* 4.1: 1–19.

Souvatzi, S., A. Baysal, and E.L. Baysal (eds.) 2019. *Time and History in Prehistory*. London: Routledge.

Spinoza, B. 1994. *A Spinoza Reader: The Ethics and Other Works*, trans. E. Curley. Princeton, NJ: Princeton University Press.

Stanislavski, K. 2010. *An Actor's Work*. New York: Routledge.

Stengers, I. 2014. *Thinking with Whitehead: A Free and Wild Creation of Concepts*, trans. M. Chase. Cambridge, MA: Harvard University Press.

Stern, W. 2007. Pyschische Präsenzzeit. *New Yearbook for Phenomenology and Phenomenological Research* 5: 310–51.

Stewart, K. 2008. Weak theory in an unfinished world. *Journal of Folklore Research* 45.1: 71–82.

Stocking, G. 1995. *After Tylor: British Social Anthropology, 1888–1951*. Madison: University of Wisconsin Press.

Strawson, G. 2009. *Selves*. Oxford: Oxford University Press.

Stroulia, A. and S.B. Sutton. 2009. Archaeological sites and local places: Connecting the dots. *Public Archaeology: Archaeological Ethnographies* 8.2–3: 124–40.

Suárez, F. 1994. *On Efficient Causality: Metaphysical Disputations 17, 18, and 19*, trans. A. Freddoso. New Haven, CT: Yale University Press.

Susskind, L. and J. Lindesay. 2004. *An Introduction to Black Holes, Information and the String Theory Revolution: The Holographic Universe*. Singapore: World Scientific Publishing.

Tamm, M. and L. Olivier. 2019. *Rethinking Historical Time: New Approaches to Presentism*. London: Bloomsbury Academic.

Trigger, B.G. 2010. *A History of Archaeological Thought*. New York: Cambridge University Press.

Tsountas, C. and J.I. Manatt. 1897. *The Mycenaean Age: A Study of the Monuments and Culture of Pre-Homeric Greece*. London: Macmillan & Co.

Twardowski, K. 1977. *On the Content and Object of Presentations: A Psychological Investigation*, trans. R. Grossmann. Dordrecht: Springer.

Uexküll, J. von. 2010. *A Foray into the Worlds of Animals and Humans, with a Theory of Meaning*, trans. J. O'Neil. Minneapolis: University of Minnesota Press.

Van Dyke, R. 2015. Materiality in practice: An introduction. In R. Van Dyke (ed.) *Practicing Materiality*. Tucson: University of Arizona Press, 3–32.

— 2021. Ethics, not objects. *Cambridge Archaeological Journal* 31.3: 487–93.

Vernant, J.-P. 1965. *Mythe et pensée chez les Grecs: études de psychologie historique*. Paris: François Maspero.

— 1976. *Religion grecque, religions antiques*. Paris: François Maspero.

Viollet-le-Duc, E. 1854. *Dictionary of French Architecture from the 11th to 16th Century*. Paris: B. Bance. English translation by Wikisource at <https://en.wikisource.org/wiki/Translation:Dictionary_of_French_Architecture_from_the_11th_to_16th_Century>.

Wace, A.J.B. 1949. *Mycenae, an Archaeological History and Guide*. Princeton: Princeton University Press.

— 1956. The last days of Mycenae. In S.S. Weinberg (ed.) *The Aegean and the Near East: Studies Presented to Hetty Goldman on the Occasion of her Seventy-fifth Birthday.* New York: J.J. Augustin Publisher, 126–35.

— and F.H. Stubbings 1962. *A Companion to Homer.* London: Macmillan.

Wallace-Hadrill, A. 2011. *Herculaneum: Past and Future.* London: Frances Lincoln.

Wandsnider, L. 2004. Solving the puzzle of the archaeological labyrinth. In S.E. Alcock and J.F. Cherry (eds.) *Side-by-Side Survey: Comparative Regional Studies in the Mediterranean World.* Oxford: Oxbow Books, 49–62.

Warren P.M. and V. Hankey. 1989. *Aegean Bronze Age Chronology.* Bristol: Bristol Classical Press.

Watkins, C. (ed.) 2000. *The American Heritage Dictionary of Indo-European Roots,* 2nd ed. Boston: Houghton Mifflin.

Webmoor, T. 2015. Archaeology: Philosophy and science. In J.D. Wright (ed.) *International Encyclopedia of the Social & Behavioral Sciences,* 2nd ed. Amsterdam: Elsevier, 891–8.

— and C. Witmore, 2008. Things are us! A commentary on human/things relations under the banner of a "social" archaeology. *Norwegian Archaeological Review* 41.1: 53–70.

White, H. 2014. *The Practical Past.* Evanston, IL: Northwestern University Press.

Whitehead, A.N. 1929. *The Aims of Education and Other Essays.* New York: The Free Press.

— 1978. *Process and Reality.* New York: Free Press.

Willerslev, R. 2011. Frazer strikes back from the armchair: A new search for the animist soul. *Journal of the Royal Anthropological Institute* 17: 504–26.

Williams, R. 2003. *Television: Technology and Cultural Form,* 3rd ed. London: Routledge.

Witmore, C. 2006. Vision, media, noise and the percolation of time: Symmetrical approaches to the mediation of the material world. *Journal of Material Culture* 11.3: 267–92.

— 2007. Landscape, time, topology: An archaeological account of the Southern Argolid, Greece. In D. Hicks, L. McAtackney, and G. Fairclough (eds.) *Envisioning Landscape: Situations and Standpoints in Archaeology and Heritage.* Walnut Creek, CA: Left Coast Press, 194–225.

— 2009. Prolegomena to open pasts: On archaeological memory practices. *Archaeologies* 5.3: 511–45.

— 2012. The realities of the past: Archaeology, object-orientations, pragmatology. In B.R. Fortenberry and L. McAtackney (eds.) *Modern Materials: Proceedings from the Contemporary and Historical Archaeology in Theory Conference 2009.* Oxford: Archaeopress, 25–36.

— 2013. Which archaeology?: A question of chronopolitics. In A. González-Ruibal (ed.) *Reclaiming Archaeology: Beyond the Tropes of Modernity*. London: Routledge, 130–44.

— 2014a. Archaeology and the new materialisms. *Journal of Contemporary Archaeology* 1: 203–46.

— 2014b. Confronting things: A Reply to Edgeworth, Hodder, Ingold and Lazzari. *Journal of Contemporary Archaeology* 1.2: 239–46.

— 2015. No past but within things: A cave and archaeology in the form of a dialogue. In M. Mircan and V.W.J. van Gerven Oei (eds.) *The Allegory of the Cave Painting Reader*. Milan: Mousse Publishing, 575–94.

— 2017a. Things are the grounds of all archaeology. In J.M. Blaising, J. Driessen, J.P. Legendre, and L. Olivier (eds.) *Clashes of Times: The Contemporary Past as a Challenge for Archaeology*. Louvain: Louvain University Press, 231–46.

— 2017b. Complexities and emergence: The case of Argos. In A.R. Knodell, and T.P. Leppard (eds.) *Regional Approaches to Society and Complexity: Studies in Honor of John F. Cherry*. Sheffield: Equinox Publishing Ltd, 268–87.

— 2018a. The end of the Neolithic? At the emergence of the Anthropocene. In S.E. Pilaar Birch (ed.) *Multispecies Archaeology*. Abingdon: Routledge, 26–46.

— 2018b. Review of Karen Bassi, *Traces of the Past: Classics between History & Archaeology*, Ann Arbor: University of Michigan Press, 2016. *Cambridge Archaeological Journal* 28.3: 515–18.

— 2020a. *Old Lands: A Chorography of the Eastern Peloponnese*. Abingdon: Routledge.

— 2020b. Objecthood. In L. Wilkie and J. Chenoweth (eds.) *A Cultural History of Objects: Modern Period, 1900 to Present*. London: Bloomsbury, 37–64.

— 2020c. Chronopolitics and archaeology. In C. Smith (ed.) *Encyclopedia of Global Archaeology*. New York: Springer.

— 2021a. Finding symmetry? Archaeology, objects, and posthumanism. *Cambridge Archaeological Journal* 31.3: 477–85.

— 2021b. Matter. In H. Callan (ed.) *The International Encyclopedia of Anthropology*. Oxford: Wiley Blackwell.

— 2022. Anthropoiesis revisited: Hominization through the incorporation of nonhumans. In F. Coolidge, K. Overmann, and T. Wynn (eds.) *The Oxford Handbook of Cognitive Archaeology*. Oxford: Oxford University Press.

— and M. Shanks. 2013. Archaeology: An ecology of practices. In W.L. Rathje, M. Shanks, and C. Witmore (eds.) *Archaeology in the Making: Conversations through a Discipline*. London: Routledge, 380–98.

Wittgenstein, L. 1922. *Tractatus Logico-Philosophicus*, trans. C.K. Ogden. New York: Harcourt, Brace & Company.

Wolfendale, P. 2014. *Object-Oriented Philosophy: The Noumenon's New Clothes*. Falmouth: Urbanomic.

Wolfson, E. 2017. *Gottwesen* and the de-divinization of the last god: Heidegger's meditation on the strange and incalculable. In M. Björk and J. Svenungsson (eds.) *Heidegger's Black Notebooks and the Future of Theology*. London: Palgrave Macmillan, 211–55.

Woolf, G. 1998. *Becoming Roman: The Origins of Provincial Civilization in Gaul*. Cambridge: Cambridge University Press.

Wylie, A. 2002. *Thinking from Things: Essays in the Philosophy of Archaeology*. Berkeley: University of California Press.

— with M. Shanks, T. Webmoor, and C. Witmore. 2013. Alison Wylie. In W.L. Rathje, M. Shanks, and C. Witmore (eds.) *Archaeology in the Making: Conversations through a Discipline*. London: Routledge, 103–31.

Yoffee, N. 2007. *Negotiating the Past in the Past: Identity, Memory, and Landscape in Archaeological Research*. Tucson: University of Arizona Press.

Young, N. 2021. Only two peas in a pod: On the overcoming of ontological taxonomies. *Symposia Melitensia* 17: 27–36.

Žižek, S. 2009. *The Parallax View*. Cambridge, MA: MIT Press.

Index